Sunset

Breads

By the Editors of Sunset Books and Sunset Magazine

Sunset Publishing Corporation □ *Menlo Park, California*

HOME-BAKED BREADS

It's hard to imagine a more versatile food than bread. Savory or sweet, filled or plain, coarse or delicate and flaky, bread offers the home baker boundless opportunities for self-expression and creativity. No matter what your preference, the range of recipes in this book is bound to entice you.

For the novice, a chapter on working with yeast explains the basics. For the bread machine enthusiast, a variety of specially tested recipes will expand your repertoire. And for the bread lover, a collection of recipes from around the world will keep you elbow-deep in flour for months. Enjoy!

For our recipes, we provide a nutritional analysis (for more information see page 5) prepared by Hill Nutrition Associates, Inc., of Florida. We thank Lynne Hill, R.D., for her advice and expertise. We also extend thanks to Fran Feldman for carefully editing the manuscript and to Geno Anderson, Evolutions, and Judy and Downing Exley of Friendship Farm Antiques for accessories used in our photographs.

Research & Text
Lisa Chaney

Coordinating Editor
Linda J. Selden

Design
Susan Sempere

Illustrations
Liz Wheaton

Photography
Peter Christiansen: 27; Keith Ovregaard: 3, 7, 11, 14, 22, 38, 46, 51, 54, 59, 62, 67, 83, 86, 91, 94, 99, 102, 107, 110, 115, 118, 123, 126; Norman A. Plate: 78; Kevin Sanchez: 35, 43, 75; Darrow M. Watt: 19, 70; Tom Wyatt: 30.

Photo Styling
Elizabeth Gamburd: 30; Bunny Martin: 3, 7, 11, 14, 22, 38, 46, 51, 54, 59, 62, 67, 83, 86, 91, 94, 99, 102, 107, 110, 115, 118, 123, 126; Susan Massey: 35, 43, 75.

Cover
Homemade breads come in a delicious array of shapes and sizes (clockwise from top left): Cherry-Almond Christmas Wreath (page 82), Dried Fig & Walnut Wheat Bread (page 121), Stretch Breadsticks (page 49), Pane Francese (page 18), Chocolate Chip Scones (page 113), and Rosemary Bread (page 34). Design and photo styling by JoAnn Masaoka Van Atta. Photography by Kevin Sanchez. Food styling by Cynthia Scheer.

About the recipes
All of the recipes in this book were tested and developed in the Sunset test kitchens.

Senior Editor (Food and Entertaining), Sunset Magazine
Jerry Anne Di Vecchio

Editor, Sunset Books: Elizabeth L. Hogan

First printing April 1994

Light and airy English Muffins (page 88) are best served split and toasted. For a delicious morning treat, spread them with plain butter or, as shown here, with Fresh Strawberry Butter (page 124).

CONTENTS

SPECIAL FEATURES

ALL ABOUT BREAD

FEW SCENTS are more appealing than the aroma of freshly baked bread. Sliced warm from the oven and spread generously with butter, bread is surely one of life's greatest—and simplest—pleasures.

To home bakers, bread baking is both art and intrigue. Although some favor a nicely rounded, evenly browned loaf, most ardent bread bakers agree that the best loaf is perfect in its imperfections. An odd shape, a thick crust, even a split on the top of the loaf only add to its earthy, homemade appeal.

The Evolution of Bread

The first bread was a thin, unleavened cake made from a mixture of grain and meal and baked on stones warmed by a hot fire. Some years later, when ancient cultures turned from a nomadic life-style based on hunting to a more settled one based on agriculture, grains such as wheat and barley evolved into dietary staples, and bread became more common.

The Egyptians were the first to turn bread baking into a skilled craft. Wheat was planted in the Nile's floodplain, where changing river levels offered natural irrigation. Once harvested, the grain was trodden by buffalo into a coarse meal used to make bread.

Although their early loaves were dense, unleavened patties, the Egyptians were probably the first to bake the lighter, leavened rounds more commonly associated with today's bread. How they discovered the efficacy of yeast is shrouded in mystery. Some attribute the discovery to a batch of fermented dough that created a starter from which other loaves were baked; others claim that the first natural leavening was derived from a yeast-rich foam skimmed from the surface of fermenting wines.

Wheat became one of Egypt's primary exports. Although it was soon found throughout the ancient world, it would be centuries before leavened bread made from wheat became common.

When commercial milling was introduced in Europe in the Middle Ages, bread making became firmly established there. Grains such as rye, barley, and oats were cultivated in northern Europe and used to make coarse, flat breads. Dry, thick slices of those breads served as plates at medieval meals, to be eaten later or given to the poor.

Early American colonists relied on corn for most of their bread making. It wasn't until later, when pioneers began to push west, that wheat became more widely cultivated and found its way into baked goods. Settlers baked their loaves directly on the hearth or in Dutch ovens buried underneath the hot coals of a camp fire.

An Array of Grains

In Caesar's time, the color of one's bread was directly related to social status: white bread was reserved strictly for the upper classes, darker loaves for the poor. These days, bread lovers delight in the wide variety of grains available to them. Although you may be familiar with many of them—wheat, corn, oats, and rye, for example—the world of grains extends far beyond those basics. On the following pages are recipes that use whole and ground millet, Italian semolina, and many different types of wheat, such as bran, bulgur, cracked wheat, and wheat berries.

Unbleached all-purpose or unbleached bread flour is often the best choice for making bread. Unbleached flour is allowed to age and whiten naturally. Although the nutrient-rich bran and germ have been removed, unbleached flours are still superior to bleached flours in nutritive value, flavor, and rising ability. For more on flours and grains, see page 13.

The Nutritive Value of Grains

Whole grains contain both the vitamin-rich germ and the fiber-rich bran valued in today's health-conscious society. However, whole grains are more difficult to digest than white flour and may lose some of their nutritive value in the digestion process.

Whole grains are a good choice for added fiber when eaten as part of a well-balanced diet. Wheat bran, whole wheat flour, corn, rye, millet, oats, and barley are grains rich in insoluble fiber, which helps keep the gastrointestinal tract healthy. Soluble fiber, which helps regulate cholesterol and fat levels, is found in oats, wheat, corn, and rice bran.

Bread Baking Today

Country loaves studded with walnuts, ladder-shaped fougasse, thick squares of focaccia topped with fresh tomato, herb-scented crusty rounds—the number of breads now available on the market is overwhelming. These breads, many of which are classic loaves in France and Italy, have spurred an interest in bread baking, as bakers strive to reproduce at home some of the new taste sensations they've been enjoying elsewhere. And many markets are responding to the demands of home bakers by offering a wider array of flours and grains than ever before.

The recipes in this book provide easy-to-understand instructions and simple illustrations to help even the novice baker. If you're using yeast for the first time, let the technique section guide you toward perfect results. If time—or the lack of it—is a major issue for you, you'll find that most recipes offer instructions for kneading with the dough hook of an electric mixer, which can cut kneading time in half. You'll even discover a selection of bread machine recipes that take virtually minutes to prepare. All you do is put the ingredients in the bread pan and press the start button, and the machine produces a delicious loaf in 3 to 5 hours.

A Word about Our Nutritional Data

For our recipes, we provide a nutritional analysis stating calorie count and percent of calories from fat; grams of protein, carbohydrates, total fat, and saturated fat; and milligrams of cholesterol and sodium. Generally, the analysis applies to a single serving, based on the number of servings given for each recipe and the amount of each ingredient. If a range is given for the number of servings and/or the amount of an ingredient, the analysis is based on an average of the figures given.

The nutritional analysis does not include optional ingredients or those for which no specific amount is stated. If an ingredient is listed with a substitution, the information was calculated using the first choice.

A mixing bowl and a few tools are all you need to make bread, but some additional equipment is helpful (clockwise from left): electric mixer with dough hook and paddle attachment, spatula, wooden spoon, whisk, thermometer, ceramic bowl, and measuring cups and spoons.

YEAST BREAD TECHNIQUES

Success in bread baking comes from understanding a few basic ingredients and knowing how to combine them to produce nicely shaped, even-textured loaves. As with most endeavors, practice makes perfect—the more you make bread, the more familiar you become with the ingredients. But if you're a novice, don't despair. Baking bread isn't difficult. Just follow the directions—and remember to allow for slight variations in amounts of flour and times for kneading and baking.

Understanding Ingredients

All it takes is a few basic ingredients to produce a delicious loaf of bread.

Leavenings. Leavenings produce the carbon dioxide gas that lightens doughs and batters. In yeast breads, yeast is the leavening. Quick breads often use chemical leavenings, such as baking soda and/or baking powder; eggs may also be used.

Yeast is a living microorganism that is sold in its inactive, or dormant, form. When activated, it gives off the bubbles of carbon dioxide that cause dough to rise.

Like any living organism, yeast needs food to grow and survive. After being activated in warm water and mixed with flour, yeast begins to eat the sugars and complex carbohydrates in the flour and reproduce at a rapid rate. The yeast produces carbon dioxide, which becomes trapped within the stretchy protein structure, called "gluten," in the dough, causing the dough to rise. When the dough is baked, the heat of the oven kills the yeast in the dough and sets the porous pattern in place, creating the spongelike texture of most yeast breads.

Yeast is available in a granular form and in a compressed cake. Granular yeast, or *active dry yeast,* is sold either in envelopes or in small jars. One envelope of dry yeast (a scant tablespoon) is roughly equal to a .06-ounce cube of fresh cake yeast. Active dry yeast can be stored in a cool, dry place (such as a refrigerator) for about a year. Be sure to check the expiration date printed on the package.

Compressed cake yeast works in much the same way as active dry yeast but is much more perishable. Stored in a refrigerator, it will remain fresh for only up to 2 weeks. Test by crumbling it—if it crumbles readily, it's still good.

Rapid-rise yeast is a new strain of low-moisture yeast that raises dough 50 percent faster than regular yeast. Although there may be a small loss of flavor and texture due to the rapid fermentation, for some people the decrease in rising time makes up for any loss of quality.

The recipes in this book call for active dry yeast. It's more widely available than the other types and is more convenient for most bakers. If you want to use compressed yeast instead, just be sure to dissolve it in lukewarm water (about 95°F) rather than the warm water (about 110°F) specified in the recipes.

Flour. It's flour that provides the structure of bread. Many kinds of flour—even ground acorns—have been kneaded into loaves over the centuries. For a description of some of the different types, see page 13.

For yeast breads, at least part of the flour must be wheat flour, which is high in gluten. When wheat flour is moistened and beaten, the gluten becomes very elastic, allowing the dough to stretch as the yeast leavens it and giving the loaf enough strength to keep its shape when baked. Some varieties of flour, such as rye, corn, and millet, contain lower amounts of gluten than wheat flour. Those flours need to be used in combination with high-gluten flours, such as whole wheat or all-purpose flour, to make yeast bread.

Liquids. Very important in bread baking, liquids are needed to dissolve and activate the yeast and to develop the gluten structure of the flour, which occurs during the kneading process.

A variety of liquids can be used in yeast breads; each imparts a different flavor and texture to the finished loaf. *Water* produces a crisp crust and coarse, chewy texture. *Milk* creates a velvety grain. *Eggs* beaten into the dough lend a rich tenderness and slightly golden tone. *Fruit juice* gives special flavor. *Buttermilk* and *sour cream* contribute a slight tang and fine texture. Many of these liquids enrich the bread with added nutrients as well.

Sugar. Sugar provides food for the yeast so it can grow. The different types of sugar lend a range of flavors and colors to bread and help brown the crust when baking. Some varieties used in these recipes are granulated sugar, brown sugar, honey, and molasses.

Salt. A natural flavor enhancer, salt also slows down the action of the yeast, keeping the dough on just the right leavening schedule for well-balanced flavor and texture. Take heed when experimenting with levels of salt in recipes: too little salt may leave bread tasting flat; too much may inhibit rising.

Fats. Fats make breads tender, moist, and palatable. They also help maintain the freshness of bread once it's baked. In bread, fats are added in the form of butter or margarine, salad oil, milk, eggs, or cheese.

Tips & Techniques for Yeast Breads

Let the following detailed information, as well as the photos on page 11, guide you as you make bread.

Dissolving yeast. Dissolving the yeast in water is the first—and one of the most important—steps in making yeast bread. Granular yeast will dissolve evenly and quickly if it's sprinkled over warm water. The temperature of the water is crucial: if the water is too hot, it will destroy the yeast and the dough won't rise; if it's too cold, the yeast will be slow to activate. For active dry yeast, the water should be about 110°F; for compressed cake yeast, it should be about 95°F. Test the water with a thermometer until you can recognize the right temperature by feel.

Most varieties of yeast should foam slightly about 5 minutes after being dissolved in water. Since different brands of yeast react to warm water in different ways, don't assume that the yeast is inactive if it fails to foam. To check whether yeast is still active, you can "proof" it by adding a generous pinch of sugar to the yeast and water mixture. In 10 to 15 minutes, a thick layer of small, foamy bubbles should be developing on the mixture's surface (see step 1 on page 11).

Mixing. The secret to a shapely, springy loaf of bread is the care and thoroughness with which you mix and knead the dough. Those are the steps that develop the gluten in the flour.

To measure flour accurately, stir it a bit in the container, lightly spoon it into a measuring cup for dry ingredients, and then level it off with a straight-edged knife. Do not pack flour into the cup or shake it down.

The amount of flour needed in the recipe will vary depending on minute amounts of moisture in the flour, as well as air temperature and humidity. The more you bake, the easier it will be to understand how the dough should look and feel at each stage.

Add flour to the yeast mixture gradually, stirring well after each addition, until the dough is evenly moistened. When enough flour has been stirred in to form a thick batter (about two-thirds the amount of flour given in a recipe), beat the batter very well with a heavy spoon or in an electric mixer on medium speed (use the paddle attachment if your mixer has one). If you beat the dough for about 5 minutes, you'll actually see the gluten developing—the batter becomes glossy and elastic, stretching with the spoon's motion. As the dough absorbs more flour, it tends to stick to itself, forming a ball. Gradually stir in enough additional flour to form a stiff dough.

Kneading. Most doughs can be kneaded either by hand or with the dough hook attachment of an electric mixer. There are pros and cons to each method. Although kneading by hand usually allows you to distinguish more clearly the development of elasticity and the changing texture of the dough as gluten develops, using a dough hook can cut the time and effort of kneading by about half.

To knead by hand, dust a smooth, clean surface (such as a wooden board) with flour. Turn the dough out onto the board and begin kneading. To knead, reach under the edge of dough farthest from you. Pull it toward you in a rolling motion (don't pull so hard that you tear the surface) and fold the dough almost in half. Then, with the heel of your palm, gently roll the ball away from you, lightly sealing the fold (see step 3 on page 11). Rotate the dough a quarter turn and continue this folding-rolling motion, turning the dough each time. Continue to knead, adding flour a little at a time to prevent the dough from sticking to the board, until the dough is smooth and elastic and no longer sticks to the board.

It's virtually impossible to overknead by hand. Although 5 minutes of kneading may be enough if you work quickly, the longer you spend at it (perhaps 20 or 30 minutes), the higher and fluffier your finished loaf will be. To test if you've kneaded enough, shape the dough into a ball, cover it, and let it rest on a lightly floured board. After 10 minutes, the dough should still be round and firm. If it's sticky and flattens significantly, knead for a few more minutes.

To knead with a dough hook, beat on high speed, adding flour a little at a time, until the dough pulls away from the sides of the bowl. Continue to beat until the dough becomes smooth, springs to the touch, and is no longer sticky (whole-grain dough will remain just slightly sticky). The kneading process usually takes 5 to 10 minutes; if the dough becomes elastic and soft during kneading and begins to cling to the bowl, turn it out onto a lightly floured board and finish kneading by hand.

Rising. Bread develops its flavor and texture while it rises. Let most breads rise in a warm place (75° to 80°F). Higher temperatures may cause fermentation, creating a slightly sour, yeasty flavor and a moist, holey dough. (Dough will rise at cooler temperatures, even in the refrigerator, but it will take longer.) Most yeast breads rise twice: the first time until doubled in bulk, the second time until almost doubled.

For the first rising, turn the dough over in a greased bowl to grease it all over. To prevent drying, cover the bowl with plastic wrap while the dough rises (plastic wrap draped loosely over the bowl and then covered with a cloth is ideal).

Like so many other aspects of bread making, rising times are variable, depending mainly on temperature. But times are also affected by the ingredients in the dough: whole-grain doughs take longer than white, and richer doughs take longer than those lower in fat. To test whether the dough has risen adequately, check it by poking two fingers about an inch into the dough. If the indentations remain when you remove your fingers, the dough has risen enough.

Punch the dough down with your fist (see step 5 on page 11). Then turn the dough out onto a lightly floured board and knead briefly (about 3 or 4 turns) to release the air bubbles. Shape the dough as directed and let it rise a second time until almost doubled. The time needed for the second rise is usually about half that of the first.

Timing & Delayed Action

Many people avoid baking yeast breads because they think it takes too much time. But there are techniques you can use to delay or even stop the rising action so you can continue at a later, more convenient time. For example, if you don't have time to shape the dough after it has risen, simply punch the dough down and let it rise again at room temperature until doubled. In fact, you can punch it down two or three times and still bake excellent bread (just watch closely—each successive rising will happen a little faster).

For a longer delay in rising time or to make dough ahead, let the dough rise overnight in the refrigerator or store it in the freezer until you're ready to bake it. To let it rise in the refrigerator, simply cover the bowl with plastic wrap. For freezing, wrap the dough in plastic wrap and then in foil; frozen dough should be thawed at room temperature and allowed to rise until doubled before you shape it.

Shaping. Dough can be shaped in a wide variety of forms. Just keep in mind that the loaf will rise both after it's shaped and during baking. Free-form loaves should be placed at least 3 inches from the edge of a baking sheet; dough in a loaf pan should have plenty of room for expansion. Dough that is braided should be done loosely, or the bread may tear at the center during baking.

In addition to the conventional loaf baked in a loaf pan, popular shapes include round or oval free-form loaves, straight or ring-shaped braided loaves, and baguettes. For other possibilities, consider clover-shaped Country Millet Bread (page 25), turban-shaped Apricot Turban Bread (page 66), and knotted and braided Orange-Saffron Bread (page 68).

After the dough is shaped, pinch any loose ends or sides together to prevent them from splitting in the oven. Place loaves seam sides down before baking.

Glazes and other finishes. Liquid glazes offer an extra embellishment when a special appearance is desired. *Egg washes* are most common: egg yolks give the dark, shiny finish often preferred on sweet, rich breads; egg whites lend a shiny finish to lean loaves, such as French bread. *Milk* and *cream* also give a dark, shiny finish. *Melted butter* and *oils* keep crusts tender and moist.

Any glaze can be used as a "glue" for solid toppings, such as nuts, seeds, herbs, granulated sugar, and sugar crystals. Just be sure the toppings reflect the ingredients of the loaf to which they're added.

Using a clean, soft brush, apply glazes to risen loaves before baking. Keep your touch light.

A range of other finishes can be applied to baked bread. For a rustic appearance, try a dusting of flour. Finish a sweet bread with a lacy topping of sifted powdered sugar or a drizzle of powdered sugar glaze.

Baking. Baking the bread is easy—just follow the recipe directions. Always preheat the oven. Remember that glass pans bake hotter than metal ones, so it's best to reduce the oven temperature by 25 degrees if you're using a glass pan. Position baking pans or sheets as much toward the center of the oven as possible. If you're baking more than one loaf at a time, you may want to switch the pans halfway through baking to ensure even browning. As soon as you take the bread from the oven, turn it out of the pan to cool on a rack unless otherwise directed in the recipe.

Storing. To store bread for a few days, let it cool completely, wrap it airtight, and store it either in the refrigerator or at room temperature. Kept in a plastic or paper bag at room temperature, savory yeast breads will remain relatively fresh for up to 3 days. Sweet yeast breads should be wrapped in plastic.

Bread also freezes beautifully for as long as 3 months. To freeze, wrap each loaf of cooled bread airtight in foil and then package in a plastic bag. When freezing sweet breads that call for glazing, apply the glaze after the bread is reheated, not before freezing.

Reheating. To reheat frozen bread, place it on a baking sheet in a 350° oven. Heat rolls and small loaves for about 15 minutes, large loaves for about 30 minutes. It's not necessary to thaw rolls and small loaves first, but large loaves should be unwrapped and allowed to thaw partially before reheating.

If the bread has a soft crust, protect it during reheating with a loose wrapping of foil; if the bread has a thick crust, leave it uncovered.

High-altitude baking. Baking at altitudes of 3,000 feet or above requires some adjustment of recipes.

Yeast bread dough rises more rapidly at higher altitudes, so you should decrease the amount of yeast you use. (The amount of leavening in quick breads should also be reduced.) To maintain flavor and texture, it's best to let the bread rise twice. Simply punch the dough down after the first rising and let it rise again until fully doubled before continuing with the recipe. You may also need to use a little more liquid in the dough, because liquid evaporates faster at high elevations and ingredients dry out more quickly.

When baking either yeast or quick breads at high altitudes, increase oven temperature to compensate for faster rising in the oven and slower heating. The lower boiling point for water also affects deep-frying methods for most breads. Below is a simple chart to guide you when baking in the high country.

Tools & Equipment

The only equipment you need for baking bread is a mixing bowl, measuring cups and spoons, a heavy spoon, and a baking pan—and even then, you could improvise if necessary. For a look at some of the most useful equipment, see page 6.

Measuring. A *thermometer* correctly measures the temperature of water or milk for dissolving yeast. For measuring ingredients, you'll need both dry and liquid *measuring cups* and *measuring spoons*.

Mixing and kneading. For mixing the dough by hand, a large, heavy *ceramic bowl* is ideal; it retains warmth and remains steady during beating. Use a

(Continued on page 12)

Guidelines for Baking at High Altitudes

	3,000 Feet	5,000 Feet	6,500 Feet and Above
Yeast	½ teaspoon less for every tablespoon (or package) at elevations above 3,000 feet		
Liquid	1 tablespoon more per cup	2 to 3 tablespoons more per cup	3 to 4 tablespoons more per cup
Sugar	1 tablespoon less per cup	2 tablespoons less per cup	3 tablespoons less per cup
Flour	1 tablespoon more per cup	2 tablespoons more per cup	3 tablespoons more per cup
Baking soda	⅛ teaspoon less per teaspoon	¼ teaspoon less per teaspoon	¼ teaspoon less per teaspoon
Baking powder	⅛ teaspoon less per teaspoon	¼ teaspoon less per teaspoon	¼ teaspoon less per teaspoon
Oven	25 degrees more for all elevations above 3,000 feet		
Deep-frying	3 degrees less for every 1,000 feet above 3,000 feet		

MAKING YEAST BREAD

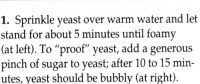

1. Sprinkle yeast over warm water and let stand for about 5 minutes until foamy (at left). To "proof" yeast, add a generous pinch of sugar to yeast; after 10 to 15 minutes, yeast should be bubbly (at right).

2. Stir in flour, 1 cup at a time, until well combined. If you stir long enough, you will see gluten developing in dough as it begins to pull in stretchy strands from sides of bowl, as shown.

3. Knead dough by pulling far end toward you in a rolling motion to fold it in half; then gently roll ball away from you with heel of your hand to seal fold, as shown.

4. Place dough in a greased bowl; turn over to grease top. Cover bowl (a loose covering of plastic wrap topped with a kitchen towel is ideal) and let dough rise until doubled.

5. Punch dough down with your fist to distribute air bubbles evenly; then turn dough out onto a lightly floured board and knead briefly to release any remaining air bubbles.

6. Shape dough as directed in recipe. When shaping dough for a loaf pan, place loaf in pan with any seams or blemishes facing down. Let rise again until almost doubled and then bake.

heavy spoon (sturdy wooden spoons are best) to beat in the flour.

An *electric mixer* is another option for mixing and kneading yeast doughs. A *paddle attachment* is often the best choice for mixing the dough, though ordinary beaters may also be used. For kneading the dough in an electric mixer, you have only one choice—a *dough hook* folds and pushes dough much like hand kneading.

Shaping and glazing. A *rolling pin* and a large, *sharp knife* are often used to shape dough. For small breads, you may need a *biscuit cutter* or *doughnut cutter*. A clean *pastry brush* is essential for glazing. Where a crusty finish is desired, a *water spray bottle* may be needed to mist bread before and during baking.

Baking. For many recipes, you'll need two 4- by 8-inch or 5- by 9-inch *loaf pans*. Although most loaf pans are made of stainless steel, there are other options. Glass and black-tinned pans are good conductors of heat and brown loaves faster; decrease oven temperature by 25 degrees when using them. Clay pans are also good heat conductors and produce crisp crusts. Cast iron makes a reliable bread pan, but it's slow to heat up and cool down. Tin and aluminum are other trustworthy choices.

Other pans that may be required include *baking sheets, cake pans* (both regular and spring-form), *tube pans, pie pans,* and *muffin tins*.

Griddle breads may require a *frying pan* or *griddle*, a *waffle iron*, and a *deep-frying thermometer*.

Cooling and slicing. A *cooling rack* will help prevent breads from getting soggy once they're out of the oven. Cut cooled breads with a long, *serrated bread knife*.

Troubleshooting Yeast Breads

Perhaps more than any other type of baking, making bread requires a sensitivity to each loaf's development from start to finish. A keen awareness of how the dough feels and looks will help you determine how much flour to add and how long to knead and bake. If you follow directions accurately and listen to your common sense, you'll have few problems producing delicious loaves of bread every time. But if problems do arise, below is a guide to help find a solution.

Troubleshooting Guidelines

Problem	Cause	Solutions
Bread flat	**1.** Dough not kneaded enough **2.** Yeast not properly dissolved **3.** Not enough flour in dough	1. Knead longer. 2. Proof yeast. 3. Let dough rest, covered, for 10 minutes after kneading. If dough is sticky and has spread sideways instead of rising, continue to knead a bit longer.
Bread collapsed in oven	**1.** Overrose in bread pan	1. Let rise for less time.
Bread collapsed while rising	**1.** Too much rising time	1. Knead dough briefly and let rise again until doubled. Continue as directed.
Bread split at sides	**1.** Too much flour in dough **2.** Too much dough in pan **3.** Uneven heat in oven	1. Decrease flour. 2. Fill pan no more than two-thirds full. 3. Use a pan that conducts heat well (see above).
Large holes in bread	**1.** Insufficient kneading **2.** Dough overrose **3.** Dough insufficiently kneaded after rising	1. Knead dough longer. 2. Punch dough down and let rise again until doubled. 3. Carefully knead (or press) out all air bubbles after dough has risen but before it's shaped.
Dense at bottom	**1.** Not enough rising time **2.** Too much flour	1. Let rise until fully doubled. 2. Decrease flour.
Bread dry and crumbly	**1.** Too much flour **2.** Dough overrose **3.** Oven temperature too low	1. Decrease flour. 2. Punch dough down and let rise again until doubled. 3. Increase oven temperature.
Skin on dough	**1.** Dough insufficiently covered while rising	1. Cover bowl with plastic wrap while rising.

FLOURS & GRAINS

OVER THE AGES, bread has been made from an array of different grains. And these days, bread bakers have a wider variety to choose from than ever before. Here are descriptions of the most common grains. Look for them in the recipes in this book or experiment with them to create recipes of your own.

All-purpose flour (regular white flour) is a blend of refined wheat flours especially suitable for making bread. It consists mainly of the starchy interior, or endosperm, of the wheat kernel after the bran and germ have been removed. Available either bleached or unbleached (the latter is stronger and creates a better-textured loaf), all-purpose flour is enriched with vitamins and minerals. Often, it's combined with a heavier whole-grain flour for added texture.

Bran is the brown outer layer of any grain, usually separated from the center of the grain during flour making. Bran is added to breads in small quantities (usually no more than a cup per recipe) for heartiness and special flavor. Most commonly derived from wheat, bran also comes from oats and rice. Bran is much coarser than flour and contributes added fiber.

Bread flour is a high-gluten flour that's been treated with potassium bromate, a conditioner that gives the dough greater tolerance during kneading and ensures a loaf with good volume and a fine grain.

Bulgur (also known as quick-cooking cracked wheat) is wheat berries from which the bran has been removed. The berries are then steamed, dried, and cracked into a variety of textures. Bulgur differs from plain **cracked wheat** in that the latter still contains the bran and germ and needs long cooking to soften the grains. Both are added in small amounts (¼ to ½ cup per recipe) to give whole-grain breads a nutty flavor and crunchy texture.

Cornmeal is ground from either white or yellow corn and comes in a variety of grinds, from fine to coarse. **Masa harina** is finely ground golden cornmeal; mixed with water into a paste, it's called "masa," the main ingredient in tortillas and tamales. **Polenta** is a coarsely ground cornmeal often used in Italian cooking to make hot cereals; it can also be added to cakes and breads.

Gluten flour is wheat flour that's been treated to remove nearly all the starch, leaving a very high gluten content. If a recipe uses a lot of a nonglutenous flour (such as soy flour), gluten flour added in small amounts will increase the bread's elasticity.

Graham flour is practically indistinguishable from regular whole wheat flour. It is stone-ground and contains noticeable flecks of the coarse bran layer.

Millet is a nutty-flavored grain available ground or whole in stores that sell bulk grain products. Because it contains only a trace of gluten, it can't replace a very high proportion of the wheat flour in breads; most recipes call for about 1 cup millet to 5 cups wheat flour.

Oatmeal comes from dehulled oats that have been ground to varying degrees of fineness. It can also be ground from rolled oats (oats that have been softened and rolled).

Rye is available in its whole-grain form (known as groats or berries), in cracked form, in light- to medium-ground flours, and in pumpernickel (the coarsest rye meal). Because rye is less glutenous than wheat, the two grains are often combined.

Semolina flour (also known as pasta flour) is the finely ground endosperm of durum wheat. Although this golden, sandlike flour is often exclusively used to make pasta, it can also add flavor and substance to some desserts and Italian-style breads.

Soy flour is ground from whole soybeans. It's rich in protein, iron, and thiamine and is a good source of dietary fiber. Because soy flour has no gluten, it must be mixed with wheat flour where yeast rising is desired. Soy flour often comes lightly toasted (toasting intensifies its flavor and improves digestibility).

Wheat germ, part of the wheat kernel, is sometimes added to breads in small quantities for nutritional enrichment and special flavor. Coarser than flour, wheat germ is rich in B and E vitamins, proteins, iron, and fat.

Whole wheat flour, ground from the entire wheat kernel, is heavier, richer in nutrients, and more perishable than all-purpose flour (unless you plan to use it up quickly, store it in the refrigerator to prevent the wheat germ from becoming rancid). Many people prefer stone-ground whole wheat to regularly milled whole wheat because the stone-ground variety is slightly coarser and has a heartier flavor.

Popular yeast breads offer a wonderful variety of flavors and textures. Here are some favorites (clockwise from left): rosemary-scented Fougasse (page 32), hearty Wheat Berry Nut Bread (page 23), S-shaped Sicilian Bread (page 33), and crusty Tuscan Olive Bread (page 32).

SAVORY YEAST BREADS

From big, hearty country loaves to dainty dinner rolls, and from the coarsest whole-grain rounds to moist batter breads, savory yeast breads offer choices to suit every baker. This chapter presents recipes for a vast array of savory breads. For the health minded, there are wholesome loaves enriched with wheat berries, bulgur, millet, and cereal mixes, such as nine-grain and muesli. Those who have enjoyed wonderful breads in distant countries will find recipes from Italy, France, Germany, Australia, Mexico, and the Middle East, among other places.

With experience will come the wish to experiment with different grains and seasonings, varied glazes and crust treatments, and unusual shapes. Creativity can be the essence of fine bread baking—the possibilities are endless. All it takes is an understanding of the basic ingredients and some practice with the techniques. For help, turn to the chapter beginning on page 7.

SUPER-FAST WHITE BREAD

This moist loaf requires no kneading and rises only once. For a finer-textured loaf, try the Basic White Bread variation; two risings give it a smaller crumb.

- 3 to 3⅓ cups all-purpose flour
- 1 package active dry yeast
- 1 tablespoon sugar
- ½ teaspoon salt
- 1¼ cups milk
- 1 tablespoon butter or margarine

1. Combine 3 cups of the flour, yeast, sugar, and salt in a food processor or large bowl; whirl (or mix) until blended.

2. Heat milk and butter to 130°F in a small pan over medium heat (butter need not melt completely).

To mix in a food processor, with motor running, pour in milk mixture and whirl until dough forms a ball and pulls away from sides of container (30 to 45 seconds); if dough clings, add more flour, 1 tablespoon at a time, and mix with short on-off bursts. Turn dough out onto a lightly floured board.

To mix with a dough hook, pour milk mixture into flour mixture. Beat on low speed, scraping flour to center of bowl with a spatula, until evenly moistened. Then beat on high speed until dough pulls away from sides of bowl (about 5 minutes), adding more flour, 1 tablespoon at a time, if dough is sticky. Turn dough out onto a lightly floured board.

To mix by hand, pour milk mixture into flour mixture and beat until dough is stretchy (5 to 7 minutes). Turn dough out onto a lightly floured board and dust lightly with more flour. Knead until smooth and satiny (about 10 minutes), adding just enough additional flour to prevent sticking.

3. Shape dough into a ball, cover with plastic wrap, and let rest for 10 minutes.

4. Uncover and press dough to release air. Pat into a 7- by 10-inch rectangle. Beginning at a short side, roll up dough, pinching edge against loaf to seal. Place seam side down in a greased 4- by 8-inch loaf pan. Cover lightly and let rise in a warm place until doubled (about 45 minutes).

5. Bake, uncovered, in a 400° oven until well browned (about 25 minutes). Turn out onto a rack and let cool. Makes 1 loaf (about 10 servings).

Per serving: 187 calories (15% from fat), 5 g protein, 34 g carbohydrates, 3 g total fat (1 g saturated fat), 7 mg cholesterol, 137 mg sodium

Basic White Bread

Follow steps 1–2 for **Super-fast White Bread** (at left). Place dough in a greased bowl and turn over to grease top. Cover with plastic wrap and let rise in a warm place until doubled (about 45 minutes). Punch dough down and knead briefly on a lightly floured board to release air.

Follow steps 3–5 (at left). Makes 1 loaf (about 10 servings).

Per serving: 191 calories (17% from fat), 5 g protein, 34 g carbohydrates, 3 g total fat (2 g saturated fat), 7 mg cholesterol, 137 mg sodium

Cheddar Cheese Pan Loaf

Follow steps 1–3 for **Super-fast White Bread** (at left) or Basic White Bread (above), but while dough is resting, melt 2 tablespoons **butter** or margarine in a small pan and have ready 1¾ cups (about 7 oz.) shredded **Cheddar cheese.**

After dough has rested, cut in half. Working with half at a time (keep remaining dough covered), cut into 8 equal pieces, shape each piece into a lumpy ball, and coat with some of the butter; arrange in a single layer in a 4- by 8-inch loaf pan and sprinkle with half the cheese. Repeat to shape remaining dough rounds, using remaining butter and cheese.

Omit step 4. Follow step 5, covering top with foil if cheese browns too quickly. Makes 1 loaf (about 10 servings).

Per serving: 287 calories (38% from fat), 10 g protein, 34 g carbohydrates, 12 g total fat (7 g saturated fat), 34 mg cholesterol, 284 mg sodium

Onion-Poppy Seed Loaf

Heat 1 tablespoon **butter** or margarine in a small pan over medium heat. Add 1 cup finely chopped **onions** and cook, stirring occasionally, until translucent (about 3 minutes); let cool.

Follow steps 1–2 for **Super-fast White Bread** (at left) or Basic White Bread (above), but add onions and 1 tablespoon **poppy seeds** after dough is mixed; whirl (or beat) until blended, adding flour as needed to prevent sticking. Follow steps 3–5. Makes 1 loaf (about 10 servings).

Per serving: 208 calories (20% from fat), 6 g protein, 35 g carbohydrates, 5 g total fat (2 g saturated fat), 10 mg cholesterol, 150 mg sodium

FRENCH BREAD

Finally, you can make a light and crusty French bread that rivals the best bakery fare. To do it, you need to know some tricks of the trade.

Professional bakers start with an unusually soft dough, so soft that it needs support from a canvas cradle while rising. To simulate cradles, the home baker can place shaped loaves side by side on a well-floured cloth (pulling the cloth up against the sides of each loaf helps maintain the shape and prevents sticking). Another secret is to let the dough rise slowly in three stages. Last, while the loaves are baking, spray them lightly with a mister, the type used for house plants; this duplicates the effect that commercial ovens' steam jets have on crusts.

> 2 packages active dry yeast
> 2½ cups tepid water (70° to 75°F)
> 2 teaspoons salt
> About 6½ cups bread flour or unbleached all-purpose flour
> Cornmeal

1. Sprinkle yeast over tepid water in large bowl of an electric mixer; let stand until foamy (about 5 minutes).

2. Add salt and 4 cups of the flour, 1 cup at a time, and beat (using a paddle attachment if you have one) on medium speed until dough begins to pull away from sides of bowl (about 10 minutes).

To knead by hand, turn out onto a floured board and gradually knead in about 2½ cups more flour, ½ cup at a time, until dough is smooth and satiny (about 15 minutes).

To knead with a dough hook, gradually beat in 2 cups more flour on low speed. Then beat on high speed until dough is springy and pulls cleanly from sides of bowl (about 8 minutes), adding more flour, 1 tablespoon at a time, if dough is sticky. Turn dough out onto a lightly floured board and knead by hand for 1 minute.

3. Place dough in a greased bowl; turn over to grease top. Cover with plastic wrap and let rise at room temperature until doubled (2 to 2½ hours).

4. Punch dough down, cover, and let rise again at room temperature until tripled (about 1½ hours).

5. Punch dough down and knead briefly on a lightly floured board to release air. Shape into a ball and cut into 3 pieces for regular loaves, 4 pieces for baguettes. Fold each piece in half. Cover and let rest for 5 minutes. Keeping remaining dough covered, pat one por-

tion into a ¾-inch-thick oval. Fold in half lengthwise and press lightly to seal edges. Turn dough seal side up and pat again into a longer ¾-inch-thick oval. Fold in half lengthwise again; with your hands, roll into a smooth loaf about 15 inches long for regular loaf, 20 inches long for baguette. Place seam side up 3 inches from long edge of a well-floured pastry cloth; pull cloth up against sides of loaf. Repeat to shape remaining dough, placing loaves on cloth and pulling cloth up against sides of each loaf.

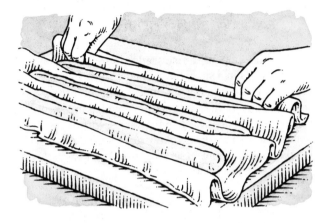

6. Cover lightly and let rise at room temperature until more than doubled (1½ to 2 hours). Meanwhile, sprinkle 2 greased baking sheets with cornmeal.

7. Turn loaves seam sides down onto sheets. With a razor blade, quickly make 3 diagonal slashes on top of each loaf. Spray loaves with water.

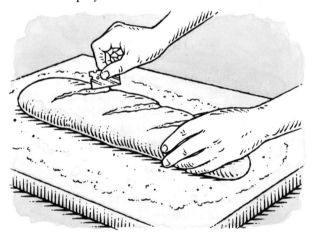

8. Bake in a 450° oven for 9 minutes, spraying loaves after 3, 6, and 9 minutes. Reduce oven temperature to 425° and bake until golden (16 to 20 more minutes), switching pan positions halfway through baking.

9. Turn oven off and leave door open for 3 minutes. Close door and let loaves stand in oven for 15 minutes.

(Continued on next page)

Transfer to racks and let cool. Makes 3 regular loaves (about 10 servings each) or 4 baguettes (about 8 servings each).

Per serving regular loaf: 115 calories (6% from fat), 4 g protein, 23 g carbohydrates, 1 g total fat (0.1 g saturated fat), 0 mg cholesterol, 148 mg sodium

---

Per serving baguette: 108 calories (6% from fat), 4 g protein, 21 g carbohydrates, 1 g total fat (0.1 g saturated fat), 0 mg cholesterol, 138 mg sodium

Seeded French Bread

. . . .

Mix 1 tablespoon *each* **anise seeds, poppy seeds,** and **sesame seeds** in a small bowl. Follow steps 1–6 for **French Bread** (page 17), but omit cornmeal. Instead sprinkle some of the seed mixture onto baking sheets. Follow step 7, but after spraying loaves, sprinkle with remaining seed mixture. Follow steps 8–9. Makes 3 regular loaves (about 10 servings each) or 4 baguettes (about 8 servings each).

Per serving regular loaf: 117 calories (9% from fat), 4 g protein, 22 g carbohydrates, 1 g total fat (0.1 g saturated fat), 0 mg cholesterol, 148 mg sodium

---

Per serving baguette: 110 calories (9% from fat), 4 g protein, 21 g carbohydrates, 1 g total fat (0.1 g saturated fat), 0 mg cholesterol, 138 mg sodium

• *Pictured on facing page* •

AUSTRALIAN DAMPER BREAD

. . . .

The original damper bread, reportedly invented by convicts of Australia's bush country, was a heavy, unleavened bread baked in camp-fire ashes. Today's version, while still a simple, rustic loaf, contains yeast, which lightens the texture and adds tangy flavor.

   1 **package active dry yeast**
 ¼ **cup warm water (about 110°F)**
   1 **cup warm milk (about 110°F)**
      About 3 cups all-purpose flour
   1 **tablespoon baking powder**
 ¾ **teaspoon salt**
   2 **tablespoons cold butter or margarine**

1. Sprinkle yeast over warm water in a small bowl; stir briefly. Let stand until foamy (about 5 minutes). Stir in milk; set aside.

2. Mix 3 cups of the flour, baking powder, and salt in

a large bowl. With a pastry blender or 2 knives, cut in butter until mixture resembles fine crumbs (or rub butter into flour mixture with your fingers). Add yeast mixture and stir until evenly moistened.

3. Turn dough out onto a lightly floured board and knead until smooth (2 to 3 minutes), adding more flour as needed to prevent sticking. Shape dough into a lumpy 5- to 6-inch round. Dust lightly with flour and place in a greased 8-inch-round cake pan. With a razor blade or sharp knife, make an X-shaped cut about ½ inch deep and 3 inches long in top of loaf.

4. Bake on lowest rack of a 375° oven until well browned (about 55 minutes). Turn out onto a rack and let cool briefly. Serve warm. Makes 1 loaf (about 10 servings).

Per serving: 181 calories (20% from fat), 5 g protein, 31 g carbohydrates, 4 g total fat (2 g saturated fat), 10 mg cholesterol, 347 mg sodium

• *Pictured on page 35* •

PANE FRANCESE

. . . .

A crisp, flour-dusted crust and a porous, chewy interior distinguish this Italian country bread. The trick to achieving the crisp, rather flat loaves is to use a wet, sticky dough (preferably prepared in a food processor) and to bake the bread in a very hot oven.

   1 **package active dry yeast**
 ¼ **cup warm water (about 110°F)**
      About 3 cups all-purpose flour
   1 **teaspoon *each* sugar and salt**
   1 **to 1¼ cups ice-cold water**

1. Sprinkle yeast over warm water in a small bowl; stir briefly. Let stand until foamy (about 5 minutes).

To mix and knead with a food processor, combine 3 cups of the flour, sugar, and salt in container. With motor running, pour in yeast mixture and slowly add 1 cup of the cold water. Whirl, scraping sides of container occasionally, until combined (if dough is dry or difficult to whirl, add more cold water, 1 to 2 teaspoons at a time). Continue to whirl until dough is shiny, elastic, and slightly sticky (3 to 4 minutes; dough should be soft and wet and form a thin, transparent skin when stretched). Sprinkle with about 2 tablespoons more flour; turn into a large bowl.

To mix and knead with a dough hook or by hand, mix 3 cups of the flour, sugar, and salt in a large bowl. Add yeast mixture and 1 cup of the cold water. Beat with an electric mixer on medium speed or with a

(Continued on page 20)

With its spongy, moist interior and extra-crisp crust, Australian Damper Bread (facing page) resembles a large, airy biscuit. It's best served warm from the oven with a generous helping of butter to melt on top.

heavy spoon until well blended. With a dough hook or heavy spoon, beat until dough is shiny, elastic, and slightly sticky (about 5 minutes with a dough hook, 10 to 20 minutes by hand), adding more cold water, 1 to 2 teaspoons at a time, if dough is dry or difficult to beat (dough should be soft and wet and form a thin, transparent skin when stretched).

2. Cover with plastic wrap. Let dough rise in a warm place until doubled (1½ to 2 hours) or in a refrigerator until next day.

3. Sprinkle dough with about 2 tablespoons more flour and turn out onto a well-floured board. Cut in half. With floured hands, lightly pat each half into a 7- by 8-inch rectangle. Beginning at a short side, roll up dough, at each turn sealing rolled edge against unrolled portion with heel of hand. Turn loaves seam sides down on board. Gently lift each loaf and generously sprinkle flour beneath; lightly dust top with flour. Cover lightly and let rest for 30 minutes.

4. Transfer loaves to a large greased baking sheet, picking up each loaf at either end (if dough sticks to board, scrape free with a spatula) and allowing dough to stretch to 12 to 14 inches long; space loaves about 4 inches apart. Cover lightly and let rise in a warm place until slightly puffy (about 15 minutes).

5. Place loaves, uncovered, in a 475° oven; immediately reduce oven temperature to 425° and bake until golden brown (20 to 30 minutes). For a crisper crust, turn off oven, prop door slightly ajar, and let loaves stand in oven for 10 minutes. Transfer to racks and let cool. Makes 2 loaves (about 6 servings each).

Per serving: 132 calories (5% from fat), 4 g protein, 27 g carbohydrates, 1 g total fat (0.1 g saturated fat), 0 mg cholesterol, 184 mg sodium

Add yeast and stir briefly; let stand until bubbly (about 10 minutes). Add salt and butter.

2. Stir in 1½ cups of the flour.

To knead by hand, beat in about ½ cup more flour, ¼ cup at a time, until dough pulls cleanly from sides of bowl. Turn dough out onto a lightly floured board and knead until smooth and elastic (10 to 20 minutes), adding more flour as needed to prevent sticking. Place in a greased bowl; turn over to grease top.

To knead with a dough hook, add ½ cup more flour and beat on high speed until dough is springy and pulls away from sides of bowl (about 8 minutes), adding more flour, a few tablespoons at a time, if dough is sticky.

3. Cover with plastic wrap and let rise in a warm place until doubled (45 to 60 minutes). Meanwhile, prepare Dutch Crunch Topping.

4. Punch dough down and knead briefly on a lightly floured board to release air. Shape into a loaf and place in a greased 4- by 8-inch loaf pan. Spread topping over dough. Let stand, uncovered, in a warm place until puffy (20 to 25 minutes).

5. Bake in a 375° oven until deep golden brown (50 to 60 minutes). Turn loaf out onto a rack and let cool. Makes 1 loaf (about 10 servings).

Dutch Crunch Topping. In a large bowl, stir together 2 teaspoons **sugar**, 2 packages **active dry yeast**, ¼ teaspoon **salt**, 6 tablespoons **white rice flour**, 1 teaspoon **salad oil**, and ⅓ cup **warm water** (about 110°F). Cover and let rise in a warm place until doubled (35 to 45 minutes). Stir well. If made ahead, cover and let stand for up to 15 minutes; stir before using.

Per serving: 153 calories (15% from fat), 4 g protein, 28 g carbohydrates, 2 g total fat (0.9 g saturated fat), 3 mg cholesterol, 177 mg sodium

DUTCH CRUNCH BREAD

This light-textured loaf with its crisp topping is especially popular for sandwiches.

> ¾ **cup warm water (about 110°F)**
> 1 **teaspoon sugar**
> 1 **package active dry yeast**
> ½ **teaspoon salt**
> 1 **tablespoon melted butter or margarine**
> 2 **to 2½ cups all-purpose flour**
>   **Dutch Crunch Topping (recipe follows)**

1. Combine warm water and sugar in a large bowl.

100% WHOLE WHEAT BREAD

Extra yeast gives this whole wheat bread a light, bouncy texture usually associated with white breads.

> 1½ **cups warm water (about 110°F)**
> 5 **tablespoons honey or molasses**
> 2 **packages active dry yeast**
> 4¾ **to 5¼ cups whole wheat flour**
> ¼ **cup butter or margarine, melted and cooled**
> 2 **teaspoons salt**
> 2 **large eggs**

1. Combine water and 1 tablespoon of the honey in a large bowl. Sprinkle with yeast; let stand until bubbly (about 10 minutes). Add 1½ cups of the flour; stir until blended. Cover with plastic wrap and let rise in a warm place until doubled (20 to 30 minutes).

2. Add butter, salt, eggs, and remaining 4 tablespoons honey to flour mixture; stir until blended. Beat in 2 cups more flour until thoroughly moistened.

3. Stir in 1¼ cups more flour.

To knead by hand, turn dough out onto a floured board and knead until smooth (about 10 minutes), adding just enough flour to prevent sticking.

To knead with a dough hook, beat on high speed until dough is springy and pulls away from sides of bowl (5 to 8 minutes), adding more flour, 1 tablespoon at a time, if dough is sticky.

4. Place dough in a greased bowl; turn over to grease top. Cover and let rise in a warm place until doubled (about 1 hour).

5. Punch dough down and knead briefly on a lightly floured board to release air. Cut dough in half. Shape each half into a loaf and place each in a greased 4- by 8-inch loaf pan. Cover lightly and let rise in a warm place until puffy (20 to 30 minutes).

6. Bake, uncovered, in a 375° oven until loaves are golden brown and sound hollow when tapped on bottoms (30 to 35 minutes). Turn out onto racks and let cool. Makes 2 loaves (about 10 servings each).

Per serving: 152 calories (21% from fat), 5 g protein, 26 g carbohydrates, 4 g total fat (2 g saturated fat), 27 mg cholesterol, 252 mg sodium

Cinnamon-Raisin Whole Wheat Bread

· ·

Follow steps 1–2 for **100% Whole Wheat Bread** (facing page), adding 1 cup **raisins** and 1 teaspoon **ground cinnamon** along with eggs. Follow steps 3–6. Makes 2 loaves (about 10 servings each).

Per serving: 174 calories (19% from fat), 5 g protein, 32 g carbohydrates, 4 g total fat (2 g saturated fat), 27 mg cholesterol, 253 mg sodium

Bulgur Wheat Bread

· ·

In a small bowl, combine ½ cup *each* **water** and **bulgur;** let stand until water is absorbed (about 45 minutes). Follow steps 1–2 for **100% Whole Wheat Bread** (facing page), adding bulgur mixture along with eggs.

Follow steps 3–6. Makes 2 loaves (about 10 servings each).

Per serving: 164 calories (20% from fat), 5 g protein, 29 g carbohydrates, 4 g total fat (2 g saturated fat), 27 mg cholesterol, 252 mg sodium

WHOLESOME NINE-GRAIN BREAD

· ·

Nine-grain cereal provides the ideal shortcut to this nubby and healthful multigrain bread.

  1½ **cups boiling water**
   1 **cup nine-grain cereal**
   1 **package active dry yeast**
  ¼ **cup warm water (about 110°F)**
  ¼ **cup butter or margarine**
  ½ **cup milk**
   2 **large eggs, beaten**
   2 **tablespoons honey**
  ½ **teaspoon salt**
   3 **cups whole wheat flour**
     About 1½ cups all-purpose flour

1. Pour boiling water over cereal in a small bowl; let stand until softened (about 1 hour).

2. Sprinkle yeast over warm water in a large bowl; stir briefly. Let stand until foamy (about 5 minutes). Meanwhile, heat butter and milk to 110°F in a small pan over medium heat. Add to yeast mixture, along with eggs, honey, salt, and cereal; stir until blended.

3. Stir in whole wheat flour and 1 cup of the all-purpose flour.

To knead by hand, turn dough out onto a floured board and knead until springy and just slightly sticky (15 to 20 minutes), adding more all-purpose flour as needed to prevent sticking.

To knead with a dough hook, beat on high speed until dough is springy and pulls away from sides of bowl (about 7 minutes), adding more all-purpose flour, a few tablespoons at a time, if dough is sticky. Turn out onto a lightly floured board and knead by hand for 2 minutes.

4. Place dough in a greased bowl; turn over to grease top. Cover with plastic wrap and let rise in a warm place until doubled (1 to 1½ hours).

5. Punch dough down and knead briefly on a lightly floured board to release air. Cut dough in half. Shape

(Continued on page 23)

*Swiss muesli, a crunchy combination of dried fruits, nuts, and oats,
joins a host of delicious ingredients to produce slightly sweet and richly flavored
Muesli Bread (facing page).*

each half into a loaf and place each in a greased 4- by 8-inch loaf pan. Cover lightly and let rise in a warm place until doubled (about 45 minutes).

6. Bake, uncovered, in a 375° oven until loaves are lightly browned and sound hollow when tapped on bottoms (35 to 40 minutes). Turn out onto racks and let cool. Makes 2 loaves (about 10 servings each).

Per serving: 143 calories (24 percent from fat), 5 g protein, 23 g carbohydrates, 4 g total fat (2 g saturated fat), 28 mg cholesterol, 89 mg sodium

• *Pictured on facing page* •

MUESLI BREAD

In Switzerland, the hearty combination of dried fruits, oats, and nuts known as *muesli* is a popular breakfast food. Different varieties of this European-style granola are now widely available in supermarkets and specialty food stores. Here, it's used in a nutty loaf that rivals even the best breakfast fare. A thick slice, toasted and spread with butter, makes a sweet and satisfying morning treat.

- ¼ **cup warm water (about 110°F)**
- 3 **tablespoons honey**
- 1 **tablespoon active dry yeast**
- 2 **tablespoons salad oil**
- 2 **tablespoons butter or margarine**
- ¾ **teaspoon ground cinnamon**
- 1 **teaspoon salt**
- ½ **cup raisins**
- 1½ **cups muesli**
- 1½ **cups boiling water**
- ⅓ **cup low-fat buttermilk**
- ½ **cup whole wheat flour**
   About 4½ cups all-purpose flour
- 3 **tablespoons milk**

1. Combine warm water and 1 tablespoon of the honey in a small bowl. Add yeast and stir briefly; let stand until bubbly (about 10 minutes). Meanwhile, combine remaining 2 tablespoons honey, oil, butter, cinnamon, salt, raisins, and 1 cup of the muesli in a large bowl. Add boiling water and stir until moistened; let stand until cereal is softened (about 5 minutes). Stir in buttermilk and yeast mixture.

2. Add whole wheat flour and 3½ cups of the all-purpose flour; stir until blended.

To knead by hand, stir in 1 cup more all-purpose flour. Turn dough out onto a floured board and knead until smooth and elastic (15 to 20 minutes), adding

more all-purpose flour as needed to prevent sticking.

To knead with a dough hook, beat in 1 cup more all-purpose flour on low speed until dough pulls away from sides of bowl. Then beat on high speed until dough is springy and no longer sticky (about 8 minutes), adding more all-purpose flour, 1 tablespoon at a time, if dough clings to sides of bowl (dough should be slightly sticky). Turn out onto a lightly floured board and knead by hand for 2 minutes.

3. Place dough in a greased bowl; turn over to grease top. Cover with plastic wrap and let rise in a warm place until doubled (about 1 hour).

4. Punch dough down and knead briefly on a floured board to release air. Cut dough in half. Shape each half into a loaf and place each in a greased 4- by 8-inch loaf pan. Soften remaining ½ cup muesli in milk; spoon over loaves. Cover lightly and let rise in a warm place until almost doubled (about 45 minutes).

5. Bake, uncovered, in a 350° oven until loaves are browned and sound hollow when tapped on bottoms (about 50 minutes); if topping browns too quickly, cover loosely with foil. Turn out onto racks and let cool. Makes 2 loaves (about 10 servings each).

Per serving: 187 calories (18% from fat), 4 g protein, 34 g carbohydrates, 4 g total fat (1 g saturated fat), 4 mg cholesterol, 138 mg sodium

• *Pictured on page 14* •

WHEAT BERRY NUT BREAD

Wheat berries are whole hulled wheat kernels. Cooked, they lend a chewy texture and slightly nutty flavor to breads and cereals. In this recipe, crunchy chopped walnuts add even more nuttiness to the bread.

- ⅓ **cup wheat berries**
- 1½ **cups tap water**
- 1 **tablespoon active dry yeast**
- 1¾ **cups warm water (about 110°F)**
- 2 **tablespoons olive oil or salad oil**
- 2 **tablespoons honey**
- 1½ **teaspoons salt**
- 1 **cup whole wheat flour**
- 3 **to 3½ cups all-purpose flour**
- 1 **cup walnuts or unsalted macadamia nuts, coarsely chopped**

1. Combine wheat berries and tap water in a small pan. Bring to a boil over high heat; remove from heat

and let stand for 1 hour. Return to heat and bring to a boil. Reduce heat, cover, and simmer for 15 minutes; drain.

2. Sprinkle yeast over ½ cup of the warm water in a large bowl; let stand until foamy (about 5 minutes). Add wheat berries, remaining 1¼ cups warm water, oil, honey, and salt; stir until blended.

3. Stir in whole wheat flour and 2½ cups of the all-purpose flour.

To knead by hand, add ½ cup more of the all-purpose flour and nuts; stir until combined. Turn dough out onto a floured board and knead until smooth and elastic (about 20 minutes), adding more all-purpose flour as needed to prevent sticking.

To knead with a dough hook, add ½ cup more all-purpose flour and beat on high speed until dough is springy and pulls away from sides of bowl (about 8 minutes), adding more all-purpose flour, a few table-spoons at a time, if dough is sticky. Add nuts and beat on low speed until evenly distributed. Turn out onto a lightly floured board and knead by hand for 1 minute.

4. Place dough in a greased bowl; turn over to grease top. Cover with plastic wrap and let rise in a warm place until doubled (about 1 hour).

5. Punch dough down and knead briefly on a lightly floured board to release air. Cut dough into thirds. Shape each piece into an oblong. Place well apart on a large greased baking sheet. Cover lightly and let rise in a warm place until doubled (about 45 minutes).

6. Bake, uncovered, in a 375° oven until loaves are browned and sound hollow when tapped on bottoms (30 to 35 minutes). Transfer to racks and let cool. Makes 3 loaves (about 8 servings each).

Per serving: 140 calories (31% from fat), 4 g protein, 21 g carbohy-drates, 5 g total fat (0.5 g saturated fat), 0 mg cholesterol, 139 mg sodium

• *Pictured on page 27* •

FRENCH WALNUT BREAD

These simple, rustic loaves have a tender, fine-grained texture and a discreet nutty flavor. Serve the bread toasted and topped with cheese and thin slices of fresh pear for a savory crostini (page 44); or, for a sweeter flavor, offer generous slices alongside Ricotta Cheese Spread with Anise Honey (page 125).

  1 **cup coarsely chopped walnuts**
  1 **package active dry yeast**

  1 **cup warm water (about 110°F)**
  ¾ **teaspoon salt**
  1 **teaspoon sugar**
  1½ **cups rye flour**
  1½ **cups all-purpose flour**
  1 **tablespoon melted butter or margarine**

1. Spread walnuts on a baking sheet and toast in a 350° oven until lightly browned (about 10 minutes). Let cool.

2. Sprinkle yeast over warm water in a large bowl; let stand until foamy (about 5 minutes). Add salt, sugar, rye flour, 1⅓ cups of the all-purpose flour, and nuts; stir until blended.

3. Turn dough out onto a floured board. Knead until smooth and no longer sticky (about 10 minutes). Cut dough in half. Shape each half into a 2- by 10-inch log. Place loaves about 4 inches apart on a greased baking sheet. Cover lightly and let rise in a warm place until puffy (30 to 40 minutes).

4. Brush with butter. Bake in a 425° oven until well browned (about 20 minutes). Transfer to racks and let cool. Makes 2 loaves (about 8 servings each).

Per serving: 138 calories (38% from fat), 3 g protein, 19 g carbohy-drates, 6 g total fat (1 g saturated fat), 2 mg cholesterol, 112 mg sodium

HONEY MULTIGRAIN HEARTH BREAD

Plump, round, and flavorful, this fine-textured bread contains a variety of grains. Look for soy flour in a specialty market or health-food store.

  1½ **cups warm water (about 110°F)**
  3 **tablespoons honey**
  1 **package active dry yeast**
  ¾ **cup milk, at room temperature**
  1½ **cups stone-ground whole wheat flour or graham flour**
      About 3¾ cups all-purpose flour
  3 **tablespoons *each* yellow cornmeal and regular rolled oats**
  3 **tablespoons *each* soy flour and salad oil**
  ½ **teaspoon salt**

1. Combine 1 cup of the warm water and honey in a large bowl. Add yeast and stir briefly; let stand until bubbly (about 10 minutes). Add milk, whole wheat flour, and ¾ cup of the all-purpose flour; stir until evenly moistened. Cover with plastic wrap and let rise in a warm place until doubled (1 to 2 hours). Meanwhile, in a small bowl, combine remaining ½ cup warm water, cornmeal, and oats; let stand until grains are softened (1 to 2 hours).

2. Add cornmeal mixture to yeast mixture; stir until blended. Stir in 2¾ cups more all-purpose flour, soy flour, oil, and salt.

To knead by hand, beat dough until stretchy. Turn dough out onto a lightly floured board and knead until smooth and elastic (about 10 minutes), adding more all-purpose flour as needed to prevent sticking. Place in a greased bowl; turn over to grease top.

To knead with a dough hook, add ¼ cup more all-purpose flour and beat on high speed until dough pulls away from sides of bowl (5 to 8 minutes), adding more all-purpose flour, 1 tablespoon at a time, if dough is sticky.

3. Cover and let rise in a warm place until doubled (about 1 hour).

4. Punch dough down and knead briefly on a lightly floured board to release air. Shape dough into a ball. Place on a greased baking sheet and pat into a 7-inch round. Cover lightly and let rise in a warm place until puffy (15 to 20 minutes).

5. Bake, uncovered, in a 350° oven until well browned (50 to 55 minutes). Transfer to a rack and let cool. Makes 1 loaf (16 to 18 servings).

Per serving: 193 calories (16% from fat), 6 g protein, 35 g carbohydrates, 4 g total fat (1 g saturated fat), 2 mg cholesterol, 71 mg sodium

COUNTRY MILLET BREAD

Since millet flour has only a trace of gluten, it's not common in bread baking. In fact, the ancient Etruscans used millet to make *puls*, a gruel or porridge still consumed today. In this clover-shaped loaf, millet combines with other flours to produce a delicately crunchy and light-textured bread.

  2 **packages active dry yeast**
  3 **cups warm water (about 110°F)**
  3 **tablespoons melted butter or margarine**
  3 **tablespoons honey**
  1 **teaspoon salt**
  1 **cup ground millet**
  ½ **cup whole millet**

  ⅔ **cup unprocessed bran or wheat germ**
  2 **cups whole wheat flour**
     About 2½ cups bread flour
     Cornmeal

1. Sprinkle yeast over warm water in a large bowl; let stand until foamy (about 5 minutes).

2. Add butter, honey, salt, ground millet, whole millet, bran, whole wheat flour, and 1 cup of the bread flour; stir until blended.

To knead by hand, stir in 1 cup more bread flour. Turn dough out onto a floured board and knead until springy and just slightly sticky (about 15 minutes), adding more bread flour as needed to prevent sticking.

To knead with a dough hook, beat in 1½ cups more bread flour on low speed. Then beat on medium speed until dough is springy and pulls away from sides of bowl (about 10 minutes; dough should be slightly sticky). Turn dough out onto a lightly floured board and knead by hand for 1 minute.

3. Place dough in a greased bowl; turn over to grease top. Cover with plastic wrap and let rise in a warm place until doubled (about 1 hour).

4. Punch dough down and knead briefly on a lightly floured board to release air. Sprinkle 2 baking sheets with cornmeal. Cut dough in half. Shape each half into a smooth round and place each on a baking sheet; lightly dust each loaf with more bread flour. Using a sharp knife, make 3 cuts through dough, starting 2 inches from center and extending to edge, to make three-leaf-clover shape. Cover lightly and let rise in a warm place until puffy (about 30 minutes).

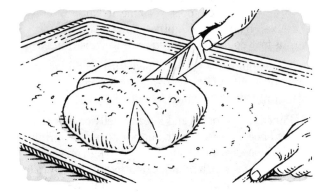

5. Bake in a 350° oven until loaves are lightly browned and sound hollow when tapped on bottoms (about 30 minutes). Transfer to racks and let cool. Makes 2 loaves (about 10 servings each).

Per serving: 176 calories (14% from fat), 5 g protein, 33 g carbohydrates, 3 g total fat (1 g saturated fat), 5 mg cholesterol, 130 mg sodium

RAISIN PUMPERNICKEL BREAD

Dense and dark, this pumpernickel bread has considerable flavor and texture appeal.

       2 packages active dry yeast
    1¼ cups warm water (about 110°F)
       1 cup *each* rye flour and whole wheat flour
     ¼ cup dark molasses
       2 tablespoons unsweetened cocoa
       1 tablespoon instant coffee powder
     ½ teaspoon salt
          About 1 cup all-purpose flour
     ½ cup raisins
       2 tablespoons cornmeal
       1 large egg white beaten with 1 tablespoon water

1. Sprinkle yeast over warm water in a large bowl; let stand until foamy (about 5 minutes).

2. Add rye flour, whole wheat flour, molasses, cocoa, coffee powder, and salt; stir until blended.

To knead by hand, stir in 1 cup of the all-purpose flour. Turn dough out onto a floured board and knead until smooth and elastic (about 5 minutes), adding just enough additional all-purpose flour to prevent sticking. Press raisins into dough and knead until well distributed.

To knead with a dough hook, beat in 1 cup of the all-purpose flour on low speed. Then beat on medium speed until dough is stretchy and pulls away from sides of bowl (about 3 minutes), adding more all-purpose flour, 1 tablespoon at a time, if dough is sticky. Turn dough out onto a lightly floured board, press raisins into dough, and knead until well distributed.

3. Place dough in a greased bowl; turn over to grease top. Cover with plastic wrap and let rise in a warm place until almost doubled (about 1 hour).

4. Punch dough down and knead briefly on a lightly floured board to release air. Shape into a ball. Sprinkle a baking sheet with cornmeal, place dough on sheet, and pat into a 6-inch round. Cover lightly and let rise in a warm place until puffy (about 30 minutes).

5. Brush loaf with egg white mixture. Bake in a 350° oven until loaf is well browned and sounds hollow when tapped on bottom (about 30 minutes). Transfer to a rack and let cool. Makes 1 loaf (12 to 14 servings).

Per serving: 140 calories (6% from fat), 4 g protein, 30 g carbohydrates, 1 g total fat (0.1 g saturated fat), 0 mg cholesterol, 94 mg sodium

• Pictured on facing page •

SUNFLOWER PUMPERNICKEL BREAD

Dark beer, rye, and three kinds of seeds contribute to the dense texture and sour flavor of this country loaf. Paired with Quick Chicken Liver Pâté (page 125) and apple slices, it becomes a delicious snack for a cold-weather picnic. (For the sourest flavor, let the beer mixture ferment for a full 48 hours before mixing and kneading the dough.)

       2 packages active dry yeast
     ¾ cup warm water (about 110°F)
     ¾ cup stout (dark, strong beer), at room temperature
       1 tablespoon sugar
     ¾ cup cracked rye
    1½ cups rye flour
     ¾ cup unsalted sunflower seeds
     ¼ cup flax seeds
       1 teaspoon salt
       2 tablespoons salad oil
          About 1½ cups all-purpose flour
       3 tablespoons sesame seeds

1. Sprinkle 1 package of the yeast over ½ cup of the warm water in a large bowl; let stand until foamy (about 5 minutes). Add beer, sugar, cracked rye, and ½ cup of the rye flour; stir until blended. Cover with plastic wrap and let stand until bubbly and sour smelling (15 to 48 hours).

2. Combine remaining 1 package yeast and remaining ¼ cup warm water in a small bowl. Stir into beer mixture. Add sunflower seeds, flax seeds, salt, and oil; stir until blended. Stir in 1½ cups of the all-purpose flour and remaining 1 cup rye flour until evenly moistened.

3. Turn dough out onto a well-floured board and knead until smooth and no longer sticky (15 to 20 minutes), adding more all-purpose flour as needed to prevent sticking.

4. Shape dough into a 6½-inch round. Sprinkle board with sesame seeds and gently roll dough in seeds. Place on a greased baking sheet. Cover lightly and let rise in a warm place until puffy (about 40 minutes).

5. Bake, uncovered, in a 350° oven until well browned (about 40 minutes). Transfer to a rack and let cool. Makes 1 loaf (about 12 servings).

Per serving: 241 calories (33% from fat), 8 g protein, 34 g carbohydrates, 9 g total fat (1 g saturated fat), 0 mg cholesterol, 187 mg sodium*

*Nutritional data for flax seeds not available.

*These country breads share the full, rich flavor and coarse texture prized
in the best peasant-style loaves (clockwise from left): Russian Cheese Bread
(page 98), seed-crusted Sunflower Pumpernickel Bread (facing page),
and French Walnut Bread (page 24).*

DARK RYE BREAD

Darkly caramelized sugar and unsweetened cocoa give this loaf its deep brown color; the sturdy texture comes from dark rye flour. Note that sugar caramelized to this degree smokes; it also spatters when water is added. Provide ample ventilation and protect your hands with heavy potholders.

    ½ **cup sugar**
    ¾ **cup boiling water**
    3 **packages active dry yeast**
    2 **cups warm water (about 110°F)**
    ¼ **cup unsweetened cocoa**
    2 **teaspoons salt**
    2 **tablespoons caraway seeds**
    2 **tablespoons melted solid vegetable shortening, butter, or margarine**
        About 3½ cups all-purpose flour
    2 **cups dark rye flour**
    2 **tablespoons cornmeal**

1. Melt sugar in a wide nonstick frying pan over medium-high heat, stirring often, until caramelized to a brown syrup (it should not be charred and burned smelling). Immediately add boiling water and cook, stirring, until liquid is reduced to ½ cup. Let cool.

2. Sprinkle yeast over warm water in a large bowl; let stand until foamy (about 5 minutes). Add sugar mixture, cocoa, salt, caraway seeds, shortening, and 2 cups of the all-purpose flour; beat until smoothly blended. Add rye flour. Using an electric mixer, beat on medium speed for 4 minutes. With your hands, work in 1 cup more all-purpose flour. Turn dough out onto a floured board, cover with plastic wrap, and let rest for 10 minutes.

3. Knead until dough is elastic and just slightly sticky (about 10 minutes), adding more all-purpose flour as needed to prevent sticking. Place in a greased bowl; turn over to grease top. Cover and let rise in a warm place until doubled (about 1 hour).

4. Punch dough down and turn over; cover and let rise again in a warm place until doubled (about 1 more hour).

5. Sprinkle a baking sheet with cornmeal. Punch dough down and knead briefly on a lightly floured board to release air. Cut dough in half. Shape each half into a ball and flatten slightly; place loaves 3 to 4 inches apart on sheet. Cover lightly and let rise in a warm place until doubled (about 1¼ hours).

6. Bake, uncovered, in a 375° oven until loaves sound hollow when tapped on bottoms (about 35 minutes).

Transfer to racks and let cool. Makes 2 loaves (8 or 9 servings each).

Per serving: 194 calories (12% from fat), 6 g protein, 38 g carbohydrates, 3 g total fat (0.6 g saturated fat), 0 mg cholesterol, 261 mg sodium

ORANGE RYE BREAD

Not your typical rye, this fine-textured bread derives its sweetness and citrus flavor from a purée of candied orange peel.

    1 **cup tap water**
    ⅓ **cup firmly packed dark brown sugar**
    ½ **cup dark corn syrup**
  1½ **teaspoons salt**
    ¼ **cup butter or margarine**
    1 **teaspoon anise seeds**
    3 **cups rye flour**
    1 **package active dry yeast**
    ¼ **cup warm water (about 110°F)**
    ½ **cup (about 3½ oz.) candied orange peel**
    1 **cup milk**
    4 **to 5 cups all-purpose flour**

1. Bring ½ cup of the tap water, brown sugar, corn syrup, and salt to a boil in a small pan; cook, stirring, until sugar is dissolved. Remove from heat; add butter and stir until melted.

2. Crush anise seeds with a mortar and pestle (or whirl in a food processor or blender). In a large bowl, stir together anise seeds, rye flour, and sugar mixture until blended; let cool.

3. Sprinkle yeast over warm water in a small bowl; stir briefly. Let stand until foamy (about 5 minutes). Meanwhile, in a food processor or blender, whirl orange peel with remaining ½ cup tap water until puréed. Add purée, yeast mixture, and milk to rye mixture; stir until blended.

4. Stir in 4 cups of the all-purpose flour until blended.

To knead by hand, turn dough out onto a lightly floured board and knead until smooth and satiny (10 to 15 minutes), adding more all-purpose flour as needed to prevent sticking. Place in a greased bowl; turn over to grease top.

To knead with a dough hook, beat on high speed until dough is springy and pulls away from sides of bowl (about 8 minutes), adding more all-purpose flour, a few tablespoons at a time, if dough is sticky.

(Continued on page 31)

COFFEE CAN BATTER BREADS

BATTER BREAD is made from very soft yeast dough, almost like a batter, as the name indicates. Vigorous beating takes the place of kneading, and the bread rises only once. The loaf is baked in an ordinary coffee can (26-ounce size). The can offers support for the soft dough during rising and also gives the bread its distinctive shape—tall, round, and domed.

Be sure your coffee can still has its plastic lid; it's useful at two different stages. First, it seals the batter in the can for freezing if you want to prepare the dough ahead of time and bake the bread later. Second, the lid tells you when the dough is ready to bake—it pops off! If the lid comes off before the dough reaches the can rim, don't worry; simply replace the lid and wait until the dough pushes it off.

Sandwich White Bread

- 1 package active dry yeast
- ⅓ cup warm water (about 110°F)
- 1 cup plus 2 tablespoons milk
- 1½ tablespoons salad oil
- 2 tablespoons sugar
- 1 teaspoon salt
  Dash of ground ginger
- 3¾ cups all-purpose flour
  Melted butter or margarine

1. Sprinkle yeast over warm water in a large bowl; let stand until foamy (about 5 minutes). Add milk, oil, sugar, salt, and ginger; stir until blended. Stir in 2¾ cups of the flour.

2. Add remaining 1 cup flour. Beat vigorously with a heavy spoon until dough pulls away from sides of bowl but is still soft and sticky.

3. Turn batter into a well-greased coffee can (26-oz. size). Cover with well-greased plastic lid. (At this point, you may freeze for up to 2 weeks.)

4. Let rise in a warm place until batter pushes off lid (1 to 1½ hours; 6 to 8 hours if frozen).

5. Bake in can, uncovered, on lowest rack of a 350° oven until crust is well browned (about 50 minutes). Lightly brush crust with butter. Let cool in can on a rack for 5 minutes; turn out onto rack and let cool upright. Makes 1 loaf (about 10 servings).

Per serving: 231 calories (20% from fat), 6 g protein, 40 g carbohydrates, 5 g total fat (2 g saturated fat), 7 mg cholesterol, 247 mg sodium

Old-fashioned Oatmeal Bread

- 1 package active dry yeast
- ¼ cup warm water (about 110°F)
- 1 cup plus 2 tablespoons warm milk (about 110°F)
- 2 tablespoons butter or margarine, at room temperature
- 2 tablespoons honey or molasses
- 1 teaspoon salt
- ½ teaspoon ground cinnamon
- 1 cup quick-cooking or regular rolled oats
- 1 large egg, lightly beaten
- 3 cups all-purpose flour
  Melted butter or margarine

1. Sprinkle yeast over warm water in a large bowl; stir briefly. Let stand until foamy (about 5 minutes).

2. Add milk, butter, honey, salt, cinnamon, oats, and egg; stir until mixture is blended. Stir in 2 cups of the flour.

3. Follow steps 2–5 for Sandwich White Bread (at left). Makes 1 loaf (about 10 servings).

Per serving: 231 calories (20% from fat), 7 g protein, 39 g carbohydrates, 5 g total fat (2 g saturated fat), 31 mg cholesterol, 265 mg sodium

Cottage Cheese–Dill Bread

- 1 package active dry yeast
- ¼ cup warm water (about 110°F)
- 2 tablespoons sugar
- 1 tablespoon dried minced onion
- 2 teaspoons dried dill weed
- 1¼ teaspoons salt
- ¼ teaspoon baking soda
- 1 cup small-curd cottage cheese
- 1 tablespoon melted butter or margarine
- 1 large egg, lightly beaten
- 2½ cups all-purpose flour
  Melted butter or margarine

1. Sprinkle yeast over warm water in a large bowl; stir briefly. Let stand until foamy (about 5 minutes). Add sugar, onion, dill weed, salt, baking soda, cheese, butter, and egg; stir until blended. Stir in 1½ cups of the flour.

2. Follow steps 2–5 for Sandwich White Bread (at left), decreasing baking time from about 50 minutes to 35 to 40 minutes. Makes 1 loaf (about 10 servings).

Per serving: 170 calories (18% from fat), 7 g protein, 28 g carbohydrates, 3 g total fat (2 g saturated fat), 28 mg cholesterol, 410 mg sodium

*Crusty Garden Vegetable Bread (facing page) bursts with fresh flavor, thanks to
a bounty of vegetables mixed into the dough. Among them are carrots, tomatoes, broccoli,
bell peppers, zucchini, eggplant, and onions.*

5. Cover with plastic wrap and let rise in a warm place until doubled (2 to 3 hours).

6. Punch dough down and knead briefly on a lightly floured board to release air. Cut dough into 3 equal pieces. Shape each piece into a loaf and place each in a greased 4- by 8-inch loaf pan. Cover lightly and let rise in a warm place until doubled (45 to 60 minutes).

7. Bake, uncovered, in a 350° oven until loaves are well browned and sound hollow when tapped on bottoms (35 to 40 minutes). Turn out onto racks and let cool. Makes 3 loaves (about 10 servings each).

Per serving: 167 calories (15% from fat), 3 g protein, 32 g carbohydrates, 3 g total fat (1 g saturated fat), 5 mg cholesterol, 140 mg sodium

• Pictured on facing page •

GARDEN VEGETABLE BREAD

Cut a slice of this herb-seasoned bread and sample a garden plot run wild! Precook the vegetables to soften their crunch and bring out their flavor; then mix them into the dough (as it rises, the dough absorbs moisture from the cooked vegetables, so you'll need to add a fair amount of flour after the first rising).

> Garden Vegetables (recipe follows)
> 1 package active dry yeast
> ¾ cup warm water (about 110°F)
> 1 large egg
> ½ to 1 teaspoon salt
> 1 tablespoon sugar
> 1 tablespoon *each* minced fresh thyme and fresh tarragon; or 1 teaspoon *each* dried thyme and dried tarragon
> ¼ cup minced fresh basil or 1½ tablespoons dried basil
> 1 tablespoon olive oil or salad oil
> ¼ cup grated Parmesan cheese
> 1 cup whole wheat flour
> About 3 cups all-purpose flour

1. Prepare Garden Vegetables; set aside.

2. Sprinkle yeast over warm water in a large bowl; let stand until foamy (about 5 minutes). Add egg, salt, sugar, thyme, tarragon, basil, oil, cheese, whole wheat flour, and 1⅔ cups of the all-purpose flour; stir until blended.

3. Beat with dough hook of an electric mixer or a heavy spoon until well blended.

To knead by hand, turn dough out onto a floured board and knead until smooth and elastic (8 to 12

minutes), adding more all-purpose flour as needed to prevent sticking.

To knead with a dough hook, beat on high speed until dough is elastic and pulls away from sides of bowl (5 to 8 minutes), adding more all-purpose flour, 1 tablespoon at a time, if dough feels sticky and clings to sides of bowl.

4. Turn dough out onto a floured board. Add ½ cup more all-purpose flour to vegetable mixture; stir gently. Gradually knead vegetables into dough (do not mash) until evenly distributed, adding more all-purpose flour as needed to prevent sticking (dough should feel sticky). Place in a greased bowl; turn over to grease top. Cover with plastic wrap and let rise in a warm place until doubled (about 1½ hours).

5. Punch dough down, turn out on a well-floured board, and sprinkle lightly with flour. Knead until dough is soft but no longer sticky, adding more all-purpose flour as needed (½ to ⅔ cup flour total) to prevent sticking. Shape into a round and place on a greased baking sheet. Cover lightly and let rise in a warm place until puffy (about 30 minutes).

6. Bake, uncovered, in a 350° oven until well browned (40 to 45 minutes). Transfer to a rack and let cool briefly. Serve warm. Makes 1 loaf (10 to 12 servings).

Garden Vegetables. Cut 1 medium-size **onion** in half lengthwise; then slice crosswise ¾ inch thick. Heat 2 tablespoons **olive oil** or salad oil in a wide frying pan over medium heat. Add onion; 2 cloves **garlic,** minced or pressed; and ½ cup 1-inch chunks **eggplant.** Cook, stirring, until eggplant is barely tender (about 10 minutes). Add ⅓ cup 1-inch chunks **pear-shaped (Roma-type) tomatoes;** cook, stirring, until tomatoes are slightly softened (1 to 2 minutes). Let cool.

Meanwhile, seed ¼ *each* medium-size **red bell pepper** and **green bell pepper** (or use half of one color pepper) and cut lengthwise into narrow strips. Cut 1 small **carrot,** 1 small stalk **celery,** and 1 small **zucchini** into ¾-inch-thick diagonal slices. Prepare ¾ cup **broccoli flowerets** and cut 2 **green onions** into 3-inch pieces.

Bring 3 cups **water** to a boil in a 1- to 2-quart pan over high heat. Cook vegetables separately, boiling carrot and broccoli for 1 minute, zucchini and bell peppers for 45 seconds, and celery and green onions for 30 seconds. Lift from pan with a slotted spoon, immerse in cold water, and drain. Pat dry and add to tomato mixture.

Per serving: 191 calories (21% from fat), 6 g protein, 32 g carbohydrates, 4 g total fat (1 g saturated fat), 16 mg cholesterol, 157 mg sodium

• *Pictured on page 14* •

FOUGASSE

Fougasse is a flat, irregular loaf originally baked directly on the hearth. In France, its shape is often that of a ladder or tree. In this classic version, rosemary and garlic flavor the soft, oval loaf, but some variations may include nuts or herbs.

> 1 package active dry yeast
> ¾ cup warm water (about 110°F)
> ½ cup olive oil
> 1 clove garlic, minced or pressed
> 1½ tablespoons chopped fresh rosemary or 2 teaspoons dried rosemary
> ¾ teaspoon salt
> About 2½ cups all-purpose flour

1. Sprinkle yeast over warm water in a large bowl; let stand until foamy (about 5 minutes). Meanwhile, combine ¼ cup of the oil, garlic, and rosemary in a small frying pan. Cook over low heat, stirring, until garlic is soft (about 2 minutes). Remove from heat and let cool briefly; pour into yeast mixture. Add salt and 2½ cups of the flour; stir until blended.

2. Turn dough out onto a lightly floured board and knead until smooth and elastic (about 15 minutes), adding more flour as needed to prevent sticking. Place in a greased bowl; turn over to grease top. Cover with plastic wrap and let rise in a warm place until doubled (about 1 hour).

3. Punch dough down and knead briefly on a lightly floured board to release air. Roll dough into a ¾-inch-thick oval about 7 by 10 inches and place on a greased baking sheet. Starting 1 inch from edge and working toward center (but without cutting through center), cut 3 diagonal slashes through dough on each long side of oval. Gently pull cuts apart. Cover lightly and let rise in a warm place until doubled (about 1 hour).

4. Brush dough with remaining ¼ cup oil. Bake in a 400° oven until lightly browned (15 to 20 minutes). Transfer to a rack and let cool. Makes 1 loaf (about 8 servings).

Per serving: 279 calories (49% from fat), 4 g protein, 31 g carbohydrates, 15 g total fat (2 g saturated fat), 0 mg cholesterol, 207 mg sodium

• *Pictured on page 14* •

TUSCAN OLIVE BREAD

In Tuscany, thick slices of spongy, slightly salty olive bread are enjoyed with country cheeses and Chianti. With its crisp, flour-dusted crust and soft interior speckled with tart green olives, this version of the rustic bread rivals the best Italian fare.

> 1 package active dry yeast
> 2 cups warm water (about 110°F)
> 1 tablespoon extra-virgin olive oil
> 1¼ teaspoons salt
> 2½ cups bread flour
> About 2½ cups all-purpose flour
> 1 cup Sicilian-style olives, coarsely chopped and patted dry

1. Sprinkle yeast over warm water in a large bowl; let stand until foamy (about 5 minutes). Add oil and salt.

2. Stir in bread flour and 2 cups of the all-purpose flour.

To knead by hand, turn dough out onto a lightly floured board. Knead until smooth and elastic (about 20 minutes), adding more all-purpose flour as needed to prevent sticking.

To knead with a dough hook, beat on medium speed until dough is springy and pulls cleanly from sides of bowl (about 8 minutes), adding more all-purpose flour, a few tablespoons at a time, if dough is sticky. Turn dough out onto a lightly floured board.

3. Press olives into dough and knead until evenly distributed. Place in a greased bowl; turn over to grease top. Cover with plastic wrap and let rise in a warm place until doubled (1 to 1½ hours).

4. Punch dough down and knead briefly on a lightly floured board to release air. Cut dough in half. Shape each half into a ball, gently pulling top surface under until smooth. Place loaves tucked sides down on lightly greased baking sheets. Dust lightly with flour. Cover lightly and let rise in a warm place until almost doubled (about 1 hour).

5. Bake in a 400° oven until loaves are lightly browned and sound hollow when tapped on bottoms (about 30 minutes). Transfer to racks and let cool. Makes 2 loaves (about 10 servings each).

Per serving: 139 calories (16% from fat), 4 g protein, 25 g carbohydrates, 2 g total fat (0.3 g saturated fat), 0 mg cholesterol, 301 mg sodium

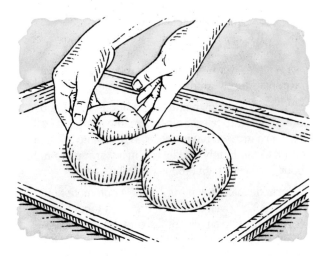

• Pictured on page 14 •

SICILIAN BREAD

Semolina is a golden flour ground from the hard part of durum wheat. Often used for making pasta, it contributes nutlike flavor to these traditional S-shaped Italian breads. The wonderfully elastic dough dries easily, so keep any unused portions well covered while shaping loaves.

   1¼ cups warm water (about 110°F)
   1 tablespoon brown sugar
   1 package active dry yeast
   1 tablespoon olive oil
   2 teaspoons salt
   2½ cups finely ground semolina
   1 cup bread flour or all-purpose flour
   1 to 2 tablespoons sesame seeds

1. Combine warm water and sugar in a large bowl. Add yeast and stir briefly; let stand until bubbly (about 10 minutes). Add oil, salt, and semolina; stir until blended.

2. Stir in bread flour.

To knead by hand, stir mixture until combined. Turn out onto a board and knead roughly until dough is smooth and very elastic (about 10 minutes).

To knead with a dough hook, beat on medium speed until dough is smooth, firm, and springy (about 5 minutes).

3. Place dough in a greased bowl; turn over to grease top. Cover with plastic wrap and let rise in a warm place until doubled (1 to 1½ hours).

4. Punch dough down and knead briefly on a board to release air. Cover and let rest for 5 minutes. Cut dough in half. Working with half at a time (keep remaining dough covered), roll each into a rope about 20 inches long. Form each rope into an S-shape by snugly coiling ends in opposite directions. Place each loaf on a greased baking sheet. Spray loaves with water and sprinkle with sesame seeds. Cover lightly and let rise in a warm place until doubled (about 1 hour).

5. Spray again with water and bake in a 425° oven for 9 minutes, spraying loaves after 3, 6, and 9 minutes. Reduce heat to 400° and continue to bake until loaves are golden brown and sound hollow when tapped on bottoms (20 to 25 more minutes), switching pan positions halfway through baking. Transfer to racks and let cool. Makes 2 loaves (about 10 servings each).

Per serving: 119 calories (15% from fat), 4 g protein, 21 g carbohydrates, 2 g total fat (0.3 g saturated fat), 0 mg cholesterol, 221 mg sodium

POLENTA CHEESE BREAD

Coarse Italian cornmeal and Cheddar cheese give this light and airy loaf its distinctive flavor. The dough is kneaded in a food processor.

   1 cup warm water (about 110°F)
   2 tablespoons sugar
   1 package active dry yeast
   4 ounces sharp Cheddar cheese, cut into small chunks
      About 3¼ cups all-purpose flour
   ½ cup polenta or yellow cornmeal
   1 teaspoon salt
   1 large egg

1. Combine warm water and 1 teaspoon of the sugar in a small bowl. Add yeast and stir briefly; let stand until bubbly (about 10 minutes). Meanwhile, combine cheese, 3¼ cups of the flour, polenta, salt, and remaining sugar in a food processor; whirl until cheese is finely chopped.

2. Add egg and whirl until combined. With motor running, slowly pour in yeast mixture and whirl until blended (about 45 seconds). Add more flour, 1 tablespoon at a time, if dough is too wet (dough should be slightly sticky). Place in a greased bowl; turn over to grease top. Cover with plastic wrap and let rise in a warm place until doubled (1 to 1½ hours).

3. Punch dough down and knead briefly on a lightly floured board to release air. Shape into a smooth ball. Place on a greased baking sheet and pat into a 7-inch round. Cover lightly and let rise in a warm place until about 2½ inches high (about 1 hour).

4. Sprinkle loaf with about 1 tablespoon more flour. Bake in a 375° oven until well browned (about 35 minutes). Transfer to a rack and let cool. Makes 1 loaf (about 10 servings).

Per serving: 245 calories (20% from fat), 9 g protein, 40 g carbohydrates, 5 g total fat (3 g saturated fat), 33 mg cholesterol, 298 mg sodium

• *Pictured on facing page* •

ROSEMARY BREAD

In Italy, different variations of this fragrant, soft-textured loaf have been popular for centuries. On the Thursday of Easter week, when it was customary for the devout to visit several different churches, vendors at church doors would sell tiny versions of the bread, each adorned with a cross on top. This larger version also bears the traditional cross. Whole wheat flour is added to the batter to produce a more flavorful, fuller-bodied loaf. The dough offers a wonderful canvas for other herbs. If you like, use dill instead of rosemary.

- 1 **package active dry yeast**
- 1 **cup warm water (about 110°F)**
- 2 **tablespoons chopped fresh rosemary or dried rosemary, crumbled**
- ½ **teaspoon sugar**
- 1 **teaspoon regular salt**
- 1 **cup whole wheat flour**
  About 2 cups all-purpose flour
  Olive oil
- 1 **large egg, lightly beaten**
- ½ **teaspoon coarse salt**

1. Sprinkle yeast over warm water in a large bowl; let stand until foamy (about 5 minutes). Add rosemary, sugar, regular salt, whole wheat flour, and about ¾ cup of the all-purpose flour. Beat with a heavy spoon or an electric mixer (using a paddle attachment if you have one) until dough pulls away from sides of bowl in stretchy strands.

2. Beat in 1¼ cups more all-purpose flour.

To knead by hand, turn dough out onto a lightly floured board and knead until smooth and springy (about 10 minutes), adding more all-purpose flour as needed to prevent sticking. Place in a greased bowl; turn over to grease top.

To knead with a dough hook, beat on medium speed until dough is springy and pulls cleanly from sides of bowl (5 to 7 minutes), adding more all-purpose flour, 1 tablespoon at a time, if dough is sticky.

3. Cover with plastic wrap and let rise in a warm place until doubled (about 1 hour).

4. Punch dough down and knead briefly on a lightly floured board to release air. Shape into a ball, gently pulling top surface under until smooth.

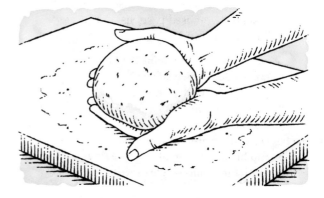

5. Place on a greased baking sheet; brush lightly with oil. Cover lightly and let rise in a warm place until doubled (about 45 minutes).

6. Brush loaf with egg. With a razor blade or very sharp knife, make a small X-shaped cut in top of loaf. Sprinkle with coarse salt. Bake in a 375° oven until loaf is browned and sounds hollow when tapped on bottom (about 45 minutes). Transfer to a rack and let cool. Makes 1 loaf (about 10 servings).

Per serving: 156 calories (14% from fat), 5 g protein, 29 g carbohydrates, 2 g total fat (0.4 g saturated fat), 21 mg cholesterol, 301 mg sodium

Dill Bread

Follow step 1 for **Rosemary Bread** (at left), but omit rosemary. Instead, add 2 tablespoons chopped **fresh dill** or 1 tablespoon dried dill weed, crumbled. Follow steps 2–6. Makes 1 loaf (about 10 servings).

Per serving: 155 calories (14% from fat), 5 g protein, 28 g carbohydrates, 2 g total fat (0.4 g saturated fat), 21 mg cholesterol, 302 mg sodium

*Luxuriate in the simple things in life: a wedge of cheese, a crisp apple or plush fig,
and freshly baked bread. For a blend of tastes and textures, offer a loaf of Rosemary Bread
(facing page) along with Italian-style Pane Francese (page 18).*

GRUYÈRE BRAID

Baked in a large braid of crusty white bread, Gruyère cheese melts temptingly into the dough. Serve the bread warm with butter; or spread thin toasted slices with Pesto Butter (page 124) and top with cured ham or prosciutto for a delicious open-face sandwich.

> 1 package active dry yeast
> ¼ cup warm water (about 110°F)
> ¾ cup dry white wine
> 1 tablespoon sugar
> About 3½ cups all-purpose flour
> ¾ cup (¼ lb. plus ¼ cup) butter or margarine, at room temperature
> 5 large eggs
> ½ pound Gruyère cheese, cut into ¼-inch cubes

1. Sprinkle yeast over warm water in a large bowl; stir briefly. Let stand until foamy (about 5 minutes). Stir in wine, sugar, and 1 cup of the flour. Using a heavy spoon or an electric mixer, gradually beat in butter. Add 4 of the eggs, one at a time, beating well after each addition.

2. Stir in 2½ cups more flour.

To knead by hand, vigorously pull dough in large handfuls from bowl and toss back repeatedly until dough pulls from hands and bowl and is satiny and smooth (about 20 minutes; dough should be soft). Press cheese into dough.

To knead with a dough hook, beat on high speed until dough is smooth, satiny, and no longer sticky (about 10 minutes). Stir in cheese.

3. Place dough in a greased bowl; turn over to grease top. Cover with plastic wrap and let rise in a warm place until doubled (about 1 hour).

4. Punch dough down and knead briefly on a lightly floured board to release air. Cut dough in half. Keeping remaining dough covered, divide one portion into 3 equal pieces, roll each piece into a rope about 15 inches long, and arrange about 1 inch apart on a greased baking sheet; braid loosely, pinching ends together and tucking under loaf. Repeat to shape remaining dough, using another baking sheet.

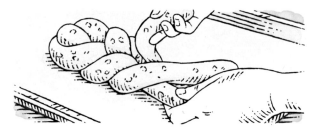

5. Cover lightly and let rise in a warm place until puffy (about 30 minutes).

6. Beat remaining egg and brush over dough. Bake in a 400° oven until golden brown (25 to 30 minutes). Transfer to racks and let cool. Makes 2 loaves (about 10 servings each).

Per serving: 217 calories (53% from fat), 7 g protein, 18 g carbohydrates, 13 g total fat (7 g saturated fat), 84 mg cholesterol, 125 mg sodium

GREEN CHILE BREAD

Soft, light textured, and subtly flavored with a purée of green chiles, this loaf makes terrific sandwich bread. Pair it with sliced jack or Cheddar cheese and brown it on a griddle or in a wide frying pan for a delicious grilled cheese sandwich. Or you can toast a slice and top it with poached eggs for a simple brunch or supper.

> 1 large can (about 7 oz.) diced green chiles
> 1 package active dry yeast
> ¼ cup warm water (about 110°F)
> ½ cup milk
> 2 tablespoons butter or margarine
> 1 teaspoon salt
> 1 tablespoon sugar
> ½ teaspoon ground red pepper (cayenne)
> About 4 cups all-purpose flour

1. Whirl chiles in a food processor or blender until puréed. Set aside.

2. Sprinkle yeast over warm water in a large bowl; stir briefly. Let stand until foamy (about 5 minutes). Meanwhile, heat milk and butter to 110°F in a small pan over low heat (butter need not melt completely); stir into yeast mixture. Add chile purée, salt, sugar, and red pepper.

3. Stir in 2 cups of the flour.

To knead by hand, stir in 1½ cups more flour until moistened; beat vigorously with a heavy spoon until stretchy (about 10 minutes). Turn out onto a lightly floured board and knead until smooth and satiny (about 8 minutes), adding more flour as needed to prevent sticking. Place in a greased bowl; turn over to grease top.

To knead with a dough hook, beat in 1½ cups more flour on low speed. Then beat on high speed until dough is springy and pulls away from sides of bowl

(7 to 10 minutes), adding more flour, 1 tablespoon at a time, if dough is sticky.

4. Cover with plastic wrap and let rise in a warm place until doubled (about 1½ hours).

5. Punch dough down and knead briefly on a lightly floured board to release air. Pat into an 8- by 12-inch rectangle. Beginning at a short side, roll up dough, pinching edge against loaf to seal. Place seam side down in a greased 5- by 9-inch loaf pan. Cover lightly and let rise in a warm place until dough is 1½ inches above pan rim (about 1 hour).

6. Bake, uncovered, in a 375° oven until golden brown (about 35 minutes). Turn out onto a rack and let cool. Makes 1 loaf (10 to 12 servings).

Per serving: 201 calories (17% from fat), 5 g protein, 36 g carbohydrates, 4 g total fat (2 g saturated fat), 7 mg cholesterol, 338 mg sodium

SOUR CREAM & CHIVE POTATO BREAD

Butter, sour cream, and chives add scrumptious flavor to plain potato bread. Shape the dough into large loaves or into rolls about the size of a baked potato.

> 1 **pound russet potatoes, peeled and quartered, or 1½ cups instant mashed potatoes**
> ¼ **cup butter or margarine, at room temperature**
> ½ **cup *each* milk and sour cream**
> 1 **teaspoon salt**
> 1 **large egg**
> ½ **cup chopped chives**
> 1 **package active dry yeast**
> ¼ **cup warm water (about 110°F)**
> 5½ **to 6½ cups all-purpose flour**

1. Place russet potatoes in a 3- to 4-quart pan; pour in water to cover. Bring to a gentle boil and boil until tender when pierced (about 25 minutes). Drain. (Or, if using instant mashed potatoes, bring 1½ cups water to a boil in a small pan; remove from heat and add potato flakes, stirring until dissolved.) In a large bowl, combine potatoes, butter, milk, sour cream, and salt. Beat with an electric mixer (or mash with a potato masher) until smooth. Beat in egg. Stir in chives.

2. Sprinkle yeast over warm water in a small bowl; stir briefly. Let stand until foamy (about 5 minutes). Add to potato mixture; stir until blended.

3. Stir in 2 cups of the flour.

To knead by hand, gradually stir in 3 cups more flour. Turn out on a floured board and knead until smooth and springy (15 to 20 minutes), adding more flour as needed to prevent sticking (dough should be soft but not sticky). Place in a greased bowl; turn over to grease top.

To knead with a dough hook, gradually beat in 3 cups more flour on low speed. Then beat on medium-high speed until dough is springy and pulls away from sides of bowl (about 8 minutes), adding more flour, a few tablespoons at a time, if dough is sticky.

4. Cover with plastic wrap and let rise in a warm place until doubled (about 1 hour).

5. Punch dough down and knead briefly on a lightly floured board to release air. Cover and let rest for 5 minutes.

6. Cut dough in half and work with half at a time (keep remaining dough covered).

To shape into rolls, cut a half into 6 equal pieces and shape into oblong rolls. Place 3 inches apart on a greased baking sheet. Repeat to shape remaining dough.

To shape into loaves, pat a half into an 8- by 12-inch rectangle. Beginning at a short side, roll up, pinching edge against loaf to seal. Place seam side down in a 5- by 9-inch loaf pan. Repeat to shape remaining dough.

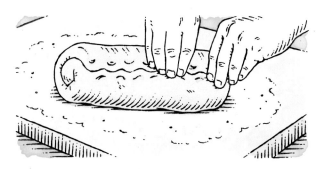

7. Cover lightly and let rise in a warm place until puffy (30 to 45 minutes).

8. Bake, uncovered, in a 375° oven until lightly browned (30 minutes for rolls, switching pan positions halfway through baking; 35 minutes for loaves). Transfer to racks and let cool. Makes 12 large rolls or 2 loaves (about 10 servings each).

Per roll: 333 calories (22% from fat), 9 g protein, 55 g carbohydrates, 8 g total fat (4 g saturated fat), 34 mg cholesterol, 242 mg sodium

Per serving: 200 calories (22% from fat), 5 g protein, 33 g carbohydrates, 5 g total fat (2 g saturated fat), 20 mg cholesterol, 145 mg sodium

A thick layer of soft white bread encloses a savory filling of spinach, bell peppers, artichoke hearts, and Gruyère. One wedge of Torte Florentine (facing page) makes a meal in itself.

• *Pictured on facing page* •

TORTE FLORENTINE

Spinach, artichoke hearts, bell peppers, and two kinds of cheese combine in a garlicky and highly seasoned filling for an old-fashioned torte. Since it can be made ahead and travels well, this crusty pie is ideal for picnics and potlucks. To reheat, warm in a 350° oven for 20 minutes.

    1   tablespoon olive oil or salad oil
    1   small onion, finely chopped
    5   large eggs
    1   package (about 10 oz.) frozen artichoke
        hearts, thawed and finely chopped
    1   package (about 10 oz.) frozen chopped
        spinach, thawed and squeezed dry
    ½   *each* medium-size red bell pepper and
        yellow bell pepper, thinly sliced
    1   tablespoon thinly sliced fresh basil
    2   large cloves garlic, minced or pressed
    3   tablespoons grated Parmesan cheese
    1   cup (about 4 oz.) grated Gruyère cheese
    1   teaspoon salt
    ½   teaspoon pepper
        Super-fast White Bread dough (page 16)
    1   tablespoon whipping cream

1. Heat oil in a small frying pan over medium heat. Add onion and cook, stirring occasionally, until translucent (about 3 minutes). In a large bowl, lightly beat 4 of the eggs. Add onion, artichokes, spinach, red bell pepper, yellow bell pepper, basil, garlic, Parmesan, Gruyère, salt, and pepper; stir until well blended. Set aside.

2. Follow steps 1–3 for Super-fast White Bread (page 16). Cut off a quarter of the dough; reserve for decoration. Cut off a third of the remaining dough for top and cover. On a lightly floured board, roll large portion into a 12-inch round. Fit dough round over bottom and up sides of a greased 2½- by 8½-inch springform pan. Spoon vegetable filling over dough, spreading evenly to edge of dough.

3. Roll remaining dough for top into an 8½-inch round. Cut a vent in center. Place dough round over filling and pinch sides over top to seal. Cover and let rise in a warm place until puffy (about 30 minutes). Meanwhile, roll out reserved dough and cut out decorative shapes. In a small bowl, beat remaining egg and cream. Lightly brush torte with egg mixture, add decorations, and brush with more egg mixture.

4. Bake in a 350° oven until browned (30 to 40 minutes). Let cool on a rack for 15 minutes. Carefully remove pan sides and let cool completely. Makes 1 torte (about 8 servings).

Per serving: 322 calories (37% from fat), 16 g protein, 35 g carbohydrates, 13 g total fat (6 g saturated fat), 158 mg cholesterol, 556 mg sodium

PITA BREAD

Steam makes the hollow in the middle of these small Middle Eastern loaves; they're ideal for filling with sliced meats, cheese, and other sandwich fixings.

    1   package active dry yeast
    1½   cups warm water (about 110°F)
    ½   teaspoon salt
    2   tablespoons olive oil
    1   cup whole wheat flour
    3 to 3½ cups all-purpose flour

1. Sprinkle yeast over warm water in a large bowl; let stand until foamy (about 5 minutes). Add salt and oil; stir until blended.

2. Stir in whole wheat flour and 2½ cups of the all-purpose flour.

To knead by hand, turn dough out onto a floured board and knead until smooth and elastic (15 to 20 minutes), adding more all-purpose flour as needed to prevent sticking.

To knead with a dough hook, add ½ cup more all-purpose flour and beat on low speed until combined. Then beat on high speed until dough is elastic and pulls cleanly from sides of bowl (about 10 minutes), adding more all-purpose flour, a few tablespoons at a time, if dough is sticky.

3. Place dough in a greased bowl; turn over to grease top. Cover with plastic wrap and let rise in a warm place until doubled (about 1 hour).

4. Punch dough down and knead briefly on a lightly floured board to release air. Cut dough into 12 equal pieces. Roll each into an ⅛-inch-thick round. Place 2 inches apart on greased baking sheets. (If using one oven, cover unbaked rounds while baking others.)

5. Bake on lowest rack of a 500° oven until puffed and speckled brown (5 to 6 minutes). Transfer to racks and let cool for 1 minute; then seal in a plastic bag to soften. Makes 12 pita breads (1 serving each).

Per serving: 191 calories (18% from fat), 5 g protein, 34 g carbohydrates, 4 g total fat (1 g saturated fat), 0 mg cholesterol, 93 mg sodium

INDIVIDUAL SAVORY PIZZAS

Choose from two savory toppings for these individual pizzas. In the classic Italian version, tomato sauce glistens under a layer of melted cheese and a sprinkling of oregano; in a more contemporary presentation, goat cheese combines with slow-cooked onions.

    1   **package active dry yeast**
1½   **cups warm water (about 110°F)**
  ½   **teaspoon salt**
       About 3 tablespoons olive oil
       About 3⅔ cups all-purpose flour
       Tomato & Cheese or Caramelized Onions & Goat Cheese topping (recipes follow)
       Salt and pepper

1. Sprinkle yeast over warm water in a large bowl; let stand until foamy (about 5 minutes). Stir in the ½ teaspoon salt and 1 tablespoon of the oil. Stir in 2¼ cups of the flour. Beat with an electric mixer (using a paddle attachment if you have one) on high speed until dough is glossy and stretchy (3 to 5 minutes).

2. Stir in 1⅓ cups more flour.

To knead by hand, turn dough out onto a lightly floured board and knead until smooth and springy (about 10 minutes), adding more flour as needed to prevent sticking. Place in a greased bowl; turn over to grease top.

To knead with a dough hook, beat on medium speed until dough is springy and pulls cleanly from sides of bowl (5 to 7 minutes), adding more flour, 1 tablespoon at a time, if dough is sticky.

3. Cover with plastic wrap. Let rise in a warm place until doubled (about 45 minutes) or in a refrigerator until next day. Meanwhile, prepare topping of your choice.

4. Punch dough down and knead briefly on a lightly floured board to release air. Cut dough into 6 equal balls. Roll each into a 7-inch round and place, 2 to a sheet, on baking sheets (if using one oven, shape only 4 pizzas; roll remaining pizzas and let stand while first batch bakes).

5. Brush rounds with remaining oil. Let rise, uncovered, in a warm place until puffy (15 to 30 minutes). Prick each several times in center with a fork.

6. Bake in a 450° oven for 5 minutes. Apply topping as directed; return to oven and continue to bake until golden brown on top and crusty on bottom (10 to 12 more minutes), switching pan positions halfway through baking. Season to taste with salt and pepper. Makes 6 servings.

Tomato & Cheese. In a blender or food processor, whirl 1½ pounds quartered **tomatoes** or 1 can (about 14½ oz.) tomatoes and their liquid until coarsely puréed. Pour into a 3- to 4-quart pan and bring to a boil; reduce heat and simmer, uncovered, until reduced to about 1 cup (about 30 minutes). Remove from heat. Spread over partially baked crusts to within ½ inch of edges. Top with 1 pound **mozzarella cheese,** thinly sliced; ¼ cup minced **fresh oregano** or 2 tablespoons dried oregano; and ¼ cup grated **Parmesan cheese.** Drizzle with **olive oil.**

Per serving: 649 calories (42% from fat), 26 g protein, 68 g carbohydrates, 31 g total fat (12 g saturated fat), 62 mg cholesterol, 539 mg sodium

Caramelized Onions & Goat Cheese. Cut 2 medium-size **onions** in half lengthwise; then slice crosswise ½ inch thick. Heat 2 tablespoons **olive oil** in an 8- to 10-inch frying pan over medium-low heat. Add onions and cook, stirring occasionally, until very soft (about 30 minutes); set aside.

In a small bowl, stir together 1 cup (about 8 oz.) **goat cheese,** ½ cup (about 4 oz.) **part-skim ricotta cheese,** and ¼ cup grated **Parmesan cheese.** Crumble over partially baked crusts. Top with onions. Sprinkle with 1 tablespoon minced **fresh thyme** or 2 teaspoons dried thyme.

Per serving: 591 calories (41% from fat), 21 g protein, 67 g carbohydrates, 27 g total fat (11 g saturated fat), 38 mg cholesterol, 467 mg sodium

HAMBURGER BUNS

A soft, light interior and a delicate crust topped with crunchy sesame seeds make these homemade buns perfect companions for ground beef patties with all the fixings. For convenience, you can store the buns airtight in a plastic bag and refrigerate or freeze.

  ½   **cup instant mashed potatoes**
    1   **cup boiling water**
    1   **package active dry yeast**
  ¼   **cup warm water (about 110°F)**
    1   **cup small-curd cottage cheese**
  ¼   **cup sugar**
    2   **tablespoons salad oil**
    2   **large eggs**
    1   **teaspoon salt**
       About 4½ cups all-purpose flour
  ¼   **cup sesame seeds or instant toasted onion**

1. Combine potatoes and boiling water in a large bowl; stir with a fork until evenly moistened. Let cool for at least 5 minutes. Meanwhile, sprinkle yeast over warm water in a small bowl; stir briefly. Let stand until foamy (about 5 minutes).

2. Add cheese, sugar, oil, 1 of the eggs, and salt to potato mixture. Stir in yeast mixture.

To knead by hand, stir in 2 cups of the flour and beat with a heavy spoon until stretchy (about 5 minutes). Stir in 2 cups more flour until evenly moistened. Turn dough out onto a well-floured board and knead until springy and no longer sticky (about 10 minutes), adding more flour as needed to prevent sticking. Place in a greased bowl; turn over to grease top.

To knead with a dough hook, gradually beat in 4½ cups of the flour on low speed. Then beat on medium speed until dough is springy and no longer sticky (about 5 minutes), adding more flour, 1 tablespoon at a time, if dough is sticky.

3. Cover with plastic wrap and let rise in a warm place until doubled (about 1½ hours).

4. Punch dough down and knead briefly on a lightly floured board to release air. Cut dough into 9 or 12 equal pieces. Lightly oil your hands. Working with one piece at a time (keep remaining dough covered), shape each into a ball, gently pulling top surface under until smooth. Place at least 2 inches apart, tucked sides down, on a greased baking sheet. Cover lightly and let rise in a warm place until puffy (about 30 minutes).

5. Beat remaining egg until blended; lightly brush tops of buns with egg. Sprinkle with sesame seeds. Bake in a 350° oven until golden brown (20 to 25 minutes). Transfer to racks and let cool. Makes nine 4-inch buns or twelve 3-inch buns.

Per 4-inch bun: 372 calories (24% from fat), 12 g protein, 58 g carbohydrates, 10 g total fat (2 g saturated fat), 51 mg cholesterol, 358 mg sodium

Per 3-inch bun: 279 calories (24% from fat), 9 g protein, 43 g carbohydrates, 7 g total fat (1 g saturated fat), 38 mg cholesterol, 268 mg sodium

POPPY SEED BOW TIES

Shaped into little bows and edged with poppy seeds, these crusty rolls make a dramatic presentation. Best of all, they're quickly kneaded in a food processor.

About 2¼ cups all-purpose flour
½ cup cornmeal
2 packages active dry yeast
1 tablespoon sugar
½ teaspoon salt
¾ cup milk
1 tablespoon butter or margarine
2 large eggs
2 tablespoons poppy seeds

1. Combine 2¼ cups of the flour, cornmeal, yeast, sugar, and salt in a food processor or large bowl; whirl (or stir) until combined.

2. Heat milk and butter to 130°F in a small pan over medium-high heat (butter need not melt completely). With motor running, pour milk mixture and 1 of the eggs into processor and whirl until dough forms a ball (about 1 minute); if dough is sticky and clings to sides of container, add more flour, 1 tablespoon at a time, and mix with short on-off bursts. (Or, to mix by hand, add milk mixture to flour mixture and beat thoroughly; add 1 of the eggs and beat with a spoon until dough is stretchy.)

3. Turn dough out onto a lightly floured board and knead for 2 minutes. (Or, if dough was mixed by hand, knead until smooth and elastic, 8 to 10 minutes.) Shape into a 12-inch log. In a small bowl, lightly beat remaining egg; brush log with egg and sprinkle with poppy seeds. With a sharp knife, cut dough into ¾-inch-thick rounds. Holding each round on opposite sides, twist half of round over to form a bow.

4. Place at least 2 inches apart on a greased baking sheet. Cover lightly and let rise in a warm place until puffy (15 to 20 minutes).

5. Bake, uncovered, in a 400° oven until well browned (15 to 20 minutes). Transfer to racks and let cool. Makes 16 rolls.

Per roll: 118 calories (21% from fat), 4 g protein, 19 g carbohydrates, 3 g total fat (1 g saturated fat), 30 mg cholesterol, 90 mg sodium

FOCACCIA MILANO

Northern Etruscans were the first to bake the large flatbreads now known to us as *focaccia*. Early versions were baked in ashes underneath large hearthstones and served with just a drizzle of olive oil for added flavor and moisture. Today's focaccia often features baked vegetables atop its springy mattress of olive oil–anointed dough. To save time, make the dough ahead and let it rise overnight in the refrigerator; or use purchased yeast bread dough.

> **Focaccia Dough (recipe follows); or 2 loaves (1 lb. *each*) frozen white bread dough, thawed and kneaded together**
> 2 **tablespoons olive oil**
> **Vegetable topping (choices follow)**
> **Salt and pepper**

1. Prepare Focaccia Dough. Coat a 10- by 15-inch rimmed baking pan with 1 tablespoon of the oil.

2. Punch dough down and knead briefly on a lightly floured board to release air. Roll into a rectangle about ½ inch thick. Place dough in pan, patting firmly to pan edges (if dough is too elastic, let rest for about 5 minutes and then continue). Cover and let rise in a warm place until almost doubled (about 45 minutes). Meanwhile, prepare vegetable topping of your choice.

3. Brush dough with remaining 1 tablespoon oil. With your fingers, gently press dimples in surface. Add topping and season to taste with salt and pepper.

4. Bake in a 400° oven until edges are well browned (30 to 40 minutes); if topping browns too quickly, cover loosely with foil. Makes 12 servings.

Focaccia Dough. In a large bowl, sprinkle 1 package **active dry yeast** over 1½ cups **warm water** (about 110°F); let stand until foamy (about 5 minutes). Stir in ½ teaspoon **salt** and 2 tablespoons **olive oil**. Add 2½ cups **all-purpose flour;** stir until blended. Beat with an electric mixer on medium speed until dough is elastic and stretchy (3 to 5 minutes).

Stir in 1⅓ cups more flour.

To knead by hand, turn dough out onto a floured board and knead until smooth and springy (5 to 10 minutes). Place dough in a greased bowl; turn over to grease top.

To knead with a dough hook, beat on medium speed until dough is stretchy and pulls cleanly from sides of bowl (5 to 7 minutes), adding more flour, 1 tablespoon at a time, if dough is sticky.

Cover with plastic wrap. Let dough rise in a warm place until doubled (about 45 minutes) or in a refrigerator until next day.

Eggplant. Seed and coarsely chop 1 large **red bell pepper.** Cut 2 medium-size **eggplants** into ¾-inch cubes. In a 10- by 15-inch rimmed baking pan, stir together bell pepper, eggplants, and 3 tablespoons **olive oil.** Spread vegetables out evenly and bake in a 450° oven, stirring once, until eggplant is lightly browned and beginning to soften (about 25 minutes).

Sprinkle 2 cups (about 8 oz.) shredded **mozzarella cheese** over dimpled dough. Spoon eggplant mixture over cheese. After baking, sprinkle focaccia with 2 tablespoons chopped **parsley.**

Per serving: 274 calories (33% from fat), 9 g protein, 37 g carbohydrates, 10 g total fat (3 g saturated fat), 15 mg cholesterol, 167 mg sodium

Tomato. Coat a 10- by 15-inch rimmed baking pan with 1 tablespoon **olive oil.** Slice 2 pounds large **pear-shaped (Roma-type) tomatoes** lengthwise ½ inch thick. Arrange in pan in a single layer, overlapping slightly if needed. Drizzle with 2 tablespoons more olive oil. Bake in a 450° oven until tomatoes look dry and pan juices have evaporated (about 25 minutes). Gently loosen from pan and arrange over dimpled dough. Sprinkle with 1 teaspoon *each* **dried basil** and **dried oregano.**

Per serving: 213 calories (26% from fat), 5 g protein, 34 g carbohydrates, 6 g total fat (1 g saturated fat), 0 mg cholesterol, 99 mg sodium

Zucchini. Slice 5 medium-size **zucchini** crosswise ⅛ inch thick. Cut 3 medium-size **pear-shaped (Roma-type) tomatoes** into ½-inch cubes. In a 10- by 15-inch rimmed baking pan, stir together zucchini, tomatoes, 1 teaspoon **dried marjoram,** and 3 tablespoons **olive oil.** Spread evenly and bake in a 450° oven, stirring once, until zucchini is slightly translucent and pan juices have evaporated (20 to 25 minutes). Sprinkle 2 cups (about 8 oz.) shredded **mozzarella cheese** over dimpled dough. Top with vegetables.

Per serving: 266 calories (35% from fat), 9 g protein, 35 g carbohydrates, 10 g total fat (3 g saturated fat), 15 mg cholesterol, 168 mg sodium

Olive. Halve 20 to 25 pitted **Spanish-style olives** (at least 1 inch long) lengthwise. Press olive halves, cut side down, into dimpled dough, spacing about 1 inch apart. Sprinkle with 1 teaspoon **dried thyme.**

Per serving: 176 calories (19% from fat), 4 g protein, 31 g carbohydrates, 4 g total fat (0.5 g saturated fat), 0 mg cholesterol, 268 mg sodium

*For a snack or light main course nearly any time of day, you can't go wrong
with the longtime Milanese specialty Focaccia Milano (facing page). Among the savory
toppings you can choose from are eggplant, olive, and tomato.*

43

CROSTINI & BRUSCHETTA

IN ITALY, meals often begin with a selection of crostini or bruschetta. Crostini, literally translated as "little crusts," are just that—small pieces of bread that are toasted and then spread with a variety of savory toppings.

Bruschetta, a heartier and larger variation of crostini, traditionally feature thick slices of country-style bread rubbed with garlic and sprinkled with olive oil; regional additions, such as vine-ripened tomatoes in Spain, roasted red peppers in Italy, and ripe olives in Greece, also exist.

The growing popularity of crostini and bruschetta has inspired a myriad of variations. As a base, you can use almost any bread that toasts well, from thick Italian focaccia and crusty Pane Francese to thin slices of French bread and nut-studded sourdough loaves. Just be sure the topping is appropriate for the bread you've chosen. In the recipes that follow, a walnut loaf makes an ideal base for Gorgonzola and fresh pears; focaccia is a delicious foundation for diced tomatoes.

Although classically prepared crostini and bruschetta are grilled over an open fire, the recipes here call for broiling them; or you can use an outdoor grill.

Olive Crostini with Melted Mozzarella

16 slices French Bread (page 17), Sourdough French Bread (page 52), or Pane Francese (page 18), *each* about 3 inches by 1½ inches by ½ inch

   About 5 tablespoons butter or margarine

1 can (about 4¼ oz.) pitted ripe olives, drained

¼ cup capers, drained and rinsed

2 teaspoons Dijon mustard

4 canned anchovy fillets

¼ teaspoon *each* cracked bay leaves and dried thyme

1 large clove garlic

1 tablespoon olive oil or salad oil

4 ounces mozzarella cheese, thinly sliced

1. Spread each bread slice with about 1 teaspoon of the butter, coating both sides. Place in a single layer on a baking sheet and broil 4 to 6 inches below heat, turning once, until edges are golden brown.

2. Combine olives, capers, mustard, anchovies, bay, thyme, garlic, and oil in a food processor or blender; whirl until puréed. Spread each bread slice with about ½ tablespoon of the mixture; top with cheese. Return to baking sheet; broil 4 to 6 inches below heat just until cheese is melted. Transfer to a serving plate and serve warm. Makes 16 pieces.

Per piece: 129 calories (51% from fat), 4 g protein, 12 g carbohydrates, 7 g total fat (3 g saturated fat), 16 mg cholesterol, 313 mg sodium

Roasted Pear & Gorgonzola Butter Crostini

16 slices French Walnut Bread (page 24) or Sourdough Whole Wheat Walnut Bread (page 58), *each* about 4 inches by 2 inches by ½ inch

1 Bartlett or d'Anjou pear

   About ½ cup Gorgonzola Butter (page 124); or 3 ounces Gorgonzola or blue-veined cheese

2 tablespoons olive oil

1. Place bread in a single layer on a baking sheet. Broil 4 to 6 inches below heat, turning once, until golden brown on both sides. Cut pear in half lengthwise and core; then cut each half crosswise into 8 equal slices.

2. Spread each bread slice with about ½ tablespoon of the butter mixture and top each with a pear slice. Brush pears lightly with oil. Broil 4 to 6 inches below heat just until pears are lightly browned. Transfer to a serving plate and serve warm. Makes 16 pieces.

Per piece: 127 calories (59% from fat), 2 g protein, 11 g carbohydrates, 9 g total fat (3 g saturated fat), 11 mg cholesterol, 92 mg sodium

Roasted Tomato-Eggplant Crostini

3 tablespoons olive oil

1 large red onion (about 12 oz.), sliced ½ inch thick

2 tablespoons balsamic or red wine vinegar

1½ pounds pear-shaped (Roma-type) tomatoes, sliced ¼ inch thick

1 medium-size eggplant (about 1 lb.), unpeeled, sliced crosswise ½ inch thick

Salt and pepper

16 slices French Bread (page 17), Sourdough French Bread (page 52), or Pane Francese (page 18), *each* about 5 inches by 2½ inches by ½ inch

1. Brush 2 rimmed baking pans with some of the oil. Arrange onion in a single layer in one of the pans; drizzle with vinegar. Arrange tomatoes over onion, overlapping tomato slices slightly. Arrange eggplant in a single layer in second pan. Brush vegetables with remaining oil.

2. Bake vegetables in a 450° oven until eggplant is browned and very soft (about 30 minutes) and tomatoes are well browned on edges (about 50 minutes).

3. Transfer vegetables to a food processor or blender; whirl until coarsely puréed. Season to taste with salt and pepper.

4. Place bread in a single layer on a baking sheet. Broil 4 to 6 inches below heat, turning once, until golden on both sides.

5. Spread each bread slice with about 3 tablespoons of the vegetable purée. Transfer to a serving plate and serve at room temperature. Makes 16 pieces.

Per piece: 105 calories (26% from fat), 3 g protein, 17 g carbohydrates, 3 g total fat (0.4 g saturated fat), 0 mg cholesterol, 81 mg sodium

White Bean & Artichoke Crostini

. . . .

1 tablespoon olive oil

1 large head garlic

½ large onion, quartered

16 slices French Bread (page 17), Sourdough French Bread (page 52), or Pane Francese (page 18), *each* about 4 inches by 2 inches by ½ inch

1 can (about 15 oz.) white beans, rinsed and drained

1 tablespoon whipping cream

½ teaspoon salt

¼ teaspoon ground white pepper

1 jar (about 5½ oz.) marinated artichoke hearts, cut into 16 slices

1. Pour oil into a small baking pan. Cut garlic in half crosswise and place, cut side down, in pan. Add onion and mix lightly until coated with oil.

2. Bake in a 350° oven until garlic is soft and golden brown on bottom (about 40 minutes). Meanwhile, place bread in a single layer on a baking sheet. Broil 4 to 6 inches below heat, turning once, until bread slices are golden on both sides.

3. Place beans, cream, salt, and white pepper in a food processor. Squeeze garlic from peel into processor; add onion. Whirl until smoothly puréed. Spread each bread slice with about 1 tablespoon of the purée and top each with an artichoke slice. Arrange on a serving plate and serve at room temperature. Makes 16 pieces.

Per piece: 120 calories (18% from fat), 5 g protein, 21 g carbohydrates, 2 g total fat (0.5 g saturated fat), 1 mg cholesterol, 195 mg sodium

Smoked Salmon Crostini

. . . .

16 slices French Bread (page 17) or Sourdough French Bread (page 52), *each* about 5 inches by 2½ inches by ½ inch

About ⅔ cup Red Radish Cheese Spread (page 125)

¼ pound thinly sliced smoked salmon

1 green onion, thinly sliced

1. Place bread in a single layer on a baking sheet. Broil 4 to 6 inches below heat, turning once, until golden on both sides; let cool.

2. Spread each bread slice with about 2 teaspoons of the cheese spread. Top with smoked salmon and garnish with green onion. Arrange on a serving plate and serve at room temperature. Makes 16 pieces.

Per piece: 90 calories (32% from fat), 4 g protein, 12 g carbohydrates, 3 g total fat (2 g saturated fat), 9 mg cholesterol, 162 mg sodium

Fresh Tomato & Basil Bruschetta

. . . .

4 medium-size pear-shaped (Roma-type) tomatoes, seeded and diced

½ cup finely diced celery

2 tablespoons *each* minced Italian parsley and minced fresh basil

2 teaspoons white wine vinegar

About ½ cup extra-virgin olive oil

Salt and pepper

1 plain Focaccia Milano (page 42) or 1 loaf Pane Francese (page 18)

Basil sprigs (optional)

1. Combine tomatoes, celery, parsley, minced basil, vinegar, and 2 tablespoons of the oil in a medium-size bowl. Stir until blended. Season to taste with salt and pepper; set aside. (At this point, you may cover and refrigerate until next day.)

2. Cut focaccia into 16 equal pieces (or cut bread into 16 slices, each about 6 inches long and 1½ inches thick). Place bread in a single layer on baking sheets and broil 4 to 6 inches below heat, turning once, until golden brown on both sides.

3. Transfer bread to a serving plate. Spoon some of the tomato mixture onto each bread slice. Garnish with basil sprigs, if desired. Serve at room temperature. Offer remaining oil to pour over each serving. Makes 16 pieces.

Per piece: 133 calories (59% from fat), 2 g protein, 12 g carbohydrates, 9 g total fat (1 g saturated fat), 0 mg cholesterol, 39 mg sodium

Classically prepared Bagels (facing page) are boiled in water before baking,
which gives them their traditional thin crust and dense, chewy interior. Bagels come
in many varieties; try seeded, onion, plain, or cinnamon-raisin whole wheat.

BAGELS

The soft, chewy texture and thin, shiny skin characteristic of bagels come from boiling the shaped dough in water before baking.

2	**packages active dry yeast**
2	**cups warm water (about 110°F)**
4	**tablespoons sugar**
3	**teaspoons salt**
5½	**to 6 cups all-purpose flour**
3	**quarts water**
	Cornmeal
1	**large egg yolk beaten with 1 tablespoon water**

1. Sprinkle yeast over warm water in a large bowl; let stand until foamy (about 5 minutes). Add 3 tablespoons of the sugar, salt, and 4 cups of the flour; beat until smooth.

2. Stir in 1¼ cups more flour.

To knead by hand, turn dough out onto a lightly floured board and knead until smooth and satiny (10 to 20 minutes), adding more flour as needed to prevent sticking (dough should be firm). Place in a greased bowl; turn over to grease top.

To knead with a dough hook, beat on high speed until dough pulls cleanly from sides of bowl (about 8 minutes), adding more flour, a few tablespoons at a time, if dough is sticky.

3. Cover with plastic wrap and let rise in a warm place until doubled (about 40 minutes).

4. Punch dough down and knead briefly on a lightly floured board to release air. Cut into 12 equal pieces. Keeping remaining dough covered, gently knead one piece into a ball. Holding ball with both hands, poke your thumbs through center. With a thumb in the hole, shape bagel like a doughnut and place on a lightly floured board. Repeat to shape remaining dough. Cover lightly and let rise in a warm place until puffy (about 20 minutes).

5. Bring water and remaining 1 tablespoon sugar to a boil in a 4- to 5-quart pan; reduce heat to keep mixture boiling gently. Sprinkle 2 greased baking sheets with cornmeal. With a slotted spatula, lower 3 or 4 bagels at a time into water and boil, turning often, for 5 minutes. Lift out, drain briefly on a towel, and place at least 2 inches apart on sheet. Let dry briefly and then brush with egg yolk mixture (don't let bagels stand for more than 5 minutes before baking).

6. Bake in a 400° oven until well browned and crusty (25 to 30 minutes), switching pan positions halfway through baking. Transfer to racks and let cool. Makes 12 bagels.

Per bagel: 257 calories (7% from fat), 7 g protein, 52 g carbohydrates, 2 g total fat (0.3 g saturated fat), 18 mg cholesterol, 553 mg sodium

Seeded Bagels

Follow steps 1–5 for **Bagels** (at left), but omit cornmeal. Instead, mix 2 tablespoons *each* **poppy seeds, sesame seeds,** and **anise seeds** (or 6 tablespoons poppy seeds or sesame seeds) in a small bowl. Sprinkle baking sheets with 2 tablespoons of the seeds. Place boiled bagels on sheets and, after brushing with egg yolk mixture, sprinkle with remaining seeds. Follow step 6. Makes 12 bagels.

Per bagel: 267 calories (10% from fat), 7 g protein, 52 g carbohydrates, 3 g total fat (0.4 g saturated fat), 0 mg cholesterol, 553 mg sodium

Onion Bagels

Follow steps 1–5 for **Bagels** (at left), but omit cornmeal. Cut 1 medium-size **onion** in half lengthwise; then cut crosswise into thin slices. Heat 1 tablespoon **olive oil** in a small frying pan over medium heat. Add onion and cook, stirring often, until translucent (about 3 minutes). Sprinkle baking sheets with some of the onion. Place boiled bagels on sheets and, after brushing with egg yolk mixture, sprinkle with remaining onion. Follow step 6. Makes 12 bagels.

Per bagel: 261 calories (9% from fat), 7 g protein, 52 g carbohydrates, 3 g total fat (0.3 g saturated fat), 0 mg cholesterol, 552 mg sodium

Whole Wheat Bagels

Follow step 1 for **Bagels** (at left), but omit sugar and the 4 cups all-purpose flour. Instead, add 3 tablespoons **honey,** 2 cups **whole wheat flour** or graham flour, 1¼ cups **all-purpose flour,** ½ cup **wheat germ,** and, if desired, 1 teaspoon **ground cinnamon** and 1 cup **raisins.** Follow steps 2–6, increasing amount of all-purpose flour in step 2 to 1½ cups. Makes 12 bagels.

Per bagel: 231 calories (8% from fat), 8 g protein, 46 g carbohydrates, 2 g total fat (0.3 g saturated fat), 0 mg cholesterol, 3 mg sodium

BOLILLOS

In Mexico, the plain white rolls called *bolillos* (pronounced bo-LEE-yos) are nearly as popular as tortillas. The crust is crisp and chewy, much like that of a French roll.

2 cups warm water (about 110°F)
1½ tablespoons sugar
1 tablespoon salt
2 tablespoons melted butter or margarine
1 package active dry yeast
5½ to 6 cups all-purpose flour
1 teaspoon cornstarch blended with ½ cup cold water

1. Combine warm water, sugar, salt, and butter in a large bowl. Add yeast and stir briefly; let stand until yeast is softened.

2. Stir in 4 cups of the flour.

To knead by hand, stir in 1 cup more flour. Turn out onto a lightly floured board and knead until smooth and satiny (5 to 20 minutes), adding more flour as needed to prevent sticking. Place in a greased bowl; turn over to grease top.

To knead with a dough hook, add 1½ cups more flour and beat on low speed until dough pulls cleanly from sides of bowl. Then beat on high speed until dough is elastic and no longer sticky (about 8 minutes), adding more flour, a few tablespoons at a time, if dough is sticky.

3. Cover with plastic wrap and let rise in a warm place until doubled (about 1½ hours).

4. Punch dough down and knead briefly on a lightly floured board to release air. Cut into 16 equal pieces. Working with one piece at a time (keep remaining dough covered), gently knead each piece into a ball. Roll and gently pull each ball from center to ends into an oblong roll about 4 inches long (center should be thicker than ends). Place 3 inches apart on greased baking sheets. Cover lightly and let rise in a warm place until almost doubled (about 35 minutes). If using one oven, refrigerate one sheet, covered, while baking others.

5. Bring cornstarch mixture to a boil in a small pan, stirring constantly; remove from heat and let cool briefly. Brush rolls with cornstarch mixture. With a razor blade or sharp knife, cut a slash about ¾ inch deep and 2 inches long down top of each roll.

6. Bake in a 375° oven until rolls are golden brown and sound hollow when tapped on bottoms (35 to 40 minutes), switching pan positions halfway through baking. Transfer to racks and let cool. Makes 16 rolls.

Per roll: 190 calories (12% from fat), 5 g protein, 36 g carbohydrates, 2 g total fat (1 g saturated fat), 4 mg cholesterol, 428 mg sodium

BULGUR WHEAT ROLLS

Bulgur gives these dinner rolls a wonderful nubby texture. Although they're best served hot out of the oven, you can make the rolls ahead and refrigerate them for up to 5 days; to reheat, cover and warm in a 325° oven for about 15 minutes.

½ cup *each* bulgur and water
1 package active dry yeast
1 cup warm milk (about 110°F)
¼ cup sugar
1 teaspoon salt
1 cup whole wheat flour
2 tablespoons butter or margarine, at room temperature
1 large egg
About 2¼ cups all-purpose flour

1. Combine bulgur and water in a small bowl; let stand until water is absorbed (about 45 minutes).

2. Sprinkle yeast over warm milk in a large bowl; let stand until softened (about 5 minutes). Add sugar, salt, whole wheat flour, butter, egg, and bulgur; stir until blended. Stir in 2 cups of the all-purpose flour.

3. Turn dough out onto a lightly floured board and knead until smooth and springy (10 to 15 minutes), adding more all-purpose flour as needed to prevent sticking. Place in a greased bowl; turn over to grease top. Cover with plastic wrap and let rise in a warm place until doubled (about 50 minutes).

4. Punch dough down and knead briefly on a lightly floured board to release air. Cut into 12 equal pieces. Working with one piece at a time (keep remaining dough covered), gently knead each piece into a smooth ball. Place at least 2 inches apart on a greased baking sheet. Cover lightly and let rise in a warm place until puffy (about 40 minutes).

5. Bake, uncovered, in a 400° oven until well browned (20 to 25 minutes). Transfer to racks and let cool. If made ahead, wrap airtight and refrigerate for up to 5 days. Makes 12 rolls.

Per roll: 202 calories (19% from fat), 6 g protein, 35 g carbohydrates, 4 g total fat (2 g saturated fat), 26 mg cholesterol, 220 mg sodium

GERMAN SOFT PRETZELS

These soft, yeasty pretzels are best served warm from the oven with ice-cold beer. Offer your favorite mustard alongside.

- 1 package active dry yeast
- 1 cup warm water (about 110°F)
- 2 tablespoons salad oil
- 1 tablespoon sugar
- 2½ to 3 cups all-purpose flour
- ⅓ cup baking soda
- 6 cups water
  Coarse salt
  Mustard (optional)

1. Sprinkle yeast over warm water in a medium-size bowl; let stand until foamy (about 5 minutes). Add oil, sugar, and 1½ cups of the flour; beat until smooth. Gradually stir in 1 cup more flour.

2. Turn dough out onto a floured board and knead until smooth and satiny (about 5 minutes), adding more flour as needed to prevent sticking. Place in a greased bowl; turn over to grease top. Cover with plastic wrap and let rise in a warm place until doubled (about 1 hour).

3. Punch dough down and knead briefly on a lightly floured board to release air. Cut dough into 12 equal pieces. Working with one piece at a time (keep remaining dough covered), roll into a smooth rope about 18 inches long and twist into a pretzel shape. Arrange slightly apart on greased baking sheets, placing loose ends underneath. Let rise, uncovered, in a warm place until puffy (about 25 minutes).

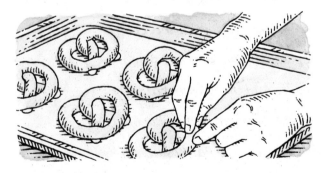

4. Bring baking soda and the 6 cups water to a boil in a 3-quart stainless steel or enamel pan (don't use aluminum); reduce heat to keep mixture boiling gently. With a slotted spatula, lower pretzels, one at a time, into water and simmer, turning once, for 10 seconds on each side; lift from water, drain, and return to baking sheet. Let dry briefly; then sprinkle with salt.

5. Bake in a 425° oven until golden brown (12 to 15 minutes). Serve warm or at room temperature. To reheat, place on baking sheets and heat, uncovered, in a 400° oven until warm (about 10 minutes). Serve with mustard, if desired. Makes 12 pretzels.

Per pretzel without salt: 130 calories (18% from fat), 3 g protein, 23 g carbohydrates, 3 g total fat (0.3 g saturated fat), 0 mg cholesterol, 158 mg sodium

• *Pictured on front cover* •

STRETCH BREADSTICKS

These crisp breadsticks—stretched into irregular, pencil-thin rods—go with just about any dish.

- 1 teaspoon sugar
- 1 cup warm water (about 110°F)
- 1 package active dry yeast
- 1 teaspoon *each* grated lemon peel and salt
- 1½ teaspoons chopped fresh rosemary or dried rosemary, crumbled
- 2 tablespoons plus 1 teaspoon olive oil
  About 2¾ cups all-purpose flour

1. Combine sugar and warm water in a large bowl. Add yeast and stir briefly; let stand until bubbly (about 10 minutes). Add lemon peel, salt, rosemary, 2 tablespoons of the oil, and 1½ cups of the flour. Beat with a heavy spoon or an electric mixer until dough is glossy and elastic (3 to 5 minutes). Stir in 1 cup more flour.

2. Turn dough out onto a lightly floured board and knead until smooth and springy (about 10 minutes), adding more flour as needed to prevent sticking. Clean off board and flour generously. Place dough on board, pat into a 6-inch square, and brush with remaining 1 teaspoon oil. Cover with plastic wrap and let rise in a warm place until puffy (about 45 minutes).

3. Rub dough with 2 more tablespoons of the flour. With a sharp knife, cut dough lengthwise into quarters. Working with a quarter at a time (keep remaining dough covered), cut lengthwise into 8 equal pieces. Stretch and roll each piece until about 15 inches long; arrange at least ½ inch apart on greased baking sheets. (If using one oven, refrigerate one sheet, covered, while baking others.)

4. Bake in a 350° oven until browned (20 to 25 minutes), switching pan positions halfway through baking. Transfer to racks and let cool. Makes 32 breadsticks.

Per breadstick: 52 calories (24% from fat), 1 g protein, 8 g carbohydrates, 1 g total fat (0.2 g saturated fat), 0 mg cholesterol, 69 mg sodium

SOURDOUGH BREADS

For centuries, dough starters have offered natural leavening, a crisp crust, and sour flavor to all kinds of baked goods. Ancient Egyptians were the first to discover the power of natural leavening by developing a bubbly dough starter to make bread. During the California gold rush, early prospectors were so fond of their all-purpose starters that the pioneers acquired the nickname "Sourdoughs."

These days, a good sour starter dough—here it's made with a mixture of yogurt, milk, and flour—remains a favorite way to add texture and piquant flavor to all types of breads, cakes, and rolls.

Look for some of your favorite sourdough recipes in this chapter. You'll find crispy baguettes, dense potato bread, and crusty sourdough rye, as well as tangy sweet breads. And, for those who might enjoy some new variations on the classics, there are loaves flavored with green onions, walnuts, sun-dried tomatoes, Parmesan, and garlic. For help with ingredients and yeast bread techniques, see page 7.

Bubbly and sour-smelling sourdough starter lends sharp flavor and moist, chewy texture to bread. Favorites include (clockwise from top left) pebbly-topped Sourdough Oatmeal Bread (page 55), several varieties of Sourdough French Bread (page 52), and Sourdough Potato Bread (page 53).

· *Pictured on page 51* ·

SOURDOUGH FRENCH BREAD

Crusty and chewy, sourdough French loaves can be made in numerous variations. Three are offered here.

> 1 **package active dry yeast**
> 1½ **cups warm water (about 110°F)**
> 1 **cup sourdough starter (page 54), at room temperature**
> **About 6 cups all-purpose flour**
> 2 **teaspoons** *each* **salt and sugar**
> **Cornmeal**
> ½ **teaspoon cornstarch blended with ½ cup cold water**

1. Sprinkle yeast over warm water in a large bowl; let stand until foamy (about 5 minutes). Add starter, 4 cups of the flour, salt, and sugar; stir until blended. Cover with plastic wrap and let rise in a warm place until doubled (about 1½ hours).

2. Stir dough down.

To knead by hand, stir in 1½ cups more flour. Turn dough out onto a lightly floured board and knead until smooth and satiny (about 10 minutes), adding more flour as needed to prevent sticking.

To knead with a dough hook, add 1¾ cups more flour and beat on high speed until dough is springy and no longer sticky (about 8 minutes), adding more flour, a few tablespoons at a time, if dough is sticky. Turn dough out onto a lightly floured board.

3. Cut dough in half. To shape into oblongs, roll each half into a 14-inch log; for rounds, shape each half into a ball, gently pulling top surface under until smooth; for baguettes, shape each half into 2 oblongs.

4. Sprinkle 2 rimless baking sheets with cornmeal. Place one large loaf (or 2 baguettes at least 4 inches apart) on each. Cover lightly and let rise in a warm place until almost doubled (about 1 hour for large loaves; 45 minutes for baguettes). If using one oven, refrigerate one sheet, covered, while baking other.

5. Bring cornstarch mixture to a boil in a small pan, stirring constantly; remove from heat and let cool briefly. Brush some of the mixture over dough. With a razor blade or sharp knife, cut ½-inch-deep slashes (diagonal slashes on oblongs, tic-tac-toe pattern on rounds) in tops of loaves.

6. Place a baking pan on lowest rack of oven and pour in boiling water to a depth of about ¼ inch. Place baking sheet on next lowest rack. Bake in a 400° oven for 10 minutes (7 minutes for baguettes); brush again with cornstarch mixture. Continue to bake until loaves are golden and sound hollow when tapped on bottoms (about 25 more minutes for large loaves; about 20 more minutes for baguettes). Transfer to racks and let cool. Makes 2 large loaves (10 to 12 servings each) or 4 baguettes (about 6 servings each).

Per serving large loaf: 150 calories (4% from fat), 4 g protein, 31 g carbohydrates, 1 g total fat (0.2 g saturated fat), 1 mg cholesterol, 205 mg sodium

Per serving baguette: 137 calories (4% from fat), 4 g protein, 28 g carbohydrates, 1 g total fat (0.2 g saturated fat), 1 mg cholesterol, 188 mg sodium

Brown & Serve Sourdough French Bread

Follow steps 1–6 for **Sourdough French Bread** (at left), but after brushing again with cornstarch mixture, bake just until surface is no longer wet (about 8 more minutes for large loaves; about 5 more minutes for baguettes). Let cool; wrap separately in foil and freeze.

Unwrap loaves and place (frozen or thawed) on a greased baking sheet. Bake in a 400° oven until loaves are golden brown and sound hollow when tapped on bottoms (about 35 minutes for large frozen loaves, 30 minutes for thawed ones; about 30 minutes for frozen baguettes, 25 minutes for thawed ones).

· *Pictured on page 51* ·

Green Onion-Nut Sourdough French Bread

Heat 1 tablespoon **olive oil** in an 8- to 10-inch frying pan over medium heat. Add 1⅓ cups chopped **green onions** and cook, stirring, until translucent (about 3 minutes). Follow steps 1–2 for **Sourdough French Bread** (at left), adding onions and 1 cup chopped **walnuts** after stirring dough down. Follow steps 3–6.

Per serving large loaf: 192 calories (22% from fat), 5 g protein, 32 g carbohydrates, 5 g total fat (1 g saturated fat), 1 mg cholesterol, 207 mg sodium

Per serving baguette: 176 calories (22% from fat), 5 g protein, 29 g carbohydrates, 4 g total fat (1 g saturated fat), 1 mg cholesterol, 189 mg sodium

· *Pictured on page 51* ·

Parmesan-Garlic Sourdough French Bread

Follow steps 1–2 for **Sourdough French Bread** (at left), adding ¼ cup grated **Parmesan cheese** and 4 medium-size cloves **garlic,** minced or pressed, after stirring dough down. Follow steps 3–6.

Per serving large loaf: 155 calories (5% from fat), 5 g protein, 31 g carbohydrates, 1 g total fat (0.4 g saturated fat), 2 mg cholesterol, 222 mg sodium

Per serving baguette: 142 calories (5% from fat), 4 g protein, 28 g carbohydrates, 1 g total fat (0.4 g saturated fat), 2 mg cholesterol, 204 mg sodium

Sun-dried Tomato Sourdough French Bread

Follow steps 1–2 for **Sourdough French Bread** (facing page), adding ½ cup chopped, **oil-packed sun-dried tomatoes,** drained and blotted dry, after stirring dough down. Follow steps 3–6.

Per serving large loaf: 165 calories (8% from fat), 5 g protein, 33 g carbohydrates, 1 g total fat (0.3 g saturated fat), 1 mg cholesterol, 209 mg sodium

Per serving baguette: 151 calories (7% from fat), 4 g protein, 30 g carbohydrates, 1 g total fat (0.3 g saturated fat), 1 mg cholesterol, 192 mg sodium

• *Pictured on page 51* •

SOURDOUGH POTATO BREAD

Instant mashed potatoes lend a soft, springy texture and delicate sweetness to these wholesome sourdough loaves. They'll remain moist and fresh-tasting for several days after they're baked. Wrap them airtight and store them at room temperature.

> **Instant mashed potatoes (amount for 2 servings) plus water, milk, butter, and salt as specified on package**
> ¾ **cup milk**
> ¼ **cup butter or margarine, melted and cooled**
> 2 **large eggs**
> 1 **cup sourdough starter (page 54), at room temperature**
> 1 **package active dry yeast**
> 5½ **to 6 cups all-purpose flour**
> ¼ **cup sugar**
> 2 **teaspoons salt**
> 1 **large egg white beaten with 2 tablespoons water**
> **Poppy seeds (optional)**

1. Prepare instant mashed potatoes according to package directions. Add the ¾ cup milk, the ¼ cup butter, the 2 eggs, and starter; stir until blended.

2. Combine yeast, 2 cups of the flour, sugar, and salt in a large bowl. Add potato mixture and beat with an electric mixer on medium speed for 2 minutes, scraping bowl occasionally. Add 1½ cups more flour and continue to beat for 2 more minutes.

3. Beat in 1½ cups more flour.

To knead by hand, turn dough out onto a lightly floured board and knead until smooth and springy (15 to 20 minutes), adding more flour as needed to prevent sticking. Place in a greased bowl; turn over to grease top.

To knead with a dough hook, add ½ cup more flour. Beat on medium-high speed until dough is very elastic and only slightly sticky (about 8 minutes), adding more flour, a few tablespoons at a time, if dough is sticky.

4. Cover with plastic wrap and let rise in a warm place until doubled (1½ to 2 hours).

5. Punch dough down and knead briefly on a lightly floured board to release air. Cut in half.

For round loaves, shape each half into a ball and place each on a greased baking sheet. With a razor blade or sharp knife, cut ½-inch-deep slashes in a tic-tac-toe pattern in tops of loaves.

For braided loaves, divide one portion into 3 equal pieces (keep remaining dough covered), roll each piece into a rope about 15 inches long, and arrange about 1 inch apart on a greased baking sheet; braid loosely, pinching ends together and tucking under loaf. Repeat to shape remaining dough, using another baking sheet.

6. Cover lightly and let rise in a warm place until almost doubled (about 45 minutes).

7. Brush with egg white mixture; sprinkle with poppy seeds, if desired. Bake in a 350° oven until richly browned (25 to 30 minutes for braided loaves; 30 to 35 minutes for round loaves), switching pan positions halfway through baking. Transfer to racks and let cool. Makes 2 loaves (12 to 14 servings each).

Per serving: 163 calories (20% from fat), 5 g protein, 28 g carbohydrates, 4 g total fat (2 g saturated fat), 24 mg cholesterol, 229 mg sodium

PROSPECTORS IN California's gold rush were among the first to popularize the tangy flavor and delicious chewy texture of first-rate sourdough bread. For them, a good sour starter for bread baking was a treasure to nurture and share.

Sourdough starters become more active and more sour as time passes. Taste also depends on the yogurt and milk you use—the lower their fat content, the tangier your starter. If yours is a young starter (less than 6 months old), it's best used in simple recipes, such as pancakes and waffles, or in breads that call for other leavening.

You can increase the tangy flavor of any bread by combining starter with yeast, flour, and water to create a moist "sponge" and letting it stand overnight before kneading.

Sourdough Starter

- 1 **cup lukewarm milk (90° to 100°F)**
- 2 **tablespoons plain yogurt**
- 1 **cup all-purpose flour**

1. Rinse a 1½-quart glass, ceramic, plastic, or stainless steel container with hot water until container is very warm; wipe dry. Add milk and yogurt; stir until blended. Cover tightly and let stand in a warm place (80° to 100°F) until a curd forms and mixture doesn't flow readily when container is slightly tilted (18 to 24 hours).

If some clear liquid rises to the top during this time, stir in. However, if liquid turns light pink, milk is beginning to break down; discard starter and begin again.

2. Add flour gradually, stirring until blended; cover tightly and let stand in a warm place (80° to 100°F) until mixture is bubbly and sour smelling (2 to 5 days).

If clear liquid forms during this time, stir in; but if liquid is pink, spoon out and discard all but ¼ cup of the starter and then stir in a mixture of 1 cup *each* lukewarm milk (90° to 100°F) and all-purpose flour. Cover tightly and let stand again in a warm place until bubbly and sour smelling.

3. Use at once or refrigerate, covered. Makes about 1½ cups.

NOTE: To maintain your supply, each time you use some of your starter, replenish with equal amounts of lukewarm milk (90° to 100°F) and all-purpose flour (for example, if you used ½ cup of the starter, stir in a mixture of ½ cup *each* milk and flour).

Cover tightly and let stand in a warm place until bubbly (several hours or until next day); then refrigerate. For consistent flavor, add same type of milk used originally.

If used and replenished regularly (about once a week), starter should stay lively and active; if not, discard about half the starter and replenish with equal amounts *each* of lukewarm milk and flour about every 2 weeks. Or freeze freshly fed starter for 1½ to 2 months; before using, let thaw at room temperature and then put in a warm place until bubbly (about 24 hours).

Before using starter, bring to room temperature.

---

1. Let milk and yogurt mixture stand until a curd forms and mixture doesn't flow readily when jar is tilted.

2. Gradually add flour to milk and yogurt mixture. Stir until smoothly blended. Cover tightly.

3. Let stand, covered, for 2 to 5 days. Mixture should become bubbly and sour smelling.

SOURDOUGH PARMESAN-PEPPER BREAD

Flavored with Parmesan and freshly ground black pepper, this bread is just as good plain as it is with a spread.

    ¾ or 1 cup lukewarm water (about 100°F)
    ½ cup sourdough starter (facing page), at
        room temperature
        About 2½ cups all-purpose flour
    1 package active dry yeast
    1 teaspoon sugar
    ½ teaspoon salt
    ¾ teaspoon freshly ground pepper
    ½ cup grated Parmesan cheese

1. Combine ½ cup of the lukewarm water, starter, and ½ cup of the flour in a small bowl; stir until blended. If very sour flavor is desired, cover with plastic wrap and let stand in a warm place until bubbly and sour smelling (12 to 24 hours).

2. Sprinkle yeast over ¼ cup more lukewarm water in a medium-size bowl; stir briefly. Let stand until foamy (about 5 minutes). Stir in sugar and sourdough mixture (if sourdough mixture has stood for more than 12 hours, add ¼ cup more water). Nest container in a bowl of ice; stir often until mixture is ice cold (15 to 20 minutes).

To mix and knead in a food processor, combine salt, pepper, cheese, and 1¾ cups more flour in container. With motor running, quickly pour in yeast mixture. Whirl until dough is elastic (1 to 1½ minutes; dough should be soft and wet and form a thin, transparent skin when stretched). Sprinkle dough with 2 tablespoons more flour. Turn into a large bowl.

To mix and knead with a dough hook or by hand, combine salt, pepper, cheese, and 1¾ cups more flour in a large bowl. Add yeast mixture and beat with an electric mixer on medium speed or with a heavy spoon until blended. Continue to beat until dough is elastic (about 5 minutes with a dough hook, about 20 minutes with a spoon; dough should be soft and wet and form a thin, transparent skin when stretched). Sprinkle dough with 2 tablespoons more flour.

3. Cover and let rise in a warm place until doubled (2 to 2¼ hours).

4. Sprinkle dough with 2 tablespoons more flour and turn out onto a well-floured board. Cut in half. Pat each half into a 7- by 8-inch rectangle. Beginning at a short side, roll up dough, pressing rolled edge against

unrolled portion with heel of hand. Pinch edge against loaf to seal.

5. Place loaves seam sides down and well apart on a generously floured board. Sprinkle lightly with more flour. Cover lightly and let stand for 30 minutes. Easing your fingers under log (if dough sticks to board, scrape free with a spatula) and letting log stretch to 14 inches, transfer each loaf to a greased baking sheet. Let rise, uncovered, in a warm place until slightly puffy (15 to 20 minutes).

6. Place loaves in a 475° oven; immediately reduce temperature to 425°. Bake until golden brown (about 20 minutes). For a crisper crust, turn off oven, prop door slightly ajar, and let loaves stand in oven for 10 minutes. Transfer to racks and let cool. Makes 2 loaves (6 to 8 servings each).

Per serving: 116 calories (10% from fat), 4 g protein, 21 g carbohydrates, 1 g total fat (1 g saturated fat), 3 mg cholesterol, 135 mg sodium

• *Pictured on page 51* •

SOURDOUGH OATMEAL BREAD

Rolled oats provide rich flavor and a slightly nubby texture to an otherwise plain sandwich bread.

    2½ cups plus 3 tablespoons regular or
        quick-cooking rolled oats
    ⅓ cup instant nonfat dry milk
    2¼ cups hot water (about 130°F)
    1 package active dry yeast
    ¾ cup sourdough starter (facing page), at
        room temperature
        About 7 cups all-purpose flour
    ¼ cup molasses or honey
    ¼ cup salad oil
    2 teaspoons salt
    1 teaspoon baking soda
    ⅓ cup milk

1. Combine 1 cup of the oats, dry milk, and hot water in a large bowl; stir until blended. Let cool to about 110°F. Meanwhile, in a food processor or blender, whirl 1½ cups more oats until reduced to a flour. Stir yeast into milk mixture and let stand until dissolved. Add starter, powdered oats, and 2½ cups of the flour; stir until blended. Cover with plastic wrap and let stand in a warm place until thickened and bubbly (about 1½ hours).

(Continued on next page)

2. Stir dough sponge down. Add molasses, oil, salt, and baking soda; stir until combined.

3. Stir in 2 cups more flour.

To knead by hand, gradually stir in 2¼ cups more flour. Turn out onto a floured board and knead until smooth and no longer sticky (about 15 minutes), adding more flour as needed to prevent sticking. Place in a greased bowl; turn over to grease top.

To knead with a dough hook, add 2¼ cups more flour and beat on low speed until combined. Then beat on high speed until dough is elastic and only slightly sticky (about 8 minutes), adding more flour, a few tablespoons at a time, if dough is sticky.

4. Cover and let rise in a warm place until doubled (about 1½ hours).

5. Punch dough down and knead briefly on a floured board to release air. Cut dough into thirds. Shape each portion into a loaf and place each in a greased 4- by 8-inch loaf pan. Cover lightly and let rise in a warm place until ½ inch above pan rims (45 to 60 minutes).

6. Soften remaining 3 tablespoons oats in milk; dot over loaves. Bake in a 375° oven until loaves are well browned (about 35 minutes). Turn out onto racks and let cool. Makes 3 loaves (about 8 servings each).

Per serving: 217 calories (15% from fat), 6 g protein, 40 g carbohydrates, 4 g total fat (1 g saturated fat), 1 mg cholesterol, 248 mg sodium

SESAME SOURDOUGH LOAVES

In this rich-flavored loaf, tahini (ground sesame paste) adds a subtle nutty taste.

> ¾ **cup sourdough starter (page 54), at room temperature**
> 2½ **to 3¼ cups bread flour**
> 1¼ **cups lukewarm water (about 90°F)**
> 1 **cup sesame seeds**
> 1 **package active dry yeast**
> 1½ **teaspoons salt**
> ¼ **cup *each* tahini, honey, and lemon juice**
> 2 **cups whole wheat flour**
> 1 **large egg white, lightly beaten**

1. Combine starter, 1 cup of the bread flour, and 1 cup of the lukewarm water in a large bowl; stir until blended. If very sour flavor is desired, cover with plastic wrap and let stand in a warm place until bubbly and sour smelling (12 to 24 hours).

2. Toast sesame seeds in a wide frying pan over medium heat, shaking pan often, until golden (about 8 minutes). Let cool. Meanwhile, sprinkle yeast over remaining ¼ cup water in a small bowl; stir briefly. Let stand until foamy (about 5 minutes).

3. Stir yeast mixture into starter mixture. Add salt, tahini, honey, lemon juice, and ½ cup of the sesame seeds; stir until blended.

4. Stir in whole wheat flour.

To knead by hand, stir in 1 cup more bread flour. Turn out onto a lightly floured board and knead until smooth and elastic (about 15 minutes), adding more bread flour as needed to prevent sticking.

To knead with a dough hook, add 1¼ cups more bread flour and beat on low speed until combined. Then beat on medium-high speed until dough is springy and pulls cleanly from sides of bowl (about 8 minutes), adding more bread flour, a few tablespoons at a time, if dough is sticky. Turn dough out onto a floured board and knead by hand for 2 minutes.

5. Place dough in a greased bowl; turn over to grease top. Cover and let rise in a warm place until doubled (1½ to 2 hours).

6. Punch dough down and knead briefly on a lightly floured board to release air. Cut dough in half. Shape each half into a flat 7-inch round and place each on a greased baking sheet. Cover lightly and let rise in a warm place until puffy (30 to 45 minutes).

7. Brush with egg white and sprinkle with remaining ½ cup sesame seeds. Bake in a 375° oven until well browned (25 to 30 minutes), switching pan positions halfway through baking. Transfer to racks and let cool. Makes 2 loaves (10 to 12 servings each).

Per serving: 187 calories (26% from fat), 6 g protein, 29 g carbohydrates, 6 g total fat (1 g saturated fat), 1 mg cholesterol, 161 mg sodium

• *Pictured on page 59* •

SOURDOUGH WHOLE-GRAIN LOAVES

For many people, the sturdy, coarse-grained texture and rich, earthy flavor of fresh whole-grain loaves are the best reason for home baking. Kneading the thick dough will give you a good workout, but the result is well worth the effort.

1 cup sourdough starter (page 54), at room temperature
1½ cups lukewarm milk (about 90°F)
3¼ to 3¾ cups bread flour
1 package active dry yeast
¼ cup warm water (about 110°F)
⅓ cup honey or firmly packed brown sugar
1½ teaspoons salt
1 large egg
2 tablespoons melted butter or margarine
½ cup *each* rolled oats, bulgur, cornmeal, and rye flour
1½ cups whole wheat flour
1 cup unprocessed wheat bran

1. Combine starter, milk, and 1½ cups of the bread flour in a large bowl. If very sour flavor is desired, cover with plastic wrap and let stand in a warm place until bubbly and sour smelling (12 to 24 hours).

2. Sprinkle yeast over warm water in a small bowl; stir briefly. Let stand until foamy (about 5 minutes). Stir into starter mixture. Add honey, salt, egg, butter, oats, bulgur, cornmeal, rye flour, whole wheat flour, and bran; stir until blended. Stir in 1½ cups more bread flour.

3. Turn out onto a well-floured board and knead until dough is smooth and springy (15 to 20 minutes), adding more bread flour as needed to prevent sticking. Place in a greased bowl; turn over to grease top. Cover and let rise in a warm place until doubled (1½ to 2½ hours).

4. Punch dough down and knead briefly on a lightly floured board to release air. Cut dough in half. Pat each half into an 8- by 9-inch rectangle; beginning at a short side, roll up dough, pinching edge against loaf to seal. Place each loaf seam side down on a greased baking sheet. Cover lightly and let rise in a warm place until puffy (25 to 45 minutes).

5. Bake, uncovered, in a 375° oven until well browned (30 to 35 minutes). Transfer to racks and let cool. Makes 2 loaves (about 12 servings each).

Per serving: 195 calories (13% from fat), 6 g protein, 37 g carbohydrates, 3 g total fat (1 g saturated fat), 15 mg cholesterol, 163 mg sodium

• *Pictured on page 59* •

CRUSTY SOURDOUGH RYE BREAD

A bubbly and sour-smelling rye "sponge" made from sourdough starter and rye flour is the secret to this rich loaf's thick, crunchy crust and soft, sour interior.

1 cup sourdough starter (page 54), at room temperature
1½ cups rye flour
1¼ cups warm water (about 110°F)
2 packages active dry yeast
1½ cups all-purpose flour
About 1½ cups whole wheat flour
1½ teaspoons salt
1 tablespoon sugar
¼ cup caraway seeds
1 teaspoon anise seeds

1. Combine starter, rye flour, and 1 cup of the warm water in a large bowl; stir until blended. If very sour flavor is desired, cover with plastic wrap and let stand in a warm place until bubbly and sour smelling (12 to 24 hours).

2. Sprinkle yeast over remaining ¼ cup warm water in a small bowl; stir briefly. Let stand until foamy (about 5 minutes). Stir into sourdough mixture. Add all-purpose flour, 1 cup of the whole wheat flour, salt, sugar, caraway seeds, and anise seeds; stir until blended.

3. Turn dough out onto a well-floured board and knead until smooth and springy (about 10 minutes), adding more whole wheat flour as needed to prevent sticking (dough should be slightly sticky). Cover and let rise in a warm place until doubled (1 to 1½ hours).

4. Punch dough down and knead briefly on a lightly floured board to release air. Shape into a round loaf and place on a greased baking sheet. Cover lightly and let rise in a warm place until almost doubled (about 45 minutes).

5. Make a small X-shaped cut about ¾ inch deep in top of loaf, using a razor blade or sharp knife. Spray loaf with water and bake in a 425° oven for 9 minutes, spraying loaf after 3, 6, and 9 minutes. Reduce oven temperature to 400° and continue to bake until loaf is well browned and sounds hollow when tapped on bottom (20 to 25 more minutes). Transfer to a rack and let cool. Makes 1 loaf (about 12 servings).

Per serving: 208 calories (7% from fat), 7 g protein, 42 g carbohydrates, 2 g total fat (0.4 g saturated fat), 2 mg cholesterol, 285 mg sodium

• *Pictured on facing page* •

SOURDOUGH WHOLE WHEAT WALNUT BREAD

. . . .

Sourdough starter gives this loaf its crispy crust and dense, chewy interior. Walnuts add crunch.

- 1 **package active dry yeast**
- 1½ **cups warm water (about 110°F)**
- 1 **cup sourdough starter (page 54), at room temperature**
- ¾ **cup rye flour**
- 1¼ **cups whole wheat flour**
  About 3½ cups all-purpose flour
- 2 **teaspoons salt**
- 1 **cup chopped walnuts**
- ¼ **cup cornmeal**
- ½ **teaspoon cornstarch blended with ½ cup cold water**

1. Sprinkle yeast over warm water in a large bowl; let stand until foamy (about 5 minutes). Add starter, rye flour, whole wheat flour, 2 cups of the all-purpose flour, and salt; beat until blended. Cover with plastic wrap and let rise in a warm place until doubled (about 1½ hours).

2. Stir in 1¼ cups more all-purpose flour.

To knead by hand, turn dough out onto a lightly floured board and knead until smooth and satiny (about 10 minutes), adding more all-purpose flour as needed to prevent sticking. Press nuts into dough and knead until evenly distributed.

To knead with a dough hook, beat on low speed until dough pulls cleanly from sides of bowl. Then beat on high speed until dough is springy and no longer sticky (about 8 minutes), adding more all-purpose flour, a few tablespoons at a time, if dough is sticky. Add nuts and beat on low speed until evenly distributed.

3. Turn dough out onto a lightly floured board. Cut into 4 equal pieces and roll each into an oblong about 15 inches long. Sprinkle 2 rimless baking sheets with cornmeal. Place 2 loaves on each sheet, spacing loaves at least 4 inches apart. Cover lightly and let rise in a warm place until puffy and almost doubled (about 45 minutes). If using one oven, refrigerate one sheet, covered, while baking other.

4. Bring cornstarch mixture to a boil in a small pan, stirring constantly; remove from heat and let cool briefly. Brush some of the mixture over dough. With a razor blade or sharp knife, cut three ½-inch-deep diagonal slashes in tops of loaves.

5. Place a baking pan on lowest rack of oven and pour in boiling water to a depth of about ¼ inch. Place baking sheet on next lowest rack. Bake in a 400° oven for 7 minutes; brush again with cornstarch mixture. Continue to bake until loaves are golden and sound hollow when gently tapped on bottoms (about 20 more minutes). Transfer to racks and let cool. Makes 4 baguettes (about 6 servings each).

Per serving: 156 calories (21% from fat), 5 g protein, 26 g carbohydrates, 4 g total fat (0.5 g saturated fat), 1 mg cholesterol, 189 mg sodium

SOURDOUGH APRICOT BREAD

. . . .

In this moist nut bread, sourdough starter blends with dried apricots for a tangy flavor and chewy crust.

- ½ **cup sourdough starter (page 54), at room temperature**
- ½ **cup lukewarm milk (about 90°F)**
- 1½ **cups all-purpose flour**
- 1 **large egg**
- ½ **cup** *each* **granulated sugar and firmly packed brown sugar**
- 3 **tablespoons salad oil**
- 1 **teaspoon baking powder**
- ½ **teaspoon salt**
- ¼ **teaspoon baking soda**
- ½ **cup** *each* **chopped dried apricots and chopped walnuts**

1. Combine starter, milk, and ½ cup of the flour in a large bowl; stir until blended. If very sour flavor is desired, cover with plastic wrap and let stand in a warm place until bubbly and sour smelling (12 to 24 hours).

2. Add egg, granulated sugar, brown sugar, and oil; stir until combined. Add baking powder, salt, baking soda, and remaining 1 cup flour; stir until blended. Stir in apricots and nuts.

3. Pour batter into a greased 5- by 9-inch loaf pan. Bake in a 350° oven until bread pulls away from sides of pan (50 to 55 minutes). Let cool in pan on a rack for 5 minutes; turn out onto rack and let cool completely. Makes 1 loaf (about 10 servings).

Per serving: 278 calories (31% from fat), 5 g protein, 44 g carbohydrates, 10 g total fat (2 g saturated fat), 24 mg cholesterol, 212 mg sodium

Add sourdough starter to nutritious whole grains and you get uncommonly good bread (clockwise from top left): Sourdough Whole Wheat Walnut Bread (facing page), Crusty Sourdough Rye Bread (page 57), and Sourdough Whole-Grain Loaves (page 56).

SOURDOUGH HOLIDAY SWIRL BREAD

. . . .

Sourdough's delicate tang cuts the intense sweetness of this horseshoe-shaped holiday bread. For more subtle flavor, substitute dried cherries for candied ones.

- ¾ cup sourdough starter (page 54), at room temperature
- ½ cup lukewarm apple juice or milk (about 90°F)
- 3¼ to 3½ cups all-purpose flour
- 1 package active dry yeast
- 5 tablespoons butter or margarine, melted and cooled
- ¼ cup granulated sugar
- 1 teaspoon grated lemon peel
- ¾ teaspoon ground cardamom
- ½ teaspoon salt
- 1 large egg
- ⅓ cup golden raisins
- ⅓ cup halved candied cherries or dried cherries
- ¼ cup chopped candied citron or candied lemon peel
- ⅓ cup firmly packed brown sugar mixed with ½ teaspoon ground cinnamon

  Lemon Icing (recipe follows)

1. Combine starter, ¼ cup of the juice, and ½ cup of the flour in a large bowl; stir until blended. If very sour flavor is desired, cover with plastic wrap and let stand in a warm place until bubbly and sour smelling (12 to 24 hours).

2. Sprinkle yeast over remaining ¼ cup juice in a small bowl; stir briefly. Let stand until foamy (about 5 minutes). Stir into starter mixture. Add 3 tablespoons of the butter, granulated sugar, lemon peel, cardamom, salt, and egg; stir until blended.

3. Stir in 2½ cups more flour.

To knead by hand, turn dough out onto a lightly floured board and knead until smooth and elastic (8 to 12 minutes), adding more flour as needed to prevent sticking. Press raisins, cherries, and citron into dough; knead until evenly distributed. Place in a greased bowl; turn over to grease top.

To knead with a dough hook, beat on high speed until smooth and elastic (about 5 minutes), adding more flour, a few tablespoons at a time, if dough is sticky. Add raisins, cherries, and citron; beat on medium-low speed until evenly distributed.

4. Cover and let rise in a warm place until doubled (1½ to 2 hours).

5. Punch dough down and knead briefly on a lightly floured board to release air. Roll into a 9- by 18-inch rectangle. Brush with remaining 2 tablespoons butter and sprinkle with brown sugar mixture. Beginning at a long side, roll up dough, pinching edge against loaf to seal. Place seam side down on a greased baking sheet, arranging in a 9-inch-wide horseshoe shape. With scissors, make cuts at 1½-inch intervals from outside of horseshoe two-thirds of the way to the center. Turn each section on its side, overlapping slightly. Cover lightly and let rise in a warm place until puffy (about 1 hour).

6. Bake, uncovered, in a 350° oven until lightly browned (about 25 minutes). Transfer to a rack and let cool for 10 minutes. Meanwhile, prepare Lemon Icing. Drizzle icing over warm bread. Makes 12 servings.

Lemon Icing. In a bowl, combine 1 cup **powdered sugar,** ½ teaspoon grated **lemon peel,** and 1½ tablespoons **lemon juice;** beat until smooth.

Per serving: 339 calories (17% from fat), 6 g protein, 65 g carbohydrates, 6 g total fat (3 g saturated fat), 32 mg cholesterol, 171 mg sodium

BUTTERY SOURDOUGH PAN ROLLS

. . . .

The soft yeast dough for these rolls requires no kneading, yet it still results in moist, airy biscuits. Serve them hot right from the oven.

- 2 packages active dry yeast
- ½ cup warm water (about 110°F)
- 4 cups all-purpose flour
- ¼ cup sugar
- 1 teaspoon salt

10 tablespoons butter or margarine, melted and cooled

1 large egg

1 cup sourdough starter (page 54), at room temperature

½ cup warm milk (about 110°F)

1. Sprinkle yeast over warm water in a small bowl; let stand until foamy (about 5 minutes). In a large bowl, mix 2 cups of the flour, sugar, and salt. Add yeast mixture, 6 tablespoons of the butter, egg, starter, and milk. Beat with an electric mixer or a heavy spoon until smooth (about 5 minutes). Gradually beat in remaining 2 cups flour. Cover with plastic wrap and let rise in a warm place until doubled (about 45 minutes).

2. Coat a 9- by 13-inch baking pan with 2 tablespoons more butter. Stir dough down. Drop into pan by large spoonfuls, making about 15 rolls. Cover lightly and let rise in a warm place until puffy (about 30 minutes).

3. Drizzle rolls with remaining 2 tablespoons butter. Bake in a 425° oven until browned (15 to 20 minutes). Turn rolls out and serve hot, pulling apart to separate. Makes about 15 rolls.

Per roll: 242 calories (34% from fat), 6 g protein, 34 g carbohydrates, 9 g total fat (5 g saturated fat), 38 mg cholesterol, 240 mg sodium

SOURDOUGH PANCAKES & WAFFLES

Some people credit the invention of sourdough to an early prospector who mixed up a bowl of pancake batter, left it for a few days while he was away from camp, and returned to find a bubbly mixture that smelled decidedly sour but made the best hotcakes he'd ever tasted. These are undoubtedly just as delicious as the original batch.

1 cup *each* whole wheat flour and all-purpose flour

½ cup sourdough starter (page 54), at room temperature

2 cups lukewarm buttermilk (about 90°F)

2 large eggs

¼ cup *each* milk and salad oil

2 tablespoons sugar

1 teaspoon baking soda

½ teaspoon salt

1. Combine whole wheat flour, all-purpose flour, starter, and buttermilk in a medium-size bowl; stir

until blended. Cover with plastic wrap. Let stand at room temperature for 45 minutes or refrigerate until next day.

2. Combine eggs, milk, and oil in a large bowl. Add buttermilk mixture and stir until blended. Stir in sugar, baking soda, and salt. Cover and let stand for 5 minutes.

For pancakes, drop batter by spoonfuls onto a moderately hot greased griddle or wide frying pan. Cook until tops are bubbly and appear dry; turn and cook until other sides are browned.

For waffles, bake in a preheated electric waffle iron, following manufacturer's directions; waffles should be richly browned. If made ahead, wrap airtight and freeze; reheat frozen waffles in a toaster.

Makes about 2 dozen 4-inch pancakes or twelve 4-inch waffles.

Per pancake: 90 calories (38% from fat), 3 g protein, 11 g carbohydrates, 4 g total fat (1 g saturated fat), 19 mg cholesterol, 128 mg sodium

Per waffle: 179 calories (38% from fat), 6 g protein, 23 g carbohydrates, 8 g total fat (1 g saturated fat), 39 mg cholesterol, 257 mg sodium

Sourdough Blueberry Pancakes & Waffles

Follow steps 1–2 for **Sourdough Pancakes & Waffles** (at left), stirring in ¾ cup fresh, canned (drained), or frozen (thawed and patted dry) **blueberries** just before cooking.

Per pancake: 92 calories (37% from fat), 3 g protein, 12 g carbohydrates, 4 g total fat (1 g saturated fat), 19 mg cholesterol, 129 mg sodium

Per waffle: 184 calories (37% from fat), 6 g protein, 24 g carbohydrates, 8 g total fat (1 g saturated fat), 39 mg cholesterol, 257 mg sodium

Sourdough Oatmeal Pancakes & Waffles

Follow step 1 for **Sourdough Pancakes & Waffles** (at left), substituting 1 cup regular or quick-cooking **rolled oats** for either whole wheat or all-purpose flour. Follow step 2.

Per pancake: 84 calories (42% from fat), 3 g protein, 10 g carbohydrates, 4 g total fat (1 g saturated fat), 19 mg cholesterol, 128 mg sodium

Per waffle: 167 calories (42% from fat), 6 g protein, 19 g carbohydrates, 8 g total fat (2 g saturated fat), 39 mg cholesterol, 257 mg sodium

*Sweetly spiced and fancifully shaped, yeast breads offer up such
mouth-watering goodness as (clockwise from top left) Pumpkin Spice Bubble Bread
(page 76), Apple-Walnut Bread (page 69), braided Orange-Saffron Bread (page 68), and
Buttery Almond Bear Claws (page 73).*

SWEET YEAST BREADS

Tender, moist, and delectable, sweet yeast breads have that melt-in-your-mouth quality that makes them perennial favorites. Because they're higher in sugar and fat than savory loaves, their flavor and texture are more refined. In this chapter you'll find buttery coffee cakes, sweet rolls, and traditional loaves for the holidays. In addition, look for some new twists on time-honored classics, such as brioche enriched with ripe bananas, Christmas braids studded with dried cherries, and sugar-dusted Italian loaves topped with fresh fruit.

Because sweet breads come in such a fantastic array of shapes and sizes, they may be challenging to the beginning baker. If the dough is too soft to be handled easily, try covering and refrigerating it until it's firm enough to shape. Or you can let the dough rise in the refrigerator overnight to shape and bake the next day. For more tips on yeast dough, turn to page 7.

PORTUGUESE SWEET BREAD

Many know this round, golden loaf as Hawaiian sweet bread, not surprising considering that Island residents have adopted the recipe as their own. In fact, Portuguese immigrants first popularized the bread in Hawaii during the late 1800s.

⅔ **cup water**
¼ **cup instant potato granules or flakes**
⅔ **cup sugar**
¼ **cup instant nonfat dry milk**
½ **cup (¼ lb.) butter or margarine, cut into pieces**
2 **packages active dry yeast**
⅓ **cup warm water (about 110°F)**
   About 5 cups all-purpose flour
4 **large eggs**
1 **teaspoon salt**
½ **teaspoon vanilla**
¼ **teaspoon lemon extract**
   Sugar (optional)

1. Bring the ⅔ cup water to a boil in a small pan. Beat in potato granules; stir in the ⅔ cup sugar, dry milk, and butter. Let cool to 110°F (butter need not melt completely).

2. Sprinkle yeast over warm water in a large bowl; stir briefly. Let stand until foamy (about 5 minutes). Stir in potato mixture. Add 2 cups of the flour and beat with an electric mixer on low speed or with a heavy spoon until blended. Beat in 3 of the eggs, salt, vanilla, and lemon extract until blended.

3. Stir in 2 cups more flour.

To knead by hand, turn dough out onto a floured board and knead until smooth, satiny, and no longer sticky (5 to 20 minutes), adding more flour as needed to prevent sticking. Place in a greased bowl; turn over to grease top.

To knead with a dough hook, add ¾ cup more flour and beat on low speed until combined. Then beat on high speed until dough is springy and no longer sticky (about 5 minutes), adding more flour, a few tablespoons at a time, if dough is sticky.

4. Cover with plastic wrap and let rise in a warm place until doubled (about 1 hour).

5. Punch dough down and knead briefly on a lightly floured board to release air. Cover and let stand for 10 minutes.

6. Cut dough in half, shape each half into a ball, and place each portion in a greased 9-inch pie pan. Gently flatten into a smooth 8-inch round. Cover lightly and let rise in a warm place until almost doubled (35 to 45 minutes).

7. Beat remaining egg and brush over loaves; sprinkle with sugar, if desired. Bake in a 350° oven until browned (25 to 30 minutes). Turn out onto racks and let cool. Makes 2 loaves (8 to 10 servings each).

Per serving: 240 calories (27% from fat), 6 g protein, 38 g carbohydrates, 7 g total fat (4 g saturated fat), 61 mg cholesterol, 197 mg sodium

SWISS EGG BRAID

Braided loaves made from a dense, egg-rich dough are called *Eier Zupfen* in Switzerland. We know them simply as egg braids. Make them plain, or add cinnamon-sugar or dried fruit and nuts.

2 **packages active dry yeast**
½ **cup warm water (about 110°F)**
1 **cup warm milk (about 110°F)**
½ **cup sugar**
1 **teaspoon salt**
   About 4½ cups all-purpose flour
½ **cup (¼ lb.) butter or margarine, melted and cooled**
3 **large eggs, lightly beaten**
1 **large egg yolk beaten with 1 tablespoon water**

1. Sprinkle yeast over warm water in a large bowl; stir briefly. Let stand until foamy (about 5 minutes). Add milk, sugar, and salt. Beat in 2 cups of the flour until smooth. Cover with plastic wrap and let stand in a warm place until light and foamy (about 45 minutes).

2. Add butter and the whole eggs; stir until well blended. Gradually beat in 2½ cups more flour. Turn dough out onto a lightly floured board, cover, and let stand for 10 minutes.

3. Knead dough until smooth and satiny (about 8 minutes), adding more flour as needed to prevent sticking. Place in a greased bowl; turn over to grease top. Cover and let rise in a warm place until doubled (about 1¾ hours).

4. Punch dough down and knead briefly on a lightly floured board to release air. Cut dough in half, cover, and let stand for 10 minutes. Keeping remaining dough covered, divide one portion into 3 equal pieces, roll each piece into a rope about 12 inches long, and place about 1 inch apart on a greased baking sheet; braid loosely, pinching ends together and tucking under loaf. Repeat to shape remaining dough, using another baking sheet.

5. Cover lightly and let rise in a warm place until almost doubled (about 1¼ hours).

6. Brush loaves with egg yolk mixture. Bake in a 350° oven until loaves are golden brown (about 35 minutes). Transfer to racks and let cool. Makes 2 loaves (10 to 12 servings each).

Per serving: 177 calories (32% from fat), 4 g protein, 25 g carbohydrates, 6 g total fat (3 g saturated fat), 51 mg cholesterol, 158 mg sodium

Giant Cinnamon Braid

Follow steps 1–4 for **Swiss Egg Braid** (facing page), but instead of cutting dough in half, cut off a third and set aside. Divide remaining dough into 3 equal pieces. Roll each into a rope about 12 inches long.

Mix ½ cup **sugar** and 1 tablespoon **ground cinnamon** on a large sheet of wax paper. Roll each rope in cinnamon-sugar. Place on a clean sheet of wax paper and braid loosely, pinching ends together and tucking under loaf. Transfer to a greased baking sheet.

Divide reserved dough into 3 equal pieces. Roll each into a rope about 12 inches long. Braid as for larger loaf. Lightly moisten top of large braid with water and place smaller braid on top. Follow steps 5–6, brushing small loaf only with egg yolk mixture and baking until a wooden skewer inserted in center comes out clean (about 45 minutes); if crust browns too quickly, cover loosely with foil. Makes 1 loaf (20 to 24 servings).

Per serving: 196 calories (29% from fat), 4 g protein, 30 g carbohydrates, 6 g total fat (3 g saturated fat), 51 mg cholesterol, 158 mg sodium

Dried Cherry & Macadamia Nut Braid

In a small bowl, soak ½ cup **golden raisins** in ¼ cup **sweet sherry;** set aside.

Follow steps 1–2 for **Swiss Egg Braid** (facing page), but add ½ cup more **flour,** ½ cup chopped **dried cherries,** ½ cup chopped **unsalted macadamia nuts,** and 1 teaspoon grated **lemon peel** to batter along with eggs. Drain raisins and stir into batter until evenly distributed. Follow steps 3–6. Makes 2 loaves (10 to 12 servings each).

Per serving: 227 calories (34% from fat), 5 g protein, 33 g carbohydrates, 9 g total fat (4 g saturated fat), 51 mg cholesterol, 159 mg sodium

BRIOCHE

Brioche is among the most popular sweet yeast breads. Here it's offered in its traditional shape—rounded with a fluted rim and topknot.

> 1 **package active dry yeast**
> ½ **cup warm water (about 110°F)**
> 2 **teaspoons sugar**
> 1¼ **teaspoons salt**
> 3 **large eggs**
> ½ **cup (¼ lb.) butter or margarine, at room temperature**
> 3½ **to 4 cups all-purpose flour**
> 1 **large egg yolk beaten with 1 tablespoon milk**

1. Sprinkle yeast over warm water in a large bowl; let stand until foamy (about 5 minutes). Add sugar, salt, and the whole eggs; stir until blended. Cut butter into small pieces and add to yeast mixture.

2. Stir in 3 cups of the flour.

To knead by hand, turn dough out onto a lightly floured board and knead until smooth and velvety (about 5 minutes), adding more flour as needed to prevent sticking. Place in a greased bowl; turn over to grease top.

To knead with a dough hook, beat on high speed until dough is springy and pulls cleanly from sides of bowl (about 5 minutes), adding more flour, 1 tablespoon at a time, if dough clings to sides of bowl.

3. Cover with plastic wrap and let rise in a warm place until doubled (1 to 2 hours).

4. Punch dough down and knead briefly on a lightly floured board to release air. Return to greased bowl, cover, and let rise in a refrigerator for 12 to 24 hours.

5. Punch dough down again and knead briefly on a lightly floured board to release air.

To shape petites brioches, cut dough into 12 equal pieces (work with one piece at a time, keeping remaining dough refrigerated).

To shape brioche à tête, leave dough whole.

6. Pinch off a sixth of each piece of dough and set aside. Shape large portion into a ball, gently pulling top surface under until smooth. Place smooth side up in a well-buttered 3- or 4-inch petite brioche pan or 3-inch muffin cup for petites brioches, or a well-buttered 9-inch fluted brioche pan or 2-quart round baking pan for brioche à tête. Press dough down to fill pan bottom. Shape small piece of dough into a teardrop shape, smoothing top. With your finger, poke a hole in center of large dough portion through to bottom of pan. Gently and evenly nest pointed end of teardrop in hole. For petites brioches, repeat to shape remaining pieces.

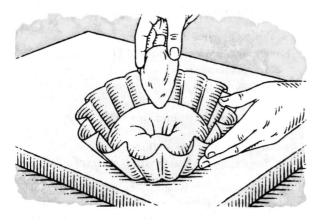

7. Cover lightly and let rise in a warm place until doubled (1 to 2 hours).

8. Brush top(s) with egg yolk mixture. Bake in a 350° oven for petites brioches, 425° for brioche à tête, until bread is well browned and a wooden skewer inserted in center comes out clean (about 20 minutes for petites brioches, 1 hour for brioche à tête); if crust browns too quickly, cover loosely with foil. Let cool in pans on racks for 5 minutes; turn out onto racks and let cool completely. Makes 12 petites brioches or 1 brioche à tête (about 8 servings).

Per petite brioche: 247 calories (37% from fat), 6 g protein, 32 g carbohydrates, 10 g total fat (5 g saturated fat), 92 mg cholesterol, 325 mg sodium

Per serving brioche à tête: 370 calories (37% from fat), 9 g protein, 48 g carbohydrates, 15 g total fat (8 g saturated fat), 138 mg cholesterol, 487 mg sodium

Banana Brioche

Follow step 1 for **Brioche** (page 65), but add ½ cup mashed ripe **banana** with eggs. Follow step 2, but add ¼ to ½ cup more **all-purpose flour** to prevent sticking or clinging to sides of bowl. Follow steps 3–8, decreasing baking time to 15 minutes for petites brioches and to 40 to 50 minutes for brioche à tête.

Per petite brioche: 270 calories (34% from fat), 7 g protein, 37 g carbohydrates, 10 g total fat (5 g saturated fat), 92 mg cholesterol, 325 mg sodium

Per serving brioche à tête: 405 calories (34% from fat), 10 g protein, 56 g carbohydrates, 15 g total fat (8 g saturated fat), 138 mg cholesterol, 487 mg sodium

• Pictured on facing page •

APRICOT TURBAN BREAD

A mélange of dried apricots, marzipan, and raisins spirals its way through this delicious loaf.

>   1 **package active dry yeast**
>   ¼ **cup warm water (about 110°F)**
>   ½ **cup milk**
>   3 **tablespoons granulated sugar**
>   ½ **teaspoon salt**
>   ¼ **cup butter or margarine, cut into ½-inch pieces**
>   **About 3½ cups all-purpose flour**
>   3 **large eggs, lightly beaten**
>   ¾ **teaspoon ground coriander or ground mace**
>   ¾ **teaspoon grated lemon peel**
>   1 **cup (about 6 oz.) chopped dried apricots**
>   7 **ounces (about 1⅓ cups) marzipan or almond paste, in ½-inch chunks**
>   ⅓ **cup golden raisins**
>   14 **sugar cubes, coarsely crushed (about 2 tablespoons)**

1. Sprinkle yeast over warm water in a large bowl; stir briefly. Let stand until foamy (about 5 minutes). Meanwhile, heat milk, granulated sugar, salt, and butter to 110°F in a small pan over low heat (butter need not melt completely). Stir into yeast mixture. Add 1½ cups of the flour; stir until evenly moistened. Reserve 1 tablespoon of the eggs; cover and refrigerate. Add remaining eggs, coriander, and lemon peel; beat with an electric mixer (using a paddle attachment if you have one) on low speed until blended.

2. Beat in 1½ cups more flour on low speed until combined.

To knead by hand, turn dough out onto a floured board and knead until smooth and no longer sticky (about 10 minutes), adding more flour as needed to prevent sticking. Place in a greased bowl; turn over to grease top.

To knead with a dough hook, beat in ¼ cup more flour on low speed. Then beat on medium speed until dough is no longer sticky and pulls cleanly from sides of bowl (about 5 minutes), adding more flour, 1 tablespoon at a time, if dough is sticky.

3. Cover with plastic wrap and let rise in a warm place until almost doubled (1 to 1½ hours).

4. Punch dough down and knead briefly on a lightly floured board to release air. Roll and stretch into a log about 16 inches long. With a floured rolling pin, roll into a thin strip about 5 inches wide and 36 inches

(Continued on page 68)

*Coffee cakes take on dazzling new dimensions. Fresh Blueberry Ring
(page 72) glimmers beside sugar-flecked Apricot Turban Bread (facing page).
Below, nuts, graham cracker crumbs, and brown sugar spiral through slices of
Walnut Coffee Roll (page 74).*

long, occasionally lifting dough and dusting board with flour to prevent sticking (let dough rest for a few minutes if too elastic).

5. Sprinkle apricots, marzipan, and raisins down center of strip. Brush long edges with water. Bring dough over filling, pinching edges together to seal. Transfer to a large greased baking sheet. To create base, coil one end of dough into a 7-inch circle, facing the seam inside. Coil remaining dough around base, gradually making loaf narrower and higher, forming a slouchy turban shape. Cover lightly and let rise in a warm place until puffy (20 to 30 minutes).

6. Brush with reserved 1 tablespoon egg. Sprinkle with crushed sugar. Bake in a 325° oven until bread is golden brown and a skewer inserted in center of thickest part comes out clean (1¼ to 1½ hours); if crust browns too quickly, cover loosely with foil. Transfer to a rack and let cool. Makes 1 loaf (about 12 servings).

Per serving: 337 calories (19% from fat), 8 g protein, 61 g carbohydrates, 7 g total fat (3 g saturated fat), 65 mg cholesterol, 156 mg sodium

• *Pictured on page 62* •

ORANGE-SAFFRON BREAD

Saffron is the dried stigmas of a crocus native to Greece. A pinch is all you need to impart an aromatic, slightly bitter flavor and a brilliant yellow color to foods.

   ¼ **teaspoon saffron threads**
   ¾ **cup milk**
   1 **package active dry yeast**
   ¼ **cup warm water (about 110°F)**
   ¼ **cup plus 1 tablespoon sugar**
   3 **tablespoons melted butter or margarine**
   2 **tablespoons honey**
   ¾ **cup orange juice**
   1 **large egg**
   2 **teaspoons grated orange peel**
   ½ **teaspoon salt**
      About 5 cups all-purpose flour
   1 **large egg white, lightly beaten**

1. Bring saffron and milk to a simmer in a small pan; let cool to about 110°F. Meanwhile, sprinkle yeast over warm water in a large bowl; stir briefly. Let stand until foamy (about 5 minutes). Add milk mixture, ¼ cup of the sugar, butter, honey, orange juice, the whole egg, orange peel, and salt; stir until blended.

2. Stir in 4 cups of the flour, 1 cup at a time, until combined.

To knead by hand, stir in ½ cup more flour. Turn dough out onto a lightly floured board and knead until smooth and elastic (10 to 20 minutes), adding more flour as needed to prevent sticking.

To knead with a dough hook, beat in ¾ cup more flour on low speed until combined. Then beat on high speed until dough is springy, is no longer sticky, and pulls cleanly from sides of bowl (about 5 minutes), adding more flour, a few tablespoons at a time, if dough clings to sides of bowl. Turn dough out onto a lightly floured board and knead for 2 minutes.

3. Place dough in a greased bowl; turn over to grease top. Cover with plastic wrap and let rise in a refrigerator for 6 to 24 hours.

4. Punch dough down and knead briefly on a lightly floured board to release air. Cut into 3 equal pieces. Let stand, covered, for 10 minutes. Then stretch and roll each piece into a smooth 30-inch rope. Braid ropes, pinching ends together. Tie a knot in center of braid; wrap ends around knot, in opposite directions, and tuck underneath to make a round loaf. Cover and let rise in a warm place until puffy (about 30 minutes).

5. Brush lightly with egg white; sprinkle with remaining 1 tablespoon sugar. Bake on lowest rack of a 350° oven until bread is golden and a skewer inserted in thickest part comes out clean (about 45 minutes); if crust browns too quickly, cover loosely with foil. Transfer to a rack and let cool. Makes 1 loaf (about 14 servings).

Per serving: 235 calories (14% from fat), 6 g protein, 44 g carbohydrates, 4 g total fat (2 g saturated fat), 24 mg cholesterol, 119 mg sodium

CINNAMON-ORANGE SWIRL BREAD

Sweetly spiced with cinnamon-sugar and scented with orange, this moist bread is delicious toasted.

   1 **package active dry yeast**
   ¼ **cup warm water (about 110°F)**
  1¼ **cups warm milk (about 110°F)**
   ¼ **cup plus 3 tablespoons butter or margarine, melted and cooled**
   ¾ **cup orange juice**
   ¼ **cup *each* sugar and honey**
   1 **large egg**
   1 **tablespoon orange zest**

6½ to 7½ cups flour

⅔ cup sugar mixed with 1½ tablespoons ground cinnamon

1. Sprinkle yeast over warm water in a large bowl; stir briefly. Let stand until foamy (about 5 minutes). Add milk, ¼ cup of the butter, orange juice, the ¼ cup sugar, honey, egg, and orange zest; stir until blended.

2. Stir in 4 cups of the flour.

To knead by hand, stir in 2 cups more flour. Turn dough out onto a lightly floured board and knead until smooth and elastic (10 to 20 minutes), adding more flour as needed to prevent sticking. Place in a greased bowl; turn over to grease top.

To knead with a dough hook, gradually beat in 2½ cups more flour on low speed. Then beat on high speed until dough is springy and no longer sticky (5 to 8 minutes), adding more flour, a few tablespoons at a time, if dough is sticky.

3. Cover with plastic wrap and let rise in a warm place until doubled (1 to 1½ hours).

4. Punch dough down and knead briefly on a lightly floured board to release air. Cut dough in half. Keeping remaining dough covered, roll one portion into an 8- by 12-inch rectangle. Brush with 1 tablespoon more butter and sprinkle evenly with half the cinnamon-sugar to within 1 inch of edges. Beginning at a short side, roll up dough, pinching edge against loaf to seal. Place seam side down in a greased 5- by 9-inch loaf pan. Repeat to shape remaining dough. Cover lightly and let rise in a warm place until puffy (about 45 minutes).

5. Brush with remaining 1 tablespoon butter. Bake in a 350° oven until loaves are browned and sound hollow when gently tapped on bottoms (40 to 45 minutes). Turn out onto racks and let cool. Makes 2 loaves (about 10 servings each).

Per serving: 270 calories (19% from fat), 6 g protein, 49 g carbohydrates, 6 g total fat (3 g saturated fat), 24 mg cholesterol, 53 mg sodium

• *Pictured on page 62* •

APPLE-WALNUT BREAD

Fresh apples sautéed in butter produce a moist, delicately flavored bread.

2 tablespoons butter or margarine

1 cup diced peeled Newtown Pippin or Granny Smith apples

½ cup apple juice

1 package active dry yeast

¼ cup warm water (about 110°F)

½ cup warm milk (about 110°F)

¼ cup honey

½ cup (¼ lb.) plus 1 tablespoon butter or margarine, melted and cooled

1 teaspoon ground cinnamon

¼ teaspoon *each* ground cloves and ground nutmeg

½ cup chopped walnuts

4 to 4½ cups all-purpose flour

1 tablespoon sugar mixed with ½ teaspoon ground cinnamon

1. Melt the 2 tablespoons butter in an 8- to 10-inch frying pan over medium heat. Add apples; cook, stirring, until soft (about 7 minutes). Transfer to a food processor or blender. Add apple juice; whirl until puréed.

2. Sprinkle yeast over warm water in a large bowl; stir briefly. Let stand until foamy (about 5 minutes). Add milk, honey, ½ cup of the butter, the 1 teaspoon cinnamon, cloves, nutmeg, nuts, and apple purée; stir well.

3. Stir in 3 cups of the flour.

To knead by hand, stir in ¾ cup more flour. Turn dough out onto a lightly floured board and knead until smooth and elastic (10 to 20 minutes), adding more flour as needed to prevent sticking. Place in a greased bowl; turn over to grease top.

To knead with a dough hook, beat in 1 cup more flour on low speed. Then beat on high speed until dough is elastic and pulls cleanly from sides of bowl (about 7 minutes), adding more flour, a few tablespoons at a time, if dough still clings to sides of bowl.

4. Cover with plastic wrap and let rise in a warm place until doubled (1 to 1½ hours).

5. Punch dough down and knead briefly on a lightly floured board to release air. Cut dough into 3 equal pieces. Gently knead each portion into a ball and place side by side in a greased 5- by 9-inch loaf pan. Cover lightly and let rise in a warm place until puffy (about 45 minutes).

6. Brush with remaining 1 tablespoon butter; sprinkle with cinnamon-sugar. Bake in a 350° oven until loaf is browned and a skewer inserted in center comes out clean (about 40 minutes); if crust browns too quickly, cover loosely with foil. Turn out onto a rack and let cool. Makes 1 loaf (10 to 12 servings).

Per serving: 353 calories (42% from fat), 6 g protein, 46 g carbohydrates, 17 g total fat (8 g saturated fat), 33 mg cholesterol, 125 mg sodium

Poached apricots glisten in a sugar-dusted yeast crust, a traditional favorite
in the Netherlands. Because it's part pie, part coffee cake, Queen's Vlaai (facing page)
is perfect for breakfast, with mid-morning coffee, or for dessert.

• *Pictured on facing page* •

QUEEN'S VLAAI

A specialty of the Limburg region in the southern part of the Netherlands, this creation is a cross between a pie and a coffee cake. The recipe's royal designation alludes to the orange color of the apricots and to the Dutch royal family's surname, van Oranje. A sprinkling of powdered sugar applied just before serving makes a lacy pattern on the top.

>   1   package active dry yeast
>   ½   cup warm water (about 110°F)
>   ⅓   cup butter or margarine, at room temperature
>   ¼   teaspoon salt
>   ¾   cup granulated sugar
>   About 1¾ cups all-purpose flour
>   3   cups (about 1 lb.) dried apricots
>   1½   cups water
>   Powdered sugar

1. Sprinkle yeast over the ½ cup warm water in a large bowl; let stand until foamy (about 5 minutes). Add butter, salt, ¼ cup of the granulated sugar, and 1 cup of the flour; beat with a heavy spoon until dough is stretchy. Add ¾ cup more flour; stir until well blended.

2. Turn dough out onto a lightly floured board and knead until smooth and elastic (8 to 10 minutes), adding just enough additional flour to prevent sticking. Place dough in a greased bowl; turn over to grease top.

3. Cover with plastic wrap and let rise in a warm place until almost doubled (1 to 1¼ hours). Meanwhile, combine apricots, remaining ½ cup granulated sugar, and the 1½ cups water in a 3- to 4-quart pan. Bring to a boil over high heat; reduce heat to low and simmer, stirring occasionally, until apricots are tender when pierced (5 to 10 minutes). With a slotted spoon, transfer apricots to a bowl and let cool. Boil syrup, uncovered, over high heat until reduced to ⅓ cup (about 5 minutes), watching closely to prevent scorching; set aside.

4. Punch dough down and knead briefly on a lightly floured board to release air. Pat into an 8-inch round. Press dough evenly over bottom and ¾ inch up sides of a well-buttered 10- to 11-inch tart pan with a removable bottom.

5. Arrange apricots, slightly overlapping, on dough. Pour syrup over fruit. Gently press edge of dough down flush with fruit.

6. Bake on lowest rack of a 375° oven until crust is evenly browned (about 40 minutes); if crust browns too quickly, cover loosely with foil. Transfer to a rack and let cool. With a knife, loosen pie from pan sides; remove rim. Just before serving, sprinkle powdered sugar over top of pie. Makes 1 pie (about 10 servings).

Per serving: 321 calories (21% from fat), 4 g protein, 62 g carbohydrates, 8 g total fat (4 g saturated fat), 18 mg cholesterol, 129 mg sodium

ITALIAN FLATBREAD WITH GRAPES

The wine-making regions of Tuscany and Umbria enjoy a unique harvest-time specialty: a flat focaccia-type loaf topped with grapes, herbs, and a little sugar. In Italy, the bread, known as *schiacciata all' uva*, uses the regions' ripe wine grapes. Here, the soft dough is topped with the common seedless red variety.

>   Pizza dough (page 40); or 2 loaves (1 lb.
>   *each*) frozen white bread dough, thawed
>   and kneaded together
>   2   tablespoons olive oil
>   2   cups seedless red grapes
>   2   tablespoons chopped fresh rosemary or
>   1 tablespoon dried rosemary, crumbled
>   2   tablespoons sugar
>   Salt (optional)

1. Follow steps 1–3 for pizza dough. After dough has risen, brush a 10- by 15-inch rimmed baking sheet with 1 tablespoon of the oil.

2. Punch dough down and knead briefly on a lightly floured board to release air. Let rest, covered, for 10 minutes. Roll into a rectangle about ½ inch thick. Place dough in pan, patting firmly to pan edges (if dough is too elastic, cover and let rest for about 5 minutes and then continue). Brush dough with remaining 1 tablespoon oil. Let rise, uncovered, in a warm place until slightly puffy (15 to 30 minutes).

3. Sprinkle with grapes, pressing fruit in lightly; sprinkle with rosemary and sugar. Season to taste with salt, if desired. Bake on lowest rack of a 450° oven until well browned (about 30 minutes). Makes 1 loaf (about 12 servings).

Per serving: 215 calories (27% from fat), 4 g protein, 35 g carbohydrates, 6 g total fat (1 g saturated fat), 0 mg cholesterol, 93 mg sodium

• Pictured on page 67 •

FRESH BLUEBERRY RING

During summer months, fresh blueberries rank among the best fruits to use in sweet breads and cakes.

- 1 package active dry yeast
- ¼ cup warm water (about 110°F)
- 2½ cups all-purpose flour
- 4 tablespoons granulated sugar
- ½ teaspoon salt
- 7 tablespoons cold butter or margarine
- ½ cup milk
- 2 large eggs, separated
- 1 teaspoon grated orange peel
- ½ cup firmly packed brown sugar
- 2 cups fresh blueberries, rinsed and dried
- 1 teaspoon ground cinnamon

1. Sprinkle yeast over warm water in a small bowl; stir briefly. Let stand until foamy (about 5 minutes). Meanwhile, in a large bowl, mix flour, 3 tablespoons of the granulated sugar, and salt. With a pastry blender or 2 knives, cut in 6 tablespoons of the butter until mixture resembles coarse crumbs. Add yeast mixture, milk, and egg yolks; stir until blended. Cover batter and egg whites separately with plastic wrap and refrigerate for 4 to 24 hours.

2. Punch dough down and knead briefly on a lightly floured board to release air. With a floured rolling pin, roll into a 12- by 22-inch rectangle. In a small bowl, beat egg whites until soft peaks form; gradually beat in orange peel and 2 tablespoons of the brown sugar. Spread meringue over dough to within 1 inch of edges. Scatter with blueberries and sprinkle with cinnamon and remaining brown sugar. Beginning at a long side, roll up dough, pinching edge against loaf to seal. Place seam side down in a well-greased 10-inch tube pan with a removable bottom, pinching ends together to seal.

3. Cover lightly and let rise in a warm place until doubled (about 1½ hours).

4. Melt remaining 1 tablespoon butter and brush over dough; sprinkle with remaining 1 tablespoon granulated sugar. Bake in a 375° oven until evenly browned (about 35 minutes). Let cool in pan on a rack for 20 minutes. Loosen bread from pan sides with a knife and remove rim. Lift bread from pan onto a serving plate. Makes 1 loaf (10 to 12 servings).

Per serving: 271 calories (32% from fat), 5 g protein, 41 g carbohydrates, 10 g total fat (5 g saturated fat), 60 mg cholesterol, 197 mg sodium

PULL-APART COFFEE CAKE

This delectable bubble loaf is an especially good choice for a make-ahead bread. Shaped and ready to bake, it can wait overnight in the refrigerator to be baked right before you want to serve it.

- Cinnamon-Nut Sugar (recipe follows)
- 1 package active dry yeast
- ¼ cup warm water (about 110°F)
- ½ teaspoon salt
- ¼ cup *each* sugar and salad oil
- ¾ cup warm milk (about 110°F)
- 1 large egg
- About 3½ cups all-purpose flour
- 1 cup raisins
- ½ cup (¼ lb.) butter or margarine, melted

1. Prepare Cinnamon-Nut Sugar; set aside.

2. Sprinkle yeast over warm water in a large bowl; stir briefly. Let stand until foamy (about 5 minutes). Add salt, sugar, oil, milk, and egg to yeast mixture; stir until blended.

3. Add 3¼ cups of the flour, 1 cup at a time, stirring after each addition.

To knead by hand, turn dough out onto a lightly floured board and knead until smooth and elastic (about 10 minutes), adding more flour as needed to prevent sticking. Press raisins into dough and knead until evenly distributed.

To knead with a dough hook, beat on high speed until dough pulls cleanly from sides of bowl (about 10 minutes), adding more flour, 1 tablespoon at a time, if dough clings to sides of bowl. Turn out onto a board, press raisins into dough, and knead until evenly distributed.

4. Cut dough into 3 equal pieces; then cut each portion into 16 equal pieces. Shape each piece into a ball; roll each ball in butter and then in sugar mixture. Stagger balls, barely touching, in layers in a greased 9- to 10-inch ring mold (about 2½-quart size). Sprinkle with remaining sugar mixture; drizzle with remaining butter. Cover lightly with plastic wrap. Let rise in a warm place until puffy (about 45 minutes) or in a refrigerator for 16 to 18 hours.

5. Bake, uncovered, in a 350° oven until well browned (30 to 35 minutes). Let cool in pan on a rack for at least 20 minutes; invert onto a serving plate. If desired, place another plate on top of cake and gently turn over (if cake comes apart, restack pieces). Makes 1 loaf (6 to 8 servings).

Cinnamon-Nut Sugar. In a small bowl, combine ¾ cup **sugar,** 1 tablespoon **ground cinnamon,** and ½ cup finely chopped **walnuts;** stir until blended.

Per serving: 688 calories (38% from fat), 11 g protein, 97 g carbohydrates, 30 g total fat (11 g saturated fat), 70 mg cholesterol, 318 mg sodium

• Pictured on page 62 •

BUTTERY ALMOND BEAR CLAWS

Rich and almondy, bear claws are usually considered a bakery specialty. But with easy refrigerator dough and this streamlined technique, you'll be able to make pastries that rival the best you can buy.

- 1 **package active dry yeast**
- ¼ **cup warm water (about 110°F)**
- 3 **large eggs**
- ¼ **cup sugar**
- ½ **teaspoon salt**
- 1 **small can (about 5 oz.) evaporated milk**
- 1 **cup (½ lb.) butter or margarine, melted and cooled**
  About 3⅓ cups all-purpose flour
  Almond Filling (recipe follows)
  About ¾ cup sliced almonds
  Sugar

1. Sprinkle yeast over warm water in a large bowl; stir briefly. Let stand until foamy (about 5 minutes). Separate eggs, reserving 2 of the whites in one bowl and remaining white in another. Stir egg yolks into yeast mixture. Add the ¼ cup sugar, salt, milk, and butter; stir until blended.

2. Add 3⅓ cups of the flour to yeast mixture. Beat with an electric mixer on low speed or with a heavy spoon until blended. Cover batter and egg whites separately with plastic wrap and refrigerate until next day or for up to 3 days.

3. Prepare Almond Filling.

4. Punch dough down and knead briefly on a floured board to release air. Roll into a 13½- by 27-inch rectangle, using a ruler to straighten edges. Cut dough lengthwise into 3 strips, each 4½ inches wide.

5. Divide filling into 3 equal portions; roll each into a 27-inch rope. Lay a rope in center of each dough strip, flattening rope slightly with your fingers. Fold long edges of dough strip over filling, pinching edges together to seal.

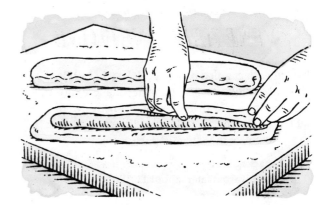

6. Cut each strip crosswise into 6 pieces, each 4½ inches long. Place seam side down on 3 large greased baking sheets and flatten slightly. With a sharp knife, make a row of cuts ¾ inch apart halfway across a long side of each piece; curve dough so cut pieces fan out.

7. Beat remaining egg white lightly and brush over dough; sprinkle evenly with almonds and sugar. Let rise, uncovered, in a warm place until puffy (about 20 minutes).

8. Bake in a 375° oven until golden brown (about 15 minutes), switching pan positions halfway through baking. Transfer to racks and let cool. Makes 18 bear claws.

Almond Filling. In a medium-size bowl, combine ½ cup (¼ lb.) **butter** or margarine, at room temperature, and 1⅓ cups **powdered sugar;** beat until smooth. Add ⅔ cup **all-purpose flour** and 8 ounces **almond paste;** stir until crumbly and evenly mixed. Beat in 1 teaspoon grated **lemon peel** and 2 of the reserved **egg whites.** Stir in ¾ cup finely chopped **blanched almonds.** Cover and refrigerate for at least 2 hours or for up to 3 days.

Per bear claw: 426 calories (53% from fat), 8 g protein, 42 g carbohydrates, 26 g total fat (11 g saturated fat), 79 mg cholesterol, 240 mg sodium

• Pictured on facing page •

VENETIAN PANETTONE

Dotted with candied orange peel, Venetian-style *panettone*, unlike its more familiar Milanese cousin, is baked in a mold that makes it distinctively tall (at home, you can use a doubled brown paper bag to approximate the same shape).

- 2 packages active dry yeast
- ¾ cup warm water (about 110°F)
- ½ cup granulated sugar
- ½ teaspoon salt
- ½ cup (¼ lb.) butter or margarine, at room temperature
- 4 large egg yolks
- 2 teaspoons vanilla
- ¾ teaspoon grated lemon peel
  About 3¼ cups all-purpose flour
- 1 tablespoon melted butter or margarine
- ¾ cup diced candied orange peel
- ¼ cup whole blanched almonds
- 1 large egg white, lightly beaten
- 6 sugar cubes, coarsely crushed

1. Sprinkle yeast over warm water in a large bowl; let stand until foamy (about 5 minutes). Add granulated sugar, salt, the ½ cup butter, egg yolks, vanilla, lemon peel, and 2 cups of the flour. Beat with an electric mixer (using a paddle attachment if you have one) on low speed until flour is evenly moistened. Then beat on high speed until dough is stretchy and glossy (5 to 10 minutes).

2. Stir in 1¼ cups more flour.

To knead by hand, turn dough out onto a floured board and knead until smooth and springy (5 to 10 minutes), adding just enough additional flour to prevent sticking (dough should be soft and slightly sticky). Place in a greased bowl; turn over to grease top.

To knead with a dough hook, beat on low speed until combined. Then beat on high speed until dough starts to pull away from sides of bowl (5 to 10 minutes), adding more flour, 1 tablespoon at a time, until dough pulls free but is still soft and slightly sticky.

3. Cover with plastic wrap. Let rise in a warm place until doubled (1½ to 2 hours) or in a refrigerator until next day. Meanwhile, line a brown paper lunch bag (3½ by 5 inches on bottom) with another bag of the same size. Fold top down to form a cuff on outside (bag should be about 6½ inches tall). Brush inside generously with melted butter. Set upright in a 4- by 8-inch loaf pan.

4. Punch dough down and knead briefly on a lightly floured board to release air. Press orange peel into dough and knead until evenly distributed.

5. Shape dough into a ball and drop into bag. Cover lightly and let rise in a warm place until almost doubled (45 to 60 minutes).

6. Reserve 2 tablespoons of the almonds; finely chop remaining nuts. Gently brush top of loaf with egg white; lightly press in reserved whole almonds. Sprinkle with chopped nuts and crushed sugar cubes.

7. Bake in a 350° oven for 30 minutes. Reduce oven temperature to 325° and continue to bake until a skewer inserted in thickest part comes out clean (25 to 30 more minutes); if crust browns too quickly, cover loosely with foil. Let cool in pan on a rack for 10 minutes. Lift bag from pan and let cool briefly on rack. Tear off bag and serve warm. Makes 1 loaf (about 10 servings).

Per serving: 385 calories (35% from fat), 7 g protein, 55 g carbohydrates, 15 g total fat (7 g saturated fat), 113 mg cholesterol, 225 mg sodium

• Pictured on page 67 •

WALNUT COFFEE ROLL

You make the dough for this lightly sweet coffee cake in advance and let it rise in the refrigerator. Then you add a filling of walnuts, graham cracker crumbs, and brown sugar. The result? Three cakes drizzled with a sugary glaze and cut into delicious spiraled rolls.

- ¼ cup granulated sugar
  About 4 cups all-purpose flour
- 1 cup (½ lb.) cold butter or margarine, cut into pieces
- 1 package active dry yeast
- 1 cup warm water (about 110°F)
- 2 large eggs
- 2 cups firmly packed brown sugar
- 1 cup *each* chopped walnuts and graham cracker crumbs
- ¾ cup powdered sugar
- 1 tablespoon cool water

1. Combine granulated sugar and 4 cups of the flour in a large bowl. With a pastry blender or 2 knives, cut in butter until mixture resembles fine crumbs.

2. Sprinkle yeast over the 1 cup warm water in a large bowl; let stand until foamy (about 5 minutes). Add eggs and beat until blended. Pour into flour mixture

(Continued on page 76)

Start the day on a festive note with cups of foamy cappuccino and wedges of sky-high Venetian Panettone (facing page). Each slice is studded with candied orange peel and crusted with crunchy almonds and coarse sugar.

and stir until evenly moistened. Cover with plastic wrap and let rise in a refrigerator for 12 to 24 hours.

3. Combine brown sugar, nuts, and cracker crumbs in a small bowl; stir until blended. Set aside.

4. Cut dough into 3 equal pieces. Keeping remaining dough covered, roll one portion on a lightly floured board into a 12-inch square and spread with a third of the crumb mixture, pressing in lightly. Roll up tightly, pinching edge against loaf to seal. Repeat to shape remaining dough.

5. Place rolls seam sides down and 2 inches apart on an ungreased baking sheet. Cover lightly and let rise in a warm place until slightly puffy (about 1 hour).

6. Bake, uncovered, in a 350° oven until richly browned (about 35 minutes). Transfer to racks and let cool briefly. Meanwhile, combine powdered sugar and the 1 tablespoon water in a small bowl; stir until smooth. Drizzle over warm rolls; cut each roll into 4 pieces. Makes 12 rolls.

Per roll: 591 calories (35% from fat), 8 g protein, 89 g carbohydrates, 23 g total fat (10 g saturated fat), 77 mg cholesterol, 243 mg sodium

Stir in 1½ cups more flour and beat until smooth. Turn dough out onto a lightly floured board and knead until smooth and elastic (8 to 10 minutes), adding more flour as needed to prevent sticking. Cover with plastic wrap and set aside.

2. Combine water, 4 tablespoons of the butter, and ½ cup of the brown sugar in a small bowl; stir until blended. Distribute mixture among twelve 2½-inch muffin cups; top evenly with pecans.

3. Roll dough on a lightly floured board into a 12- by 15-inch rectangle. Brush with remaining 2 tablespoons butter. Mix cinnamon with remaining ¼ cup brown sugar and sprinkle over dough. Beginning at a short side, roll up dough, pinching edge against loaf to seal. Cut crosswise into 12 equal pieces. Place each piece cut side down in a muffin cup. Let rise, uncovered, in a warm place until doubled (about 1½ hours).

4. Bake in a 350° oven until golden (about 25 minutes). Immediately invert pan onto a serving plate; let pan remain briefly on rolls so syrup can drizzle down. Let cool for at least 10 minutes. Makes 12 rolls.

Per roll: 320 calories (39% from fat), 5 g protein, 44 g carbohydrates, 14 g total fat (5 g saturated fat), 16 mg cholesterol, 296 mg sodium

UPSIDE-DOWN PECAN ROLLS

These sweet breakfast pastries require just one rising. Let them cool briefly before you eat them—right out of the oven, the caramel-pecan topping is hot enough to burn your fingers and tongue.

  ¼ **teaspoon baking soda**
  ¼ **cup granulated sugar**
  1 **teaspoon salt**
  1 **package active dry yeast**
    About 3 cups all-purpose flour
  1 **cup buttermilk**
  3 **tablespoons salad oil**
  ¼ **cup water**
  6 **tablespoons butter or margarine, melted and cooled**
  ¾ **cup firmly packed brown sugar**
  ¾ **cup chopped pecans**
  1 **teaspoon ground cinnamon**

1. Mix baking soda, granulated sugar, salt, yeast, and 1 cup of the flour in a large bowl. In a small pan, heat buttermilk and oil to 110°F over medium-low heat. Add buttermilk mixture to flour mixture and beat with an electric mixer on high speed for 2 minutes.

• Pictured on page 62 •

PUMPKIN SPICE BUBBLE BREAD

Inverted onto a platter, this richly glazed dessert bread makes an impressive presentation.

  2 **teaspoons ground cinnamon**
  1 **teaspoon *each* ground cloves, ground ginger, and ground nutmeg**
  2 **packages active dry yeast**
  1 **cup warm water (about 110°F)**
  1¼ **cups sugar**
  ½ **cup (¼ lb.) butter or margarine, melted and cooled**
  1 **teaspoon salt**
  ½ **cup instant nonfat dry milk**
  1 **cup canned pumpkin**
    About 5½ cups all-purpose flour
  ½ **cup finely chopped walnuts**

1. Combine cinnamon, cloves, ginger, and nutmeg in a small bowl; stir until blended. Set aside.

2. Sprinkle yeast over warm water in a large bowl; let stand until foamy (about 5 minutes). Stir in ½ cup of the sugar, 3 tablespoons of the butter, salt, dry milk,

(Continued on page 79)

GOLDEN TEDDY BEAR BREADS

Soft, plump breads shaped like teddy bears add a touch of whimsy and imagination to your holiday table. Easy to make, the dough is smooth and firm—just right for shaping. Each recipe makes enough for four teddy bears, complete with arms, legs, and ears. The rich egg breads can be frozen, so you can bake the bears ahead if you like.

If you want to use the teddy bears as a project at a children's holiday party, simply mix up the dough in advance; then let the children shape the bears. Once the dough has risen, bake the breads—they'll be ready for the kids to take home at the end of the party.

Teddy Bear Breads

- 1 **package active dry yeast**
- ¼ **cup warm water (about 110°F)**
- ½ **cup (¼ lb.) butter or margarine, at room temperature**
- ½ **cup sugar**
- 2 **tablespoons vanilla**
- ⅓ **cup warm milk (about 110°F)**
- ½ **teaspoon salt**
- 5 **large eggs**
  About 4¾ cups all-purpose flour
- 1 **large egg beaten with 1 tablespoon milk**

1. Sprinkle yeast over warm water in a large bowl; stir briefly. Let stand until foamy (about 5 minutes). Add butter, sugar, vanilla, milk, salt, and the 5 eggs; beat until combined. Stir in 3 cups of the flour; beat with an electric mixer (using a paddle attachment if you have one) on high speed until dough is smooth and stretchy (about 6 minutes).

2. Add 1¾ cups more flour.

To knead by hand, stir with a heavy spoon until flour is combined.

To knead with a dough hook, beat on high speed until dough pulls cleanly from sides of bowl (about 5 minutes).

3. Cover with plastic wrap and let rise in a warm place until doubled (about 1 hour) or in a refrigerator until next day.

4. Turn dough out onto a lightly floured board and knead briefly to release air. Cut into 4 equal pieces. Working with one piece at a time (keep remaining dough covered), divide each piece as follows: 3 tablespoons for arms, ½ cup for body, about ¼ cup for head, and 1 to 1½ tablespoons total for ears, face features, and belly button.

Roll arm and leg pieces into 8-inch-long ropes. Shape into arcs and place on a greased baking sheet, spacing arcs 1 inch apart at centers. Press center 3 inches of arcs flat; brush flattened portions with egg mixture.

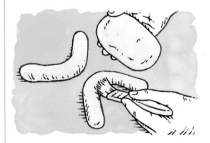

Shape body dough into an oval 5 inches long, gently pulling top surface under until smooth. Place body smooth side up on flattened part of arcs. Press and tuck bottom of trunk underneath arc to secure. If necessary, pull arms and legs until they are 2½ inches long.

Shape head into a ball, pulling top surface under until smooth. Press into a 2½-inch circle. Press top ½ inch of body to flatten; brush with egg mixture. Place head smooth side up on baking sheet so head overlaps flat part of body; press to seal.

Shape two-thirds of remaining dough into 2 ears. Flatten 2 spots on top sides of head, about ¼ inch in; brush with egg mixture. Press ears in place.

Roll remaining dough into 4 or 5 balls: 2 for eyes, 1 for belly button, 1 for nose, and 1 for snout, if desired (make nose and snout pieces slightly bigger). With your finger, poke small holes in bear for dough pieces. Brush holes with egg mixture. Place dough in holes.

5. Cover lightly and let rise in a warm place until puffy (25 to 30 minutes).

6. Brush gently with remaining egg mixture. Bake in a 350° oven until golden (16 to 18 minutes). Let cool on sheets for 10 minutes; transfer to racks and let cool completely. Makes 4 bear breads (2 or 3 servings each).

Per serving: 332 calories (30% from fat), 9 g protein, 48 g carbohydrates, 11 g total fat (6 g saturated fat), 128 mg cholesterol, 206 mg sodium

A crisp, wafer-thin fringe decorates the top of raisin-studded
Costa Rican Fringed Spice Bread (facing page). In its native land, this aromatic
loaf is often enjoyed on special occasions.

Pumpkin Spice Bubble Bread (continued)

and pumpkin. Add 2 teaspoons of the cinnamon mixture and 2 cups of the flour. Beat with an electric mixer (using a paddle attachment if you have one) on low speed or with a heavy spoon until blended. Gradually beat in 2½ cups more flour until combined.

3. Turn dough out onto a floured board and knead until smooth (about 5 minutes), adding more flour as needed to prevent sticking. Place in a greased bowl; turn over to grease top. Cover with plastic wrap and let rise in a warm place until doubled (about 1½ hours). Meanwhile, combine remaining cinnamon mixture and remaining ¾ cup sugar in a small bowl; stir until blended. Set aside.

4. Punch dough down and knead briefly on a lightly floured board to release air. Cut into 3 equal pieces. Roll each piece into a smooth rope about 18 inches long; then cut each rope into 18 equal pieces. Shape each piece into a ball; roll in remaining butter and then in sugar mixture.

5. Arrange 18 balls in a single layer in a greased 10-inch tube pan (if pan has a removable bottom, line bottom and sides with foil and grease foil before adding balls). Sprinkle with a third of the nuts. Repeat, making 2 more layers and sprinkling each layer with nuts. Cover lightly and let rise in a warm place until very puffy (about 45 minutes).

6. Bake, uncovered, in a 350° oven until golden brown (about 55 minutes). Let cool in pan on a rack for 20 minutes; invert onto a serving plate. Makes 1 loaf (about 12 servings).

Per serving: 424 calories (26% from fat), 9 g protein, 71 g carbohydrates, 12 g total fat (5 g saturated fat), 21 mg cholesterol, 281 mg sodium

• *Pictured on facing page* •

COSTA RICAN FRINGED SPICE BREAD

In Costa Rica, this springy, flavorful bread is called *pan bon* (good bread). Richly scented with spices and studded with dried fruit, it easily lives up to its name. Caramelized sugar and Cheddar cheese give the loaf its warm hue; a strip of dough cut like a fringe decorates the top.

    1   cup sugar
    ½   cup (¼ lb.) butter or margarine, cut into pieces
    1½ cups boiling water
    1   tablespoon vanilla
    2   packages active dry yeast
    ¼   cup warm water (about 110°F)
    1½ teaspoons *each* ground ginger and ground cinnamon
    ½   teaspoon *each* ground nutmeg and salt
    5   to 5½ cups all-purpose flour
    1   cup (about 4 oz.) shredded sharp Cheddar cheese
    ½   cup *each* raisins and chopped dried apricots

1. Melt sugar in a wide frying pan over medium heat, stirring often, until caramelized to a brown syrup (it should not be charred and burned smelling). Add butter and the 1½ cups boiling water. Reduce heat to low and cook, stirring, until sugar is dissolved and butter is melted. Remove from heat and let cool to 110°F. Add vanilla.

2. Sprinkle yeast over the ¼ cup warm water in a large bowl; stir briefly. Let stand until foamy (about 5 minutes). Add sugar mixture, ginger, cinnamon, nutmeg, and salt; stir until blended.

3. Stir in 4 cups of the flour.

To knead by hand, stir in 1 cup more flour until evenly moistened. Turn dough out onto a floured board and knead until smooth and elastic (about 10 minutes), adding just enough additional flour to prevent sticking. Pinch off 3 tablespoons of the dough, cover, and set aside. Press cheese, raisins, and apricots into remaining dough and knead until evenly distributed. Place in a greased bowl; turn over to grease top.

To knead with a dough hook, beat in 1 cup more flour on low speed. Then beat on high speed until dough is stretchy and pulls cleanly from sides of bowl (about 3 minutes), adding more flour, 1 tablespoon at a time, if dough is sticky. Pinch off 3 tablespoons of the dough, cover, and set aside. On low speed, gradually beat cheese, raisins, and apricots into remaining dough just until incorporated.

4. Cover with plastic wrap and let rise in a warm place until almost doubled (2 to 2½ hours).

5. Punch dough down and knead briefly on a lightly floured board to release air. Cut dough in half. Shape each half into a ball. Place each on a greased baking sheet and flatten into a 6-inch round.

6. Divide reserved dough in half. Roll each piece into a 12-inch rope. With a floured rolling pin, roll each rope into a 2- by 14-inch strip. Along one side of each strip, make 1½-inch-long slashes about ¼ inch apart. Coil a strip over top of each loaf. Cover lightly and let rise in a warm place until almost doubled (1½ to 2 hours).

(Continued on next page)

7. Bake in a 325° oven until tops of loaves spring back when gently pressed in center (40 to 45 minutes). Transfer to racks and let cool. Makes 2 loaves (about 8 servings each).

Per serving: 313 calories (25% from fat), 7 g protein, 52 g carbohydrates, 9 g total fat (5 g saturated fat), 23 mg cholesterol, 173 mg sodium

CROISSANTS

The secret to achieving delicate, flaky croissants is in keeping the dough cold while you work.

> 1 **package active dry yeast**
> ¼ **cup warm water (about 110°F)**
> ¾ **cup warm milk (about 110°F)**
> 1 **tablespoon sugar**
> ½ **teaspoon salt**
> ⅓ **cup gluten flour**
> 2¼ **cups bread flour**
> 1 **cup (½ lb.) cold unsalted butter**
> **Filling (optional; suggestions follow)**
> 1 **large egg yolk beaten with 1 tablespoon milk**

1. Sprinkle yeast over warm water in a large bowl; stir briefly. Let stand until foamy (about 5 minutes). Stir in milk, sugar, salt, and gluten flour. Gradually add 2 cups of the bread flour, beating with an electric mixer (using a paddle attachment if you have one) on high speed for 5 minutes (or beating vigorously by hand for 15 minutes) until dough is elastic and pulls away from sides of bowl in stretchy strands. Cover with plastic wrap and let rise in a warm place until doubled (about 1½ hours).

2. Turn dough out onto a lightly floured baking sheet; cover with plastic wrap and refrigerate until dough is very cold (about 30 minutes). Meanwhile, cut butter into thin slices and refrigerate until cold.

3. Sprinkle about 1 tablespoon more bread flour on a cool surface. Roll dough into a rectangle about ¼ inch thick. Arrange butter slices, slightly overlapping, in center third of dough rectangle. Fold sides over butter.

4. Turn dough a quarter turn and roll again into a rectangle about ⅜ inch thick (if necessary, occasionally lift dough and dust surface with just enough additional flour to prevent sticking).

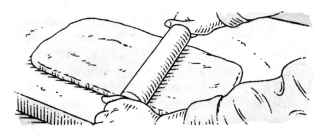

5. Fold dough in thirds again, forming a squarish rectangle. Turn dough a quarter turn. Then roll dough again into a rectangle about ¼ inch thick. Fold in thirds. Wrap dough in plastic wrap and refrigerate for 30 minutes.

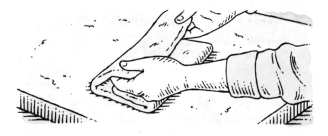

6. Roll dough about ¼ inch thick again and fold in thirds. Turn a quarter turn and then roll and fold one more time. Wrap dough in plastic wrap and refrigerate until firm (15 to 30 minutes). Meanwhile, prepare filling of your choice as directed on facing page, if desired. Roll dough into a rectangle ⅛ inch thick. Using a sharp knife, cut into triangles measuring about 6 inches at base and 8 inches long.

7. Place filling, if used, in center of each triangle near base. Starting at base, roll up triangles and arrange point down on 2 baking sheets, spacing croissants at least 1½ inches apart.

8. Curve ends of roll inward to form a crescent shape. Cover lightly and let rise in a warm place until very puffy and doubled (about 2 hours).

9. Brush croissants with egg yolk mixture. Bake in a 400° oven until golden brown (20 to 25 minutes), switching pan positions halfway through baking. Transfer to racks and let cool. Makes about 16 croissants.

Per croissant: 202 calories (56% from fat), 4 g protein, 19 g carbohydrates, 13 g total fat (8 g saturated fat), 46 mg cholesterol, 77 mg sodium

Almond Filling. In a food processor or blender, whirl ⅓ cup unblanched **whole almonds** until finely ground. Add ⅓ cup *each* **all-purpose flour** and **powdered sugar;** whirl until blended. Using food processor or a fork, work in ⅓ cup firm **unsalted butter** and ¼ teaspoon **almond extract.** Fill each croissant with 1 tablespoon of the filling rolled into a 3-inch log. After brushing with egg yolk mixture, sprinkle with **sliced almonds.** Bake as directed. If desired, sprinkle with **powdered sugar** while still hot.

Per croissant: 271 calories (59% from fat), 4 g protein, 24 g carbohydrates, 18 g total fat (10 g saturated fat), 56 mg cholesterol, 78 mg sodium

Chocolate Filling. Break each of 4 **semisweet chocolate bars** (about 1½ oz. each) into 12 small rectangles; fill each croissant with 3 rectangles, overlapping slightly. Bake as directed. If desired, sprinkle with **powdered sugar** while still hot.

Per croissant: 253 calories (55% from fat), 4 g protein, 25 g carbohydrates, 16 g total fat (9 g saturated fat), 46 mg cholesterol, 78 mg sodium

Jam Filling. Fill each croissant with 1 tablespoon **fruit preserves.** Bake as directed. If desired, sprinkle with **powdered sugar** while still hot.

Per croissant: 251 calories (45% from fat), 4 g protein, 32 g carbohydrates, 13 g total fat (8 g saturated fat), 46 mg cholesterol, 85 mg sodium

Chile & Cheese Filling. Fill each croissant with 2 tablespoons shredded **jack cheese** and 1 teaspoon **diced green chiles.**

Per croissant: 257 calories (59% from fat), 7 g protein, 19 g carbohydrates, 17 g total fat (10 g saturated fat), 61 mg cholesterol, 153 mg sodium

Ham & Cheese Filling. Fill each croissant with 1 tablespoon thin julienne strips **ham,** turkey, or roast beef and 2 teaspoons shredded **jack,** Cheddar, or Swiss **cheese.**

Per croissant: 233 calories (57% from fat), 6 g protein, 19 g carbohydrates, 15 g total fat (9 g saturated fat), 55 mg cholesterol, 196 mg sodium

BUCCELLATO

In the medieval town of Lucca in Northern Italy, this sweet, anise-scented bread is a source of local pride. Laced with raisins soaked in grappa, it maintains a sweet-tart appeal that has made it a favorite in other places as well. For a special occasion, serve it with strawberry sauce and a generous dollop of whipped cream.

- ½ cup raisins
- ¼ cup grappa (Italian brandy) or sweet or dry marsala
- 1 package active dry yeast
- 1½ tablespoons anise seeds
- ¾ cup warm milk (about 110°F)
- ½ cup (¼ lb.) butter or margarine, at room temperature
- ½ cup sugar
- 5 large eggs
- 1 teaspoon *each* vanilla and grated orange peel
- ½ teaspoon *each* anise extract and salt
  About 4½ cups all-purpose flour
  Strawberry-Marsala Sauce (optional; recipe follows)
  Sweetened whipped cream (optional)
  Whole strawberries (optional)

1. Combine raisins and grappa in a small bowl; let stand for 30 minutes. Set aside.

2. Sprinkle yeast and anise seeds over warm milk in another small bowl; let stand until yeast is softened (about 5 minutes). Meanwhile, combine butter and sugar in a large bowl; beat with a heavy spoon or an electric mixer until light and fluffy. Add 4 of the eggs, one at a time, beating well after each addition. Stir in vanilla, orange peel, anise extract, and salt. Add yeast mixture. Drain grappa from raisins into batter; set raisins aside.

3. Stir in 4½ cups of the flour.

To knead by hand, turn dough out onto a lightly floured board and knead until smooth and springy (about 15 minutes), adding just enough additional flour to prevent sticking (dough should be soft). Press raisins into dough and knead until evenly distributed.

To knead with a dough hook, beat on high speed until dough is springy and pulls away from sides of bowl (10 to 12 minutes), adding more flour, 1 tablespoon at a time, if dough is sticky (dough should be soft). Add raisins, beating on low speed until evenly distributed.

4. Place dough in a greased bowl; turn over to grease

top. Cover with plastic wrap. Let rise in a warm place until doubled (about 1 hour) or in a refrigerator until next day.

5. Punch dough down and knead briefly on a lightly floured board to release air. Cut dough in half. Shape each half into a 20-inch log. Place each log on a greased baking sheet, join ends to form a ring, and pinch together to seal. Cover lightly and let rise in a warm place until puffy (about 30 minutes).

6. Beat remaining egg until blended and brush over dough. Bake in a 350° oven until richly browned (25 to 35 minutes). Meanwhile, prepare Strawberry-Marsala Sauce, if desired. Transfer rings to racks and let cool. Offer with sauce, whipped cream, and strawberries, if desired. Makes 2 rings (about 10 servings each).

Per serving: 215 calories (31% from fat), 5 g protein, 31 g carbohydrates, 7 g total fat (4 g saturated fat), 67 mg cholesterol, 123 mg sodium

Strawberry-Marsala Sauce. In a food processor or blender, combine 2½ cups hulled **strawberries**, 6 tablespoons **sweet** or dry **marsala,** and 2 tablespoons **sugar;** whirl until puréed. Makes about 1¾ cups.

Per tablespoon: 12 calories (5% from fat), 0.1 g protein, 2 g carbohydrates, 0.1 g total fat (0 g saturated fat), 0 mg cholesterol, 0.4 mg sodium

• *Pictured on facing page* •

CHERRY-ALMOND CHRISTMAS WREATH

Special cutting and shaping expose a colorful filling and give this bread its distinctive swirled appearance.

> 1 package active dry yeast
> ¼ cup warm water (about 110°F)
> ½ cup warm milk (about 110°F)
> 3 tablespoons sugar
> ¼ cup butter or margarine, at room temperature
> 1½ teaspoons salt
> ½ teaspoon ground cardamom
> 2 large eggs
> 1 teaspoon grated lemon peel
> About 3½ cups all-purpose flour
> Cherry-Almond Filling (recipe follows)
> Sugar Glaze (recipe follows)

1. Sprinkle yeast over warm water in a large bowl; stir briefly. Let stand until foamy (about 5 minutes). Stir in milk, sugar, butter, salt, cardamom, eggs, and lemon peel. With an electric mixer (using a paddle attach-ment if you have one) or a heavy spoon, add 2 cups of the flour, 1 cup at a time, beating well after each addition. Then beat on medium speed for 3 minutes (or beat by hand for 10 minutes). Add 1¼ cups more flour; beat until combined.

2. Scrape dough out onto a lightly floured board and knead until smooth (5 to 10 minutes), adding more flour as needed to prevent sticking. Place in a greased bowl; turn over to grease top. Cover with plastic wrap and let rise in a warm place until doubled (about 1½ hours). Meanwhile, prepare Cherry-Almond Filling.

3. Punch dough down and knead briefly on a lightly floured board to release air. Roll into a 9- by 30-inch rectangle. Crumble filling over dough to within 1 inch of edges. Beginning at a long side, tightly roll up dough, pinching edge against loaf to seal. With a sharp knife, cut roll in half lengthwise, carefully turn cut sides up, and loosely twist ropes around each other, keeping cut sides up.

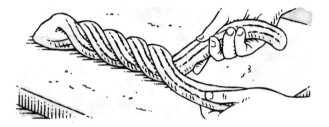

4. Transfer to a greased and floured baking sheet and shape into a 10-inch ring, pinching ends together to seal. Let rise, uncovered, in a warm place until puffy (45 to 60 minutes).

5. Bake in a 375° oven until lightly browned (about 20 minutes). Transfer to a rack and let cool briefly. Meanwhile, prepare Sugar Glaze; drizzle over warm bread. Makes 1 wreath (about 18 servings).

Cherry-Almond Filling. In a medium-size bowl, combine ¼ cup **butter** or margarine, at room temperature; ¼ cup **all-purpose flour;** and 2 tablespoons **sugar.** Beat until smooth. Stir in ⅔ cup finely chopped **blanched almonds,** ¼ cup *each* chopped **red** and **green candied cherries** or ½ cup dried cherries, ½ teaspoon grated **lemon peel,** and ¾ teaspoon **almond extract.** Cover and refrigerate.

Sugar Glaze. In a small bowl, combine ⅔ cup **powdered sugar,** 1½ teaspoons **lemon juice,** and 1 tablespoon **water;** stir until smooth.

Per serving: 240 calories (35% from fat), 5 g protein, 34 g carbohydrates, 9 g total fat (4 g saturated fat), 38 mg cholesterol, 247 mg sodium

Christmas breads are as much a part of the holiday season as gift giving.
This international lineup of favorites includes (clockwise from top left) St. Lucia Buns
from Sweden (page 85), Cherry-Almond Christmas Wreath (facing page), and
Germany's Dresden-style Stollen (page 84).

CHRISTMAS TREE BREAD

For this delicious holiday loaf, you shape a long, fruit-filled dough rope into a shape resembling a Christmas tree. The sweetly spiced filling—laden with almonds, raisins, apricots, and apples—twists deliciously through the lemon-scented bread.

   2 **packages active dry yeast**
   ½ **cup warm water (about 110°F)**
   ½ **cup (¼ lb.) butter or margarine, cut into pieces**
   1 **cup milk**
   3 **large eggs**
   ¼ **cup sugar**
   2 **teaspoons vanilla**
   1 **teaspoon grated lemon peel**
   ½ **teaspoon ground cardamom or ground mace**
   ½ **teaspoon salt**
      About 5½ cups all-purpose flour
      Fruit Filling (recipe follows)
   1 **large egg yolk beaten with 1 tablespoon water**
      Orange Glaze (recipe follows)

1. Sprinkle yeast over warm water in a large bowl; stir briefly. Let stand until foamy (about 5 minutes). Heat butter and milk to 110°F in a small pan over medium heat. Stir into yeast mixture. Add the whole eggs, sugar, vanilla, lemon peel, cardamom, salt, and 3 cups of the flour. Beat with an electric mixer (using a paddle attachment if you have one) on medium speed until dough is stretchy and glossy (5 to 8 minutes).

2. Stir in 2¼ cups more flour.

To knead by hand, turn dough out onto a lightly floured board and knead until smooth and elastic (about 10 minutes), adding just enough additional flour to prevent sticking. Place dough in a greased bowl; turn over to grease top.

To knead with a dough hook, beat on high speed until dough pulls cleanly from sides of bowl (5 to 8 minutes), adding more flour, 1 tablespoon at a time, if dough still clings to sides of bowl.

3. Cover with plastic wrap and let rise in a warm place until doubled (about 1 hour). Meanwhile, prepare Fruit Filling.

4. Punch dough down and knead briefly on a lightly floured board to release air. Cut off ⅓ cup of the dough; set aside. Roll remaining dough into a 10- by 36-inch rectangle. Spread filling to within ½ inch of long sides. Beginning at a long side, roll up dough, pinching edge against loaf to seal. Place seam side down on a greased baking sheet and arrange in a

zigzag pattern, narrow at the top and broad at the base. Shape reserved dough into a ball and attach at middle of base.

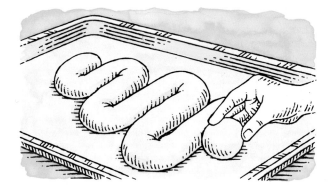

5. Cover lightly and let rise in a warm place until puffy (about 25 minutes).

6. Brush dough gently with egg yolk mixture. Bake in a 350° oven until golden brown (40 to 45 minutes). Let cool on sheet for 15 minutes. Meanwhile, prepare Orange Glaze; spoon over warm bread. Transfer to a serving platter. Makes 1 loaf (12 to 16 servings).

Fruit Filling. In a small bowl, soak 1 cup **golden raisins** in 3 tablespoons **orange juice** and 2 tablespoons **brandy** or vanilla for 30 minutes. Meanwhile, spread ¾ cup **slivered almonds** on a baking sheet and toast in a 350° oven, stirring occasionally, until golden (about 10 minutes).

    In a food processor or blender, combine raisin mixture, almonds, 1 cup *each* coarsely chopped peeled **apples** and coarsely chopped **dried apricots,** 2 teaspoons **ground cinnamon,** and 1 teaspoon grated **orange peel;** whirl until finely chopped.

Orange Glaze. In a small bowl, combine 1¼ cups **powdered sugar** and 2 tablespoons **orange juice;** stir until smooth.

Per serving: 445 calories (27% from fat), 10 g protein, 72 g carbohydrates, 13 g total fat (5 g saturated fat), 81 mg cholesterol, 172 mg sodium

• *Pictured on page 83* •

DRESDEN-STYLE STOLLEN

Of the many versions of Germany's famous stollen, this one from Dresden is among the most popular. The rich, buttery dough is studded with candied orange peel, almonds, raisins, and currants.

½ cup milk

1 cup (½ lb.) butter or margarine, cut into pieces

½ cup granulated sugar

2 packages active dry yeast

½ cup warm water (about 110°F)

½ teaspoon salt

1 teaspoon *each* grated lemon peel and almond extract

About 5¼ cups all-purpose flour

2 large eggs

⅓ cup finely chopped candied orange peel

½ cup *each* dark raisins, golden raisins, currants, and slivered almonds

1 large egg white beaten with 1 teaspoon water

¼ cup butter or margarine, melted and cooled

⅓ cup powdered sugar

1. Combine milk, the 1 cup butter, and granulated sugar in a small pan over medium-low heat. Heat to 120°F, stirring to dissolve sugar and melt butter. Let cool to lukewarm.

2. Sprinkle yeast over warm water in a large bowl; stir briefly. Let stand until foamy (about 5 minutes). Add milk mixture, salt, lemon peel, almond extract, and 3 cups of the flour; beat until blended. Add the whole eggs, one at a time, beating well after each addition. Gradually stir in orange peel, dark raisins, golden raisins, currants, almonds, and 2 cups more flour.

3. Turn dough out onto a floured board and knead until smooth and satiny (about 10 minutes), adding more flour as needed to prevent sticking. Place dough in a greased bowl; turn over to grease top. Cover with plastic wrap and let rise in a warm place until doubled (about 1½ hours).

4. Punch dough down and knead briefly on a floured board to release air. Cut dough in half and place each portion on a lightly greased baking sheet. Shape each into a 7- by 9-inch oval about ¾ inch thick. Brush with some of the egg white mixture. Crease each oval lengthwise, slightly off center, and fold so top edge is about an inch back from bottom edge. Brush with remaining egg white mixture. Cover lightly and let rise in a warm place until puffy and almost doubled (35 to 45 minutes).

5. Bake, uncovered, in a 375° oven until richly browned (about 25 minutes). Brush loaves with melted butter and dust with powdered sugar. Return to oven and continue to bake for 3 more minutes. Transfer to racks and let cool. Makes 2 loaves (8 to 10 servings each).

Per serving: 367 calories (40% from fat), 7 g protein, 49 g carbohydrates, 16 g total fat (9 g saturated fat), 59 mg cholesterol, 207 mg sodium

• *Pictured on page 83* •

ST. LUCIA BUNS

St. Lucia ushers in the Swedish holiday season with the festival of light. At daybreak on December 13, it's traditional for the youngest daughter in the family to don a wreath-crown adorned with candles and serve her family these cardamom buns.

1 package active dry yeast

1 cup warm milk (about 110°F)

⅔ cup sugar

⅓ cup butter or margarine, at room temperature

2 large eggs

½ teaspoon salt

2 teaspoons ground cardamom or crushed, hulled cardamom seeds

About 3¾ cups all-purpose flour

About ¼ cup raisins

1. Sprinkle yeast over warm milk in a large bowl; let stand until softened (about 5 minutes). Stir in sugar, butter, 1 of the eggs, salt, and cardamom.

2. Stir in 3½ cups of the flour, 1 cup at a time.

To knead by hand, turn dough out onto a well-floured board and knead until smooth and elastic (about 10 minutes), adding just enough additional flour to prevent sticking. Place in a greased bowl; turn over to grease top.

To knead with a dough hook, beat on high speed until dough pulls cleanly from sides of bowl (about 6 minutes), adding more flour, 1 tablespoon at a time, if dough still clings to sides of bowl.

3. Cover with plastic wrap and let rise in a warm place until doubled (about 1½ hours).

4. Punch dough down and knead briefly on a lightly floured board to release air. Keeping remaining dough covered, pinch off a 1½-inch ball of dough, roll into a rope about 10 inches long, and form into an S-shape by snugly coiling ends in opposite directions; place on a lightly greased baking sheet. Repeat to shape remaining buns, placing about 2 inches apart on sheets. Put a raisin in center of each coil. Cover lightly and let rise in a warm place until almost doubled (about 25 minutes).

5. Beat remaining egg and brush over buns. Bake in a 350° oven until golden (15 to 20 minutes), switching pan positions halfway through baking. Transfer to racks and let cool. Makes about 36 buns.

Per bun: 92 calories (24% from fat), 2 g protein, 15 g carbohydrates, 2 g total fat (1 g saturated fat), 17 mg cholesterol, 55 mg sodium

Morning beckons when these delectable treats are on the breakfast menu.
The choices are (clockwise from left) golden Puffy Pear Pancake (page 92), plump
Cinnamon Twists (page 89), Spiced Cake Doughnuts—and holes—with a variety of
coatings (page 89), and Oatmeal Buttermilk Pancakes with fresh fruit (page 93).

GRIDDLE BREADS

Baked right on the griddle or in a frying pan, tasty griddle breads are a wonderful alternative to oven baking. Actually, griddle breads are nothing new. Bakers around the world have been making them for centuries. You'll find some of the best choices in this chapter: flour and corn tortillas from Mexico, puffy Dutch babies from Germany, and paper-thin crêpes from France, plus the familiar English muffins, doughnuts, waffles, and pancakes.

Country of origin is not the only way in which these breads differ. Some are leavened with yeast and some with baking powder or baking soda; some are unleavened flatbreads. The sweet ones lend themselves to breakfast or dessert; others are perfect for enclosing a savory filling. You can also choose between plain breads of airy lightness and breads chunky with fresh fruit or whole grains.

FLOUR TORTILLAS

Introduced to Mexico by the Spanish in the 16th century, wheat flour was quickly translated by the Mexicans into tortillas. Today, flour tortillas remain an important culinary staple in Mexico.

3 cups all-purpose flour
2 teaspoons baking powder
¾ teaspoon salt
About 1 cup warm water (90° to 110°F)

1. Mix flour, baking powder, and salt in a large bowl. Gradually stir in enough of the warm water so dough is crumbly; work dough with your hands until it holds together. Turn out onto a board and knead until smooth. Divide into 12 equal pieces and shape each into a smooth ball.

2. Cover lightly with plastic wrap and let rest for 15 minutes. Keeping remaining dough covered, flatten a ball of dough into a 4- to 5-inch round. Using a floured rolling pin and working from center to edges, roll into a 9-inch round, turning tortilla often and stretching dough as you carefully peel it off the board. Repeat to shape remaining dough.

3. Heat a griddle or wide frying pan over medium-high heat. When griddle is hot, add a tortilla (tiny blisters should appear almost immediately). Turn tortilla over and immediately press a wide spatula gently but firmly all over top (blister will form over most of surface). Turn over again and continue to cook, pressing down, until blisters turn golden brown (tortilla should remain soft). Place tortilla in a folded cloth towel inside a plastic bag. Repeat to cook remaining tortillas, stacking cooked tortillas in bag.

4. Close bag and let tortillas steam. Serve when softened. If made ahead, let cool, remove from bag, and wrap airtight; refrigerate for up to a week or freeze for longer storage. Makes 12 tortillas.

Per tortilla: 117 calories (2% from fat), 3 g protein, 25 g carbohydrates, 0.3 g total fat (0.1 g saturated fat), 0 mg cholesterol, 219 mg sodium

CORN TORTILLAS

Generally, corn tortillas are made in a special press, but a rolling pin works just as well. To make your tortilla a perfect circle, trim the edges with a knife, using the rim of a coffee can as a guide, if you like.

2 cups dehydrated masa flour
1¼ to 1⅓ cups warm water (about 100°F)

1. Mix flour with enough of the warm water so dough holds together well. Shape into a smooth ball. Divide into 12 equal pieces and shape each into a ball. Cover with a damp paper towel. Keeping remaining dough covered, place a ball of dough between 2 pieces of wax paper. Flatten slightly with your hand; then flatten with a rolling pin, turn dough over, and roll into a 6-inch circle. Carefully peel off top paper, leaving bottom paper attached; if desired, trim edges with a knife. Repeat to shape remaining dough.

2. Heat a griddle or wide frying pan over medium-high heat. When griddle is hot, lift a tortilla, supporting it with paper, and turn over onto griddle. At once, peel off paper. Cook tortilla until bottom is flecked with brown (about 30 seconds); turn over and continue to cook for 1 more minute. Remove from pan and cover with foil. Repeat to cook remaining tortillas. Serve immediately. If made ahead, let cool, wrap airtight, and refrigerate for up to a week; freeze for longer storage. Makes 12 tortillas.

Per tortilla: 69 calories (9% from fat), 2 g protein, 14 g carbohydrates, 1 g total fat (0.1 g saturated fat), 0 mg cholesterol, 1 mg sodium

• Pictured on page 3 •

ENGLISH MUFFINS

English muffins are not really English, but rather a Yankee interpretation of Britain's griddle-baked crumpets. Many variations of this breakfast favorite are made with milk and whole egg, but these muffins achieve their dramatic rise and "holey" interior thanks to beaten egg whites and baking soda. They'll keep well stored in a plastic bag in the refrigerator.

1 package active dry yeast
1¼ cups warm water (about 110°F)
½ teaspoon baking soda
1½ teaspoons salt
3½ to 4 cups bread flour
2 small egg whites
Cornmeal

1. Sprinkle yeast over warm water in a large bowl; let stand until foamy (about 5 minutes). Add baking soda, salt, and 2 cups of the flour; beat until smooth.

2. Beat egg whites until stiff, moist peaks form. Fold into batter. With an electric mixer or a heavy spoon, beat in about 1 cup more flour, ¼ cup at a time, until dough pulls away from sides of bowl in stretchy strands. Turn out onto a well-floured board and knead until smooth and slightly springy (about 5 minutes; dough should be soft and sticky). Place in a greased bowl; turn over to grease top. Cover with plastic wrap and let rise in a warm place until doubled (about 1 hour).

3. Punch dough down and knead briefly on a lightly floured board to release air. With a floured rolling pin, roll dough ½ inch thick. Using a 3-inch-round cookie cutter, cut out muffins and place slightly apart on a board lightly sprinkled with cornmeal; sprinkle muffins with more cornmeal. Reroll scraps and cut. Cover lightly and let rise in a warm place until almost doubled (about 45 minutes).

4. Heat a griddle or wide frying pan over medium heat. When griddle is hot, grease lightly. Cook muffins, 2 or 3 at a time, turning once, until muffins are golden brown on top and bottom and a skewer inserted in sides comes out clean (8 to 10 minutes). Makes about 12 muffins.

Per muffin: 192 calories (16% from fat), 6 g protein, 33 g carbohydrates, 3 g total fat (0.4 g saturated fat), 0 mg cholesterol, 335 mg sodium

• Pictured on page 86 •

CINNAMON TWISTS

These twists, spicy with cinnamon, are perennial favorites.

    2 **packages active dry yeast**
   ¼ **cup warm water (about 110°F)**
1½ **cups milk**
   ½ **cup sugar**
   1 **teaspoon salt**
   ½ **teaspoon ground cinnamon**
   ⅓ **cup butter or margarine, cut into pieces**
   2 **large eggs**
      About 5¼ cups all-purpose flour
      Salad oil
   1 **cup sugar mixed with 4 teaspoons ground cinnamon**

1. Sprinkle yeast over warm water in a large bowl; stir briefly. Let stand until foamy (about 5 minutes). Meanwhile, heat milk, the ½ cup sugar, salt, the ½ teaspoon cinnamon, and butter to about 110°F in a medium-size pan over medium heat (butter need not melt completely).

2. Stir butter mixture into yeast mixture. Add eggs

and 2 cups of the flour; stir until blended. With an electric mixer or a heavy spoon, beat in 3 cups more flour until smooth (dough should be soft and sticky). Cover with plastic wrap and let rise in a warm place until almost doubled (about 1 hour).

3. Beat dough briefly with a heavy spoon to release air. Turn out onto a well-floured board and roll to coat evenly with flour. With a floured rolling pin, roll into an 8- by 18-inch rectangle. Cut dough crosswise into 1-inch strips. Working with one strip at a time (keep remaining dough covered), fold in half crosswise and, starting at fold, loosely twist strands around each other; press ends together to seal.

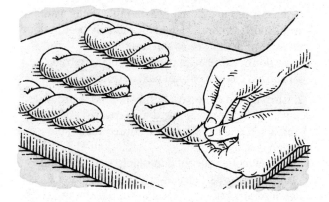

4. Arrange twists at least 4 inches apart on a floured baking sheet. Cover lightly and let rise in a warm place until almost doubled (20 to 30 minutes).

5. Pour oil to a depth of 1½ to 2 inches in a deep frying pan or 5-quart pan. Heat to 365° to 375°F. With a slotted spatula, lower twists, a few at a time, into oil; cook, turning often, until golden brown (about 3 minutes). Lift out and let drain on paper towels.

6. Place cinnamon-sugar in a plastic bag. Add warm twists, 1 or 2 at a time, and shake until coated. Makes 18 twists.

Per twist: 272 calories (24% from fat), 5 g protein, 46 g carbohydrates, 7 g total fat (3 g saturated fat), 36 mg cholesterol, 175 mg sodium

• Pictured on page 86 •

SPICED CAKE DOUGHNUTS

Cakelike and accented with nutmeg, cloves, and mace, doughnuts like these have been popular for years.

      About 3½ cups all-purpose flour
   3 **teaspoons baking powder**

(Continued on next page)

    1   teaspoon *each* salt and ground nutmeg
  ¼ teaspoon *each* ground cloves and mace
    4 large eggs
  ⅔ cup sugar
  ⅓ cup milk
  ⅓ cup butter or margarine, melted and cooled
    1 teaspoon *each* vanilla and grated lemon peel
       Salad oil
       Glaze or coating (optional; choices follow)

1. Mix 3 cups of the flour, baking powder, salt, nutmeg, cloves, and mace in a medium-size bowl. In large bowl of an electric mixer, beat eggs on high speed until very light and fluffy. Gradually add sugar, beating until mixture is thickened and lemon colored. Reduce speed to low and beat in milk, butter, vanilla, and lemon peel until blended. Gradually beat in flour mixture (if dough seems soft, beat in about ¼ cup more flour). Cover with plastic wrap and refrigerate for at least 2 hours or until next day.

2. Turn dough out onto a lightly floured board. Cut in half. Keeping remaining dough covered and refrigerated, roll one portion with a floured rolling pin until dough is ½ inch thick. Using a well-floured 3-inch doughnut cutter, cut out doughnuts and holes and place slightly apart on a lightly floured baking sheet. Reroll scraps and cut. Repeat to cut remaining dough. Let rest, uncovered, at room temperature for 15 to 20 minutes.

3. Pour oil to a depth of 2 inches in a deep frying pan or 5-quart pan. Heat to 375° to 400°F. With a slotted spatula, lower doughnuts and holes, a few at a time, into oil. Cook, turning often, until golden brown (1½ to 2 minutes). Lift out and let drain on paper towels. If desired, prepare and apply glaze or coating. Makes about 24 doughnuts and holes.

Per doughnut and hole: 150 calories (36% from fat), 3 g protein, 21 g carbohydrates, 6 g total fat (2 g saturated fat), 43 mg cholesterol, 191 mg sodium

Sugar Glaze with Nuts. Finely chop ¾ cup **walnuts**; set aside. In a small bowl, combine 2 cups **powdered sugar**, 1 teaspoon **vanilla**, and 2 tablespoons plus 2 teaspoons **water**; stir until smooth. Dip top of each doughnut and hole into glaze and sprinkle with about ½ tablespoon of the nuts.

Per doughnut and hole: 214 calories (35% from fat), 4 g protein, 31 g carbohydrates, 8 g total fat (2 g saturated fat), 43 mg cholesterol, 192 mg sodium

Chocolate Glaze. Melt 6 ounces **unsweetened chocolate**, ½ cup (¼ lb.) **butter** or margarine, and 1 tablespoon **light corn syrup** in a small pan over low

heat or heat in a microwave oven on MEDIUM (50%) for 2 minutes (do not overheat). Remove from heat and let stand, stirring occasionally, until mixture is of good dipping consistency. Dip top of each doughnut and hole into glaze.

Per doughnut and hole: 240 calories (42% from fat), 4 g protein, 32 g carbohydrates, 11 g total fat (6 g saturated fat), 50 mg cholesterol, 221 mg sodium

Powdered Sugar Coating. Place 2 cups **powdered sugar** in a plastic bag. Add doughnuts and holes, 1 or 2 at a time, and shake until coated.

Per doughnut and hole: 189 calories (28% from fat), 3 g protein, 31 g carbohydrates, 6 g total fat (2 g saturated fat), 43 mg cholesterol, 191 mg sodium

Cinnamon-Sugar Coating. Mix 1½ cups **sugar** and 2 tablespoons **ground cinnamon** in a plastic bag. Add doughnuts and holes, 1 or 2 at a time, and shake until coated.

Per doughnut and hole: 200 calories (27% from fat), 3 g protein, 34 g carbohydrates, 6 g total fat (2 g saturated fat), 43 mg cholesterol, 191 mg sodium

• Pictured on facing page •

STRAWBERRY DUTCH BABY

This easy-to-make pancake puffs impressively in the oven, forming a light and airy "bowl" that's perfect for sliced strawberries and fresh strawberry sauce.

    3 tablespoons butter or margarine
  ¾ cup *each* all-purpose flour and milk
    3 large eggs
    2 teaspoons sugar
       Strawberry Sauce (recipe follows)
    3 cups sliced strawberries
       Powdered sugar
       Lemon wedges

1. Place 1½ tablespoons of the butter in each of two 8- to 10-inch ovenproof frying pans. Set pans in a 425° oven until butter is melted (3 to 4 minutes); swirl to coat surface. Meanwhile, in a blender or food processor, whirl flour, milk, eggs, and sugar until blended.

2. Pour batter equally into hot pans. Bake until deep golden brown (18 to 20 minutes). Meanwhile, prepare Strawberry Sauce.

3. Spoon sliced strawberries into each pancake and drizzle with sauce. Sprinkle with powdered sugar. Offer with lemon wedges. Makes 4 servings.

(Continued on page 92)

About 20 minutes before you plan to sit down to eat, pop Strawberry Dutch Baby (facing page) into the oven. The pancake puffs up dramatically as it bakes and forms an edible bowl for sliced fresh strawberries topped with strawberry sauce. A sprinkling of powdered sugar dusts the top.

91

Strawberry Sauce. In a food processor or blender, combine 1 cup rinsed, hulled **strawberries,** 2 tablespoons **sugar,** and 2 teaspoons **lemon juice.** Whirl until puréed.

Per serving: 338 calories (38% from fat), 10 g protein, 43 g carbohydrates, 15 g total fat (8 g saturated fat), 189 mg cholesterol, 160 mg sodium

BASIC CRÊPES

Versatile crêpes enclose a myriad of fillings, from leftover turkey to berries with cream. Make the crêpes ahead and freeze them. When you're ready, thaw them and add your choice of filling.

> 3 **large eggs**
> ⅔ **cup all-purpose flour**
> 1 **cup milk**
> **About 4 teaspoons butter or margarine**

1. Combine eggs and flour in a blender or food processor; whirl until smooth. Add milk and whirl until blended.

2. Heat a 6- to 7-inch crêpe pan or other flat-bottomed frying pan over medium heat. When pan is hot, add ¼ teaspoon of the butter, swirling to coat surface. Stir batter and pour in about 2 tablespoons all at once, tilting pan so batter flows quickly over bottom. Cook, turning once, until surface looks dry and edge is lightly browned. Repeat to cook remaining crêpes, adding butter as needed to prevent sticking.

3. Stack crêpes between pieces of wax paper. If made ahead, let cool, wrap airtight, and refrigerate for up to a week; freeze for longer storage. Bring to room temperature, unwrapped, before filling. Makes about 18 crêpes.

Per crêpe: 45 calories (44% from fat), 2 g protein, 4 g carbohydrates, 2 g total fat (1 g saturated fat), 40 mg cholesterol, 26 mg sodium

• *Pictured on page 86* •

PUFFY PEAR PANCAKE

This light pancake is akin to a thick French soufflé. Turned out onto a serving plate, it reveals fresh pears that have caramelized at pan bottom.

> 2 **tablespoons butter or margarine**
> 1 **teaspoon anise seeds (optional)**

> 3 **large ripe Bartlett or d'Anjou pears (1¼ to 1½ lbs. *total*), peeled, cut in half lengthwise, and cored**
> 5 **large eggs, separated**
> ½ **cup sugar**
> ½ **teaspoon vanilla**
> ¼ **cup all-purpose flour**

1. Heat butter and, if desired, anise seeds in an 8- to 10-inch ovenproof frying pan over medium heat. Add pears and cook, turning occasionally, until lightly browned on both sides (about 10 minutes). Remove pan from heat and arrange pears, cut sides down and spaced evenly apart, in pan; keep warm.

2. Beat egg whites in a large bowl until foamy; gradually beat in sugar until stiff, moist peaks form. In another large bowl, beat yolks until doubled in volume; add vanilla and flour and beat until blended. Stir about a quarter of the whites into yolk mixture; then fold yolk mixture gently into whites. Pour over warm pears, pushing batter down between fruit with a slender spatula.

3. Cook over medium heat until pancake is golden brown on bottom. Transfer to a 300° oven and bake until top is lightly browned and center is set (about 15 minutes). Gently loosen pancake from pan sides with a knife; invert onto a serving plate. Makes 6 servings.

Per serving: 237 calories (31% from fat), 6 g protein, 36 g carbohydrates, 8 g total fat (4 g saturated fat), 187 mg cholesterol, 92 mg sodium

SPICED PUMPKIN PANCAKES

These hearty pancakes make a good choice for a holiday breakfast.

> 2 **cups all-purpose flour**
> 2 **tablespoons sugar**
> 2 **teaspoons baking powder**
> 1 **teaspoon *each* baking soda and ground cinnamon**

½ teaspoon ground nutmeg

¼ teaspoon salt

1¾ cups nonfat milk

1 cup canned pumpkin

2 large eggs

2 tablespoons salad oil

Butter or margarine

Warm maple syrup

1. Mix flour, sugar, baking powder, baking soda, cinnamon, nutmeg, and salt in a medium-size bowl. In another medium-size bowl, beat milk, pumpkin, eggs, and oil until blended. Add milk mixture to flour mixture; stir just until moistened.

2. Heat a griddle or wide frying pan over medium heat. When griddle is hot, grease lightly. For each pancake, spoon about ¼ cup of the batter onto griddle, spacing pancakes about 1 inch apart. Cook until tops are bubbly and appear dry; turn and continue to cook until other sides are browned. Offer with butter and syrup. Makes about twenty 4-inch pancakes.

Per pancake: 92 calories (31% from fat), 3 g protein, 13 g carbohydrates, 3 g total fat (1 g saturated fat), 22 mg cholesterol, 157 mg sodium

• *Pictured on page 86* •

OATMEAL BUTTERMILK PANCAKES

Top these pancakes with butter, syrup, and fresh fruit.

1 cup all-purpose flour

½ cup *each* yellow cornmeal and quick-cooking rolled oats

⅓ cup oat bran

¼ cup sugar

1½ teaspoons baking soda

1 teaspoon baking powder

¼ teaspoon salt

2 cups buttermilk

½ cup sour cream

2 large eggs

2 tablespoons melted butter or margarine

Butter or margarine

Maple syrup

Fresh berries, sliced peaches, or sliced bananas

1. Mix flour, cornmeal, rolled oats, oat bran, sugar, baking soda, baking powder, and salt in a large bowl. In another large bowl, beat buttermilk, sour cream, eggs, and the 2 tablespoons melted butter until com-

bined. Add egg mixture to flour mixture; stir until blended.

2. Heat a griddle or wide frying pan over medium heat. When griddle is hot, grease lightly. For each pancake, spoon about ¼ cup of the batter onto griddle, spacing pancakes about 1 inch apart. Cook until tops are bubbly and appear dry; turn and continue to cook until the other sides are browned. Offer with butter, syrup, and berries. Makes about eighteen 4-inch pancakes.

Per pancake: 117 calories (37% from fat), 3 g protein, 15 g carbohydrates, 5 g total fat (2 g saturated fat), 31 mg cholesterol, 214 mg sodium

APPLE OATMEAL WAFFLES

Chock-full of apples, raisins, and oatmeal, these waffles are a good choice for a hearty breakfast.

1 cup regular rolled oats

1⅔ cups all-purpose flour

2½ teaspoons baking powder

1 teaspoon ground cinnamon

½ teaspoon salt (optional)

1 cup nonfat milk

¼ cup maple syrup

¼ cup orange or apple juice

1 large egg

3 large egg whites

¾ cup finely chopped tart apple

½ cup raisins

Butter or margarine

Maple syrup

1. Spread oats on a baking sheet; toast in a 350° oven, stirring occasionally, until golden (12 to 15 minutes). Mix oats, flour, baking powder, cinnamon, and, if desired, salt in a large bowl. In a medium-size bowl, beat milk, syrup, juice, egg, and egg whites until blended. Stir in apple and raisins. Add egg mixture to flour mixture; stir until evenly moistened.

2. Preheat a waffle iron following manufacturer's directions. Grease iron; fill three-quarters full of batter. Bake until golden and crisp (6 to 8 minutes). Transfer to a plate and keep warm in a 200° oven while making remaining waffles. Offer with butter and syrup. Makes about twelve 4-inch-square waffles.

Per waffle: 156 calories (10% from fat), 5 g protein, 30 g carbohydrates, 2 g total fat (0.3 g saturated fat), 18 mg cholesterol, 133 mg sodium

These quick breads really do live up to their name! Beautiful to look at, they each take less than 30 minutes to prepare. Teatime treats are (clockwise from left) Irish Soda Bread studded with currants (page 97), Old-fashioned Lemon Bread (page 104), Spicy Gingerbread (page 105), and Apricot-Blackberry Cornmeal Kuchen (page 108).

QUICK BREADS

Quick breads are among the simplest breads to bake because they're leavened with baking soda or baking powder instead of yeast. All you do is prepare the batter, add the flavoring ingredients, and bake the bread. Considering the wide range of muffins, biscuits, fruit and nut breads, and savory loaves you can make, it's easy to understand why quick breads are so popular with home bakers.

Whether they're large loaves or smaller scones or biscuits, quick breads are delicious served either warm or at room temperature. Whole loaves should be cooled briefly before slicing. In fact, if you wait a day before serving them, they're not only easier to slice but also more flavorful. To store, wrap the cooled loaves airtight and place them in the refrigerator; they'll keep for up to a week. You can also freeze them. To serve them warm so you can recapture the full flavor and wonderful aroma of fresh-baked breads, reheat them in a warm oven.

• *Pictured on page 99* •

CHORIZO BREAD

Chorizo is a chile-spiced Spanish sausage that's significantly hotter than most American sausages. In bread, it adds a pleasing spice and chunkiness. This golden brown loaf is best served warm, cut into thick slices.

- 3 cups all-purpose flour
- 3 tablespoons grated Parmesan cheese
- 2 tablespoons brown sugar
- 4½ teaspoons baking powder
- 1 teaspoon fennel seeds or caraway seeds
- ½ teaspoon salt
- ¼ teaspoon baking soda
- 1 small package (3 oz.) plus 1 large package (8 oz.) cream cheese, at room temperature
- 1 cup milk
- 2 large eggs
- ¼ cup butter or margarine, melted and cooled
- 1 cup coarsely chopped dry chorizo or pepperoni sausage (about 5½ oz.), casing removed

1. Mix flour, Parmesan cheese, sugar, baking powder, fennel seeds, salt, and baking soda in a large bowl. In another large bowl, beat cream cheese until smooth; stir in milk. Add eggs, one at a time, beating well after each addition. Stir in butter and sausage. Add egg mixture to flour mixture; stir just until moistened.

2. Spoon batter into a greased 5- by 9-inch loaf pan. Bake in a 375° oven until loaf is browned and begins to pull away from sides of pan (about 55 minutes). Let cool in pan on a rack for 5 minutes; turn out onto rack. Serve warm or at room temperature. If made ahead, wrap airtight and store at room temperature until next day; freeze for longer storage. To reheat, place, uncovered, in a 350° oven until warm (about 15 minutes). Makes 1 loaf (10 to 12 servings).

Per serving: 378 calories (55% from fat), 11 g protein, 31 g carbohydrates, 23 g total fat (12 g saturated fat), 96 mg cholesterol, 792 mg sodium

SPICED CORNBREAD

Spread this fluffy cornbread, enlivened by a liberal sprinkling of Mexican spices, with a creamy chili-spiked butter.

- 1 cup *each* yellow cornmeal and all-purpose flour
- 1 tablespoon baking powder
- 2 tablespoons sugar
- ½ teaspoon salt
- 1½ teaspoons *each* ground coriander and ground cumin
- ⅓ cup cold butter or margarine, cut into pieces
- 1 large egg
- 1 cup milk
  Basil-Chili Butter (recipe follows)

1. Mix cornmeal, flour, baking powder, sugar, salt, coriander, and cumin in a large bowl. With a pastry blender or 2 knives, cut in butter until mixture resembles coarse crumbs. Add egg and milk; stir until evenly moistened.

2. Spread batter in a greased 8-inch-square baking pan. Bake in a 400° oven until deep golden (about 30 minutes). Meanwhile, prepare Basil-Chili Butter.

3. Let bread cool on a rack. Serve warm or at room temperature with flavored butter. Makes 6 servings.

Per serving: 313 calories (39% from fat), 7 g protein, 41 g carbohydrates, 14 g total fat (8 g saturated fat), 68 mg cholesterol, 562 mg sodium

Basil-Chili Butter. In a small bowl, combine ½ cup (¼ lb.) **butter** or margarine, at room temperature; 2 teaspoons **chili powder;** and 2 tablespoons minced **fresh basil** or 2 teaspoons dried basil. Stir until blended. Makes about ⅔ cup.

Per tablespoon: 84 calories (97% from fat), 0.2 g protein, 0.5 g carbohydrates, 9 g total fat (6 g saturated fat), 25 mg cholesterol, 99 mg sodium

OLD-FASHIONED BROWN BREAD

Before yeast became widely available, hearty, coarse-textured brown breads like this one were among the most popular loaves on the table. For a satisfying supper, serve thick slices of this bread alongside a hearty, steaming stew and a wedge of cheese. Or slice it thinly and spread with cream cheese or butter.

- 2 cups graham or whole wheat flour
- 1 cup all-purpose flour
- 1 teaspoon baking soda
- ½ teaspoon salt
- 1 cup *each* dark molasses and buttermilk
- ½ cup low-fat milk

1. Mix graham flour, all-purpose flour, baking soda, and salt in a medium-size bowl. In a large bowl, combine molasses, buttermilk, and low-fat milk; stir until blended. Add flour mixture to milk mixture; stir until well blended.

2. Pour batter into a greased 5- by 9-inch loaf pan. Bake in a 325° oven until bread begins to pull away from sides of pan and a skewer inserted in center comes out clean (1 to 1¼ hours). Let cool in pan on a rack for 10 minutes; turn out onto rack and let cool completely. Serve warm or at room temperature. Makes 1 loaf (10 to 12 servings).

Per serving: 204 calories (6% from fat), 5 g protein, 44 g carbohydrates, 1 g total fat (0.4 g saturated fat), 2 mg cholesterol, 261 mg sodium

• *Pictured on page 94* •

IRISH SODA BREAD

In Ireland, soda bread is traditionally cooked over a smoldering peat fire. Irish cooks claim it gives the bread its distinctive flavor. In Dublin today, rounds of soda bread still accompany every meal. Although these simple loaves are often made without embellishment, our version is studded with tiny currants.

        3 cups all-purpose flour
        ½ cup sugar
        1 tablespoon baking powder
        1 teaspoon baking soda
        1½ cups dried currants or raisins
        1¾ cups buttermilk
        2 large eggs
        3 tablespoons melted butter or margarine
        ½ teaspoon vanilla

1. Mix flour, sugar, baking powder, baking soda, and currants in a large bowl. In a small bowl, beat buttermilk, eggs, 2 tablespoons of the butter, and vanilla until blended. Add egg mixture to flour mixture; stir until evenly moistened.

2. Spread batter in a greased 10-inch ovenproof frying pan or cheesecake pan with a removable bottom. Drizzle with remaining 1 tablespoon butter. Bake in a 350° oven until bread is browned and pulls away from sides of pan (about 45 minutes). Let cool in pan on a rack for 10 minutes. Remove rim. Serve warm or at room temperature. Makes 1 loaf (about 10 servings).

Per serving: 304 calories (16% from fat), 7 g protein, 57 g carbohydrates, 6 g total fat (3 g saturated fat), 54 mg cholesterol, 368 mg sodium

PROSCIUTTO BISCUIT TWISTS

Sprinkled with cinnamon-sugar and rolled with thin strips of prosciutto, these biscuit twists feature a tantalizing mixture of sweet and savory. They're a natural accompaniment to a frothy mug of beer, but they're equally delicious served on their own.

           About 2 cups all-purpose flour
        4 teaspoons baking powder
        ½ teaspoon salt
        5 tablespoons cold butter or margarine, cut into pieces
        ¾ cup milk
        2 tablespoons melted butter or margarine
        3 tablespoons sugar
        ½ teaspoon ground cinnamon
        2 tablespoons minced fresh jalapeño chiles
        ⅛ pound thinly sliced prosciutto or cooked ham, cut into thin strips
        1 large egg white, lightly beaten

1. Mix 2 cups of the flour, baking powder, and salt in a large bowl. With your fingers, rub in the 5 tablespoons butter until fine crumbs form. With a fork, stir in milk until evenly moistened.

2. Shape dough into a ball and knead on a lightly floured board until smooth (10 to 12 turns). Roll into a 12- by 15-inch rectangle and brush with the 2 tablespoons melted butter. In a small bowl, mix 2 tablespoons of the sugar, cinnamon, chiles, and prosciutto. Starting at a short side, sprinkle mixture evenly over half the dough. Fold dough in half over filling. Cut through fold into 8 equal pieces; twist each 3 times. Arrange on a large baking sheet.

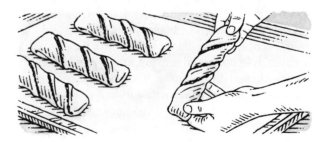

3. Brush twists with egg white. Sprinkle with remaining 1 tablespoon sugar. Bake in a 450° oven until deep golden (about 15 minutes). Transfer twists to a rack and let cool completely. Serve at room temperature. Makes 8 twists.

Per twist: 260 calories (42% from fat), 7 g protein, 31 g carbohydrates, 12 g total fat (7 g saturated fat), 36 mg cholesterol, 639 mg sodium

• *Pictured on page 27* •

RUSSIAN CHEESE BREAD

This cheese-filled loaf from southern Russia, known as *khachapuri,* is substantial enough to serve as an entrée. For the most authentic flavor, use a full pound of the goat cheese. Traditional accompaniments include parsley, cilantro or green onions, and a dry, fruity white wine.

½ to 1 pound goat cheese, such as bûcheron or Montrachet
1 to 2 packages (8 oz. *each*) Neufchâtel cheese or cream cheese (if using 1 lb. goat cheese, use only 8 oz.)
  About 3 cups all-purpose flour
½ teaspoon salt
1 teaspoon baking soda
1 tablespoon baking powder
1¾ cups sour cream
1 large egg yolk beaten with 1 teaspoon water

1. Beat goat cheese and Neufchâtel in a large bowl until blended; set aside.

2. Mix 3 cups of the flour, salt, baking soda, and baking powder in a large bowl. Add sour cream; stir until evenly blended.

3. Turn dough out onto a well-floured board and knead until fairly smooth (5 to 10 minutes). Reserve a third of the dough; cover with plastic wrap and set aside. Roll remaining dough into a 14-inch round; trim edge to make a circle, adding scraps to reserved dough. Fold dough round into quarters and place in a greased 10-inch ovenproof frying pan. Unfold dough and line pan, allowing edges to overhang pan rim.

4. Pat cheese mixture evenly over dough. On a floured board, roll reserved dough into a 9-inch round and place over filling. Brush top with some of the egg yolk mixture. Fold bottom edge over top and press edges together to seal. Brush rim with remaining egg yolk mixture. Prick top all over with a fork.

5. Bake in a 400° oven until well browned (about 30 minutes). Let cool on a rack for 5 minutes. With a knife, gently loosen bread from sides of pan. Turn out onto a plate; then turn upright onto a rack. Let cool for 10 more minutes. Serve warm or at room temperature. If made ahead, let cool completely; then wrap airtight and refrigerate for up to 2 days. Makes 1 loaf (8 to 10 servings).

Per serving: 498 calories (56% from fat), 18 g protein, 38 g carbohydrates, 31 g total fat (20 g saturated fat), 102 mg cholesterol, 795 mg sodium

• *Pictured on facing page* •

CORNHUSK MUFFINS

Cornhusks make a crisp, papery cup for little cornbread muffins. Before eating, simply peel off the husks.

6 to 8 dry cornhusks (*each* 6 to 8 inches long)
2 cups all-purpose flour
¾ cup yellow cornmeal or dehydrated masa flour
1 tablespoon baking powder
½ teaspoon salt
1⅓ cups (about 5 oz.) shredded jack cheese with chiles
1 large egg
¼ cup butter or margarine, melted and cooled
2 tablespoons honey
1 cup milk

1. Separate cornhusks and place in a large bowl. Pour in boiling water to cover; let husks soak until soft and pliable (about 10 minutes). Drain and pat dry. Tear lengthwise into 1½- to 2-inch-wide strips; set aside.

2. Mix flour, cornmeal, baking powder, salt, and ¾ cup of the cheese in a large bowl. In a small bowl, combine egg, butter, honey, and milk; beat until blended. Add egg mixture to flour mixture; stir just until evenly moistened.

3. Arrange 2 or 3 husks in each of 12 greased 2½-inch muffin cups, crossing centers in bottom of each cup and fanning ends out sides. As each cup is lined, fill with batter. Sprinkle evenly with remaining cheese.

4. Bake in a 375° oven until golden (about 25 minutes). Turn out onto a rack and let cool. Serve warm or at room temperature. Makes 12 muffins.

Per muffin: 225 calories (40% from fat), 7 g protein, 27 g carbohydrates, 10 g total fat (5 g saturated fat), 43 mg cholesterol, 331 mg sodium

• *Pictured on facing page* •

CHILE-CHEESE SCONES

Unlike most scones, these offer robust, savory flavor instead of sweetness, thanks to a combination of Cheddar cheese and spicy dried red chiles.

2 cups all-purpose flour
½ cup yellow cornmeal
1 tablespoon baking powder
1 to 2 teaspoons crushed dried hot red chiles

(Continued on page 101)

These simple, rustic quick breads are redolent with the flavors of Mexico and the American Southwest. From top, hot red chiles accent cheese-laden Chile-Cheese Scones (facing page), dried husks enclose sweet Cornhusk Muffins (facing page), and chunks of spicy pork sausage dot thick slices of Chorizo Bread (page 96).

BREADS FOR GIFT GIVING

AT HOLIDAY TIME, a gift of freshly baked bread is one of the season's greatest pleasures. If you're the one baking during this time, you'll appreciate the streamlined technique below. It allows you to bake three different varieties of fruit and nut bread all at once.

You simply distribute the flour mixture among three bowls, make a well in each, and crack an egg into the well. After choosing your flavor variations, you add the ingredients for each variation to one of the bowls. Then you bake the batter and you're finished!

Flour Mixture

7½   cups all-purpose flour
2¼   cups sugar
4½   teaspoons baking powder
1½   teaspoons *each* baking soda
      and salt
3   large eggs
      Flavor variations (recipes follow)

1. Use three large mixing bowls. In each bowl, mix 2½ cups of the flour, ¾ cup of the sugar, 1½ teaspoons of the baking powder, ½ teaspoon of the baking soda, and ½ teaspoon of the salt. Make a well in center of the flour mixture. Crack 1 of the eggs into each well.

2. Choose three of the flavor variations. Add each mixture to one of the bowls as directed.

3. Spoon each batter into one greased and floured 5- by 9-inch loaf pan, two 4- by 8-inch loaf pans, or three 3½- by 5-inch loaf pans.

4. Bake in a 350° oven until a skewer inserted in center comes out clean (about 55 minutes for 5- by 9-inch loaves; 40 to 45 minutes for 4- by 8-inch loaves; 30 to 35 minutes for 3½- by 5-inch loaves). Let cool in pans on racks for 5 minutes; turn out onto racks and let cool completely. If made ahead, wrap in plastic wrap and store at room temperature for up to a week; freeze for longer storage. Makes 3 large loaves (about 2 lbs. each), 6 medium-size loaves (about 1 lb. each), or 9 small loaves (about 10 oz. each).

• Pictured on page 126 •

Almond Spice Bread

Follow step 1 for **Flour Mixture** (at left). To well in one bowl, add ½ cup **vegetable oil,** ¾ cup **milk,** ¼ cup **sherry,** 1½ teaspoons **almond extract,** and ½ teaspoon *each* **ground cinnamon, ground cloves,** and **ground nutmeg.** With a fork, beat liquid mixture until blended. With a heavy spoon, stir liquid mixture into flour mixture until smooth. Crumble 4 ounces **almond paste** into batter; stir well. Follow steps 3–4.

Per ounce: 96 calories (39% from fat), 1 g protein, 13 g carbohydrates, 4 g total fat (1 g saturated fat), 7 mg cholesterol, 90 mg sodium

• Pictured on page 126 •

Cranberry Nut Bread

Follow step 1 for **Flour Mixture** (at left). To well in one bowl, add ½ cup *each* **orange juice** and **milk,** ¼ cup **vegetable oil,** and 1 teaspoon **orange zest.** With a fork, beat liquid mixture until blended. With a heavy spoon, stir liquid mixture into flour mixture until smooth. Stir in 1½ cups **fresh** or frozen **cranberries,** cut in half, and 1 cup chopped **walnuts.** Follow steps 3–4.

Per ounce: 104 calories (39% from fat), 2 g protein, 14 g carbohydrates, 5 g total fat (1 g saturated fat), 7 mg cholesterol, 89 mg sodium

Apricot-Ginger Bread

Follow step 1 for **Flour Mixture** (at left). To well in one bowl, add ¼ cup **vegetable oil,** 1 cup **milk,** and 1 teaspoon *each* grated **lemon peel** and **ground nutmeg.** With a fork, beat liquid mixture until blended. With a heavy spoon, stir liquid mixture into flour mixture until smooth. Stir in 3 tablespoons **crystallized ginger** and ¾ cup coarsely chopped **dried apricots.** Follow steps 3–4.

Per ounce: 91 calories (23% from fat), 2 g protein, 16 g carbohydrates, 2 g total fat (0.5 g saturated fat), 8 mg cholesterol, 91 mg sodium

• Pictured on page 126 •

Pumpkin Nut Bread

Follow step 1 for **Flour Mixture** (at left). To well in one bowl, add 1 more **large egg,** ½ teaspoon more **baking soda,** 1 cup **canned pumpkin,** ¾ cup **vegetable oil,** ⅓ cup **water,** and 1 teaspoon *each* **ground allspice** and **ground cinnamon.** With a fork, beat liquid mixture until blended. With a heavy spoon, stir liquid mixture into flour mixture until smooth. Stir in 1 cup chopped **walnuts.** Follow steps 3–4.

Per ounce: 130 calories (54% from fat), 2 g protein, 13 g carbohydrates, 8 g total fat (1 g saturated fat), 13 mg cholesterol, 108 mg sodium

½ **teaspoon ground cumin**
¼ **cup cold butter or margarine, cut into pieces**
1 **cup (about 4 oz.) shredded Cheddar cheese**
2 **large eggs**
½ **cup milk**

1. Combine flour, cornmeal, baking powder, chiles, and cumin in a food processor or large bowl; whirl or mix until blended. Add butter; whirl or rub with your fingers until mixture resembles coarse crumbs. Add cheese; whirl or stir just until combined. In a small bowl, beat eggs and milk until blended; reserve 2 tablespoons of the mixture. Add remaining egg mixture to flour mixture; whirl or stir just until evenly moistened.

2. Turn dough out onto a floured board and knead until dough holds together (about 6 turns). Divide in half. Pat each half into a round about ¾ inch thick. Place well apart on a large greased baking sheet. Using a knife, cut each round not quite through into 6 equal wedges. Brush with reserved egg mixture.

3. Bake in a 400° oven until golden brown (about 18 minutes). Let cool in pan on a rack for 5 minutes. Break into wedges. Serve warm or at room temperature. Makes 12 scones.

Per scone: 195 calories (41% from fat), 6 g protein, 22 g carbohydrates, 9 g total fat (5 g saturated fat), 57 mg cholesterol, 236 mg sodium

HARVEST POPOVERS

Here's a popover recipe with an appealing twist: to a basic batter, you add your choice of savory flavoring. If you prefer plain popovers, just omit the added ingredients and bake as directed.

Harvest flavoring (optional; choices and directions follow)
2 **large eggs**
1 **cup all-purpose flour**
¼ **teaspoon salt**
1 **cup milk**

1. Prepare flavoring mixture of your choice, if desired; set aside.

2. Combine eggs, flour, salt, and milk in a large bowl; beat with an electric mixer until smoothly blended. Stir in flavoring mixture, if used.

3. Ladle batter equally into 8 greased 2½-inch muffin cups or heavy 2- to 2½-inch popover cups, or 6 to 8

greased 4- to 5-ounce custard cups, filling cups no higher than ¼ inch below rims (if using individual cups, set well apart in a large baking pan).

4. Bake in a 375° oven until popovers are well browned and firm to the touch (about 50 minutes). Using a knife, gently loosen from sides of pan and turn out onto a rack. Serve hot. For extra-crisp popovers, return popovers to pans, tilting them at an angle. Pierce sides with a skewer and return to turned-off oven for 5 to 10 minutes. If made ahead, let cool completely; cover and store at room temperature until next day. To reheat, place popovers slightly apart in a 10- by 15-inch baking pan and heat, uncovered, in a 375° oven until warm (about 5 minutes). Makes 6 to 8 popovers.

Per popover: 119 calories (31% from fat), 5 g protein, 15 g carbohydrates, 4 g total fat (1 g saturated fat), 66 mg cholesterol, 113 mg sodium

Wild Rice–Parmesan. Rinse 3 tablespoons **wild rice** with water; drain. In a small pan, bring rice and 1 cup **water** to a boil over high heat; reduce heat, cover, and simmer, stirring occasionally, until rice is tender to bite (about 50 minutes). Drain and let cool. In a small bowl, mix rice with ¼ cup grated **Parmesan cheese** and 1 teaspoon grated **orange peel.**

Per popover: 148 calories (31% from fat), 7 g protein, 19 g carbohydrates, 5 g total fat (2 g saturated fat), 68 mg cholesterol, 166 mg sodium

Bran-Cheddar. In a small bowl, mix ⅓ cup **bran flakes,** ¼ cup shredded **sharp Cheddar cheese,** and ¾ teaspoon **dried rosemary.**

Per popover: 142 calories (35% from fat), 6 g protein, 17 g carbohydrates, 5 g total fat (2 g saturated fat), 70 mg cholesterol, 155 mg sodium

Oat-Hazelnut. Spread ¼ cup chopped **hazelnuts** or almonds on a baking sheet and toast in a 350° oven, stirring occasionally, until lightly browned (5 to 8 minutes). In a small bowl, mix nuts, ⅓ cup **quick-cooking rolled oats,** and ½ teaspoon **ground allspice.**

Per popover: 160 calories (39% from fat), 6 g protein, 19 g carbohydrates, 7 g total fat (2 g saturated fat), 66 mg cholesterol, 113 mg sodium

Cornmeal–Green Onion. In a small bowl, mix ⅓ cup **yellow cornmeal,** ⅓ cup thinly sliced **green onions,** and 1 clove **garlic,** minced or pressed.

Per popover: 134 calories (20% from fat), 5 g protein, 21 g carbohydrates, 3 g total fat (1 g saturated fat), 66 mg cholesterol, 114 mg sodium

*Out on the range, flaky breads like these Whole Wheat Beer Biscuits (facing
page) are served alongside hearty one-pot meals. Why not enjoy the same treat at home?
Offer these moist morsels hot from the oven with a generous pat of butter.*

WHOLE WHEAT BEER BISCUITS

In the cattle lands of the Rocky Mountains, where this recipe originated, hearty whole-grain biscuits like these are baked in a Dutch oven over an open fire.

      About 2 cups all-purpose flour
    1 **cup whole wheat flour**
    2 **tablespoons sugar**
  4½ **teaspoons baking powder**
    1 **teaspoon salt**
    ¾ **teaspoon cream of tartar**
    ¾ **cup (¼ lb. plus ¼ cup) cold butter or margarine, cut into pieces**
    1 **large egg, lightly beaten**
    1 **cup beer**

1. Mix all-purpose flour, whole wheat flour, sugar, baking powder, salt, and cream of tartar in a large bowl. With a pastry blender or 2 knives, cut in butter until mixture resembles coarse crumbs. Add egg and beer; stir with a fork just until dough holds together.

2. Turn dough out onto a well-floured board and knead briefly until smooth (2 or 3 turns). Pat dough 1 inch thick. Using a floured 2½- to 2¾-inch-round cookie cutter, cut out biscuits. Gently pat scraps together; cut out remaining biscuits.

3. Arrange biscuits slightly apart on a large greased baking sheet. Bake in a 425° oven until browned (18 to 20 minutes). Transfer biscuits to a rack. Serve warm or at room temperature. Makes 8 or 9 biscuits.

Per biscuit: 324 calories (47% from fat), 6 g protein, 37 g carbohydrates, 17 g total fat (10 g saturated fat), 65 mg cholesterol, 654 mg sodium

PIZZA SNACK MUFFINS

When you want the savory flavor of homemade pizza without the fuss, try these tasty treats.

    2 **cups all-purpose flour**
    2 **teaspoons baking powder**
    1 **teaspoon** *each* **crumbled dried basil and dried oregano**
    ¾ **cup nonfat milk**
    1 **large egg**
    2 **tablespoons salad oil**
    ½ **cup chopped tomatoes**
    ½ **cup (about 2 oz.) finely chopped pepperoni**
    1 **can (2¼ oz.) sliced ripe olives, drained**
    ¾ **cup (about 3 oz.) shredded mozzarella cheese**

1. Mix flour, baking powder, basil, and oregano in a large bowl. Add milk, egg, and oil; stir until blended. Stir in tomatoes, pepperoni, olives, and half the cheese.

2. Spoon batter equally into 10 greased 2- to 2½-inch muffin cups; top with remaining cheese. Bake in a 350° oven until well browned (30 to 35 minutes). Turn out onto a rack. Serve warm or at room temperature. Makes 10 muffins.

Per muffin: 202 calories (43% from fat), 7 g protein, 22 g carbohydrates, 10 g total fat (3 g saturated fat), 33 mg cholesterol, 318 mg sodium

CHEDDAR CHEESE CRACKERS

To make these crispy crackers, you roll the dough very thin; then you cut it into strips with a pastry wheel.

    2 **tablespoons butter or margarine, at room temperature**
    1 **large egg**
    ½ **teaspoon paprika**
    ⅛ **teaspoon ground black pepper**
      Pinch of ground red pepper (cayenne)
    2 **cups (about 8 oz.) finely shredded extra-sharp Cheddar cheese**
    1 **cup all-purpose flour**
      Cracked pepper

1. Beat butter in a medium-size bowl with an electric mixer until creamy. Beat in egg, paprika, ground black pepper, and ground red pepper. Add cheese, a third at a time, beating until combined. Stir in flour.

2. Shape dough into a ball; divide in half. Evenly roll each half between 2 sheets of wax paper into a 7- by 14-inch rectangle. With a pastry wheel or knife, cut dough crosswise into ½-inch strips. Place slightly apart on a baking sheet. Sprinkle with cracked pepper, lightly pressing pepper into dough.

3. Bake in a 400° oven until deep golden (6 to 8 minutes). Transfer to racks and let cool for 5 minutes. Serve warm. If made ahead, let cool completely, wrap airtight, and store at room temperature for up to a week. Makes 56 crackers.

Per cracker: 29 calories (57% from fat), 1 g protein, 2 g carbohydrates, 2 g total fat (1 g saturated fat), 9 mg cholesterol, 30 mg sodium

APRICOT-DATE PUMPKIN BREAD

This hearty, orange-scented pumpkin loaf is laden with dried fruit, nuts, and spices. To store, wrap in a plastic bag and refrigerate for up to 5 days.

- 2 **large eggs**
- 1 **cup** *each* **sugar and canned pumpkin**
- ½ **cup** *each* **salad oil and orange juice**
- 2 **cups all-purpose flour**
- 1 **teaspoon baking soda**
- ½ **teaspoon** *each* **baking powder, ground cinnamon, ground cloves, ground nutmeg, and ground ginger**
- ½ **cup** *each* **chopped walnuts and chopped dates**
- ¼ **cup chopped dried apricots**

1. Beat eggs, sugar, pumpkin, oil, and orange juice in a large bowl until blended. In a medium-size bowl, mix flour, baking soda, baking powder, cinnamon, cloves, nutmeg, and ginger. Add flour mixture to egg mixture; stir until blended. Stir in nuts, dates, and apricots.

2. Pour batter into a greased 5- by 9-inch loaf pan. Bake in a 350° oven until a skewer inserted in center comes out clean (about 1 hour). Let cool in pan on a rack for 15 minutes; turn out onto rack and let cool completely. Serve at room temperature. Makes 1 loaf (10 to 12 servings).

Per serving: 336 calories (39% from fat), 5 g protein, 48 g carbohydrates, 15 g total fat (2 g saturated fat), 39 mg cholesterol, 151 mg sodium

• *Pictured on page 94* •

OLD-FASHIONED LEMON BREAD

While it's still hot from the oven, you poke this loaf with a skewer until it's full of holes and then drizzle a sweet, lemony glaze over the top.

- 1½ **cups all-purpose flour**
- 1 **cup sugar**
- 1 **teaspoon baking powder**
- ½ **teaspoon salt**
- 2 **large eggs**
- ½ **cup** *each* **milk and salad oil**
- 1½ **teaspoons grated lemon peel**
  Lemon Glaze (recipe follows)

1. Mix flour, sugar, baking powder, and salt in a large bowl. In a small bowl, beat eggs, milk, oil, and lemon peel until blended. Add egg mixture to flour mixture; stir just until blended.

2. Pour batter into a greased and floured 5- by 9-inch loaf pan. Bake in a 350° oven until a skewer inserted in center comes out clean (40 to 45 minutes). Meanwhile, prepare Lemon Glaze. Leaving loaf in pan, use a long skewer to poke numerous holes all the way to bottom of loaf. Slowly drizzle hot glaze over top.

3. Let bread cool in pan on a rack for 10 minutes; turn out onto rack and let cool completely. Serve at room temperature. Makes 1 loaf (10 to 12 servings).

Lemon Glaze. In a small pan, combine 4½ tablespoons **lemon juice** and ⅓ cup **sugar**. Cook over medium heat, stirring constantly, until sugar is dissolved. Remove from heat and keep warm.

Per serving: 271 calories (39% from fat), 3 g protein, 39 g carbohydrates, 12 g total fat (2 g saturated fat), 40 mg cholesterol, 163 mg sodium

BANANA BRAN BREAD

This variation of popular banana nut bread is enriched with oat bran and accented with a hint of lemon.

- 1 **cup all-purpose flour**
- ¾ **cup oat bran**
- 1¼ **teaspoons baking powder**
- ½ **teaspoon baking soda**
- ¼ **teaspoon salt**
- 1 **teaspoon grated lemon peel**
- ⅓ **cup butter or margarine**
- ⅔ **cup sugar**
- 2 **large eggs**

1 cup mashed ripe bananas (about 2
   medium-size)
½ cup chopped walnuts

1. Mix flour, oat bran, baking powder, baking soda, and salt in a small bowl. In a large bowl, beat lemon peel, butter, and sugar until blended. Add eggs, one at a time, beating well after each addition. Add flour mixture, bananas, and nuts to egg mixture; stir until evenly moistened.

2. Pour batter into a greased 4- by 8-inch loaf pan. Bake in a 350° oven until bread begins to pull away from sides of pan and a skewer inserted in center comes out clean (about 55 minutes). Let cool in pan on a rack for 10 minutes; turn out onto rack and let cool completely. Serve at room temperature. Makes 1 loaf (8 to 10 servings).

Per serving: 274 calories (41% from fat), 5 g protein, 38 g carbohydrates, 13 g total fat (5 g saturated fat), 65 mg cholesterol, 282 mg sodium

LEMON ZUCCHINI BREAD

Tart and refreshing, lemon adds life to this zucchini bread. This recipe makes two loaves.

    3 cups all-purpose flour
    1 tablespoon baking powder
    1 cup chopped walnuts
    1 cup salad oil
    2 cups sugar
    2 tablespoons grated lemon peel
    ¼ cup lemon juice
    3 large eggs
    1 pound zucchini (about 4 medium-size), grated

1. Mix flour, baking powder, and nuts in a medium-size bowl. In a large bowl, beat oil, sugar, lemon peel, and lemon juice until blended. Add eggs, one at a time, beating well after each addition. Gradually stir in flour mixture until blended. Add zucchini; stir until combined.

2. Pour batter into 2 greased and floured 4- by 8-inch loaf pans. Bake in a 350° oven until a skewer inserted in center comes out clean (about 50 minutes). Let cool in pans on racks for 10 minutes; turn out onto racks and let cool completely. Serve at room temperature. Makes 2 loaves (about 8 servings each).

Per serving: 379 calories (47% from fat), 5 g protein, 46 g carbohydrates, 20 g total fat (3 g saturated fat), 40 mg cholesterol, 106 mg sodium

• *Pictured on page 94* •

SPICY GINGERBREAD

A longtime favorite, this moist spice cake can be made with ground, fresh, or crystallized ginger. To create a delicate snowflake design on top, place a decorative stencil or doily on the cooled cake, sift with powdered sugar, and carefully remove the stencil.

    ¼ cup butter or margarine, at room temperature
    ¼ cup granulated sugar
    1 large egg
    ½ cup light molasses
    1¼ cups all-purpose flour
    1 teaspoon baking soda
    ¼ teaspoon *each* ground nutmeg and salt
    1 teaspoon ground ginger, 1 tablespoon minced fresh ginger, or 3 tablespoons minced crystallized ginger
    ½ cup hot water
      About 1 tablespoon powdered sugar

1. Beat butter, granulated sugar, and egg in a large bowl until blended. Stir in molasses. In a small bowl, mix flour, baking soda, nutmeg, salt, and ginger. Add flour mixture to egg mixture alternately with water; stir until smooth.

2. Spread batter in a greased and floured 8- to 9-inch-round cake pan. Bake in a 350° oven until a skewer inserted in center comes out clean (25 to 30 minutes). Let cool in pan on a rack for 15 minutes; turn out onto a serving plate. Serve warm or at room temperature. Just before serving, lay a decorative stencil or doily on bread and sift with powdered sugar. Carefully remove stencil. Makes 6 servings.

Per serving: 298 calories (29% from fat), 4 g protein, 50 g carbohydrates, 10 g total fat (5 g saturated fat), 56 mg cholesterol, 400 mg sodium

EASY APPLE COFFEE CAKE

A buttery "crust" and a filling reminiscent of apple pie top this moist and light coffee cake.

- 2 cups all-purpose flour
- 1 cup granulated sugar
- 2 teaspoons baking powder
- ¼ teaspoon salt
- 1 large egg, lightly beaten
- 1 cup milk
- 2 tablespoons salad oil
- 2 large Golden Delicious apples, peeled, cored, and thinly sliced
- 1 cup firmly packed brown sugar
- 1 teaspoon ground cinnamon
- ⅓ cup butter or margarine, melted and cooled
- ½ cup chopped walnuts

1. Mix flour, granulated sugar, baking powder, and salt in a large bowl. Add egg, milk, and oil; stir until well moistened. Spoon batter into a greased and floured 9- by 13-inch baking pan, evenly smoothing top. Arrange apple slices in rows over batter. In a small bowl, mix brown sugar, cinnamon, and butter; crumble over apples. Sprinkle with nuts.

2. Bake in a 350° oven until cake begins to pull away from sides of pan (about 45 minutes). Let cool in pan on a rack for 10 minutes. Serve warm or at room temperature. Makes 10 servings.

Per serving: 414 calories (31% from fat), 5 g protein, 68 g carbohydrates, 15 g total fat (2 g saturated fat), 25 mg cholesterol, 251 mg sodium

ROCKY MOUNTAIN APPLE BREAD

This chunky, hearty loaf is dense with fresh apples, raisins, and chopped walnuts.

- 4 large eggs
- 2 cups sugar
- ½ cup *each* buttermilk and mayonnaise
- 1 teaspoon vanilla
- 3½ cups all-purpose flour
- ¼ teaspoon salt
- ½ teaspoon baking soda
- 1 teaspoon *each* baking powder and ground cinnamon
- 2 medium-size Newtown Pippin or other tart green apples
- 1 cup *each* raisins and chopped walnuts

1. Beat eggs, sugar, buttermilk, mayonnaise, and vanilla in a large bowl until smooth. In another large bowl, mix flour, salt, baking soda, baking powder, and cinnamon. Add flour mixture to egg mixture; stir just until combined.

2. Core and chop apples. Add to batter with raisins and nuts; stir just until combined. Spread batter in 2 greased and floured 5- by 9-inch loaf pans.

3. Bake in a 375° oven until a skewer inserted in center comes out clean (about 1 hour and 10 minutes). Let cool in pans on racks for 10 minutes; turn out onto racks and let cool completely. Serve at room temperature. Makes 2 loaves (about 10 servings each).

Per serving: 290 calories (30% from fat), 5 g protein, 47 g carbohydrates, 10 g total fat (1 g saturated fat), 46 mg cholesterol, 135 mg sodium

MANGO BREAD

The secret to this moist bread's mellow flavor is baking soda. When mixed with the mango purée, it neutralizes the fruit's acid, giving the bread a rich flavor.

- 1 cup mango purée (about 1 ripe 1-lb. mango)
- ¾ teaspoon baking soda mixed with 2 teaspoons water
- 1 cup sugar
- 2 large eggs
- ½ cup sweetened flaked coconut, minced
- ¼ cup salad oil
- 2½ cups all-purpose flour
- 1½ teaspoons baking powder

1. Combine mango purée and baking soda mixture in a large bowl; stir until blended. Let stand for 5 minutes. Add sugar, eggs, coconut, and oil; beat until combined. Stir in flour and baking powder until blended. Pour batter into a greased 5- by 9-inch loaf pan.

2. Bake in a 350° oven until bread is richly browned and begins to pull away from sides of pan (50 to 55 minutes). Let cool in pan on a rack for 10 minutes; turn out onto rack. Serve warm or at room temperature. Makes 1 loaf (10 to 12 servings).

Per serving: 270 calories (25% from fat), 4 g protein, 47 g carbohydrates, 8 g total fat (2 g saturated fat), 39 mg cholesterol, 174 mg sodium

Apples are a popular addition to breads and cakes because they soften and become sweeter as they bake. These quick breads use the flavorful fruit in two different ways: coarsely chopped for Rocky Mountain Apple Bread (top) and thinly sliced atop Easy Apple Coffee Cake (bottom). The recipes are on the facing page.

• Pictured on page 94 •

APRICOT-BLACKBERRY CORNMEAL KUCHEN

Cornmeal gives this Austrian coffee cake a slightly grainy texture. Topped with fresh apricots and blackberries, it makes a delicious morning or mid-afternoon treat.

- ½ cup *each* yellow cornmeal and all-purpose flour
- 1½ teaspoons baking powder
- 1 large egg
- ¼ cup firmly packed brown sugar
- ½ cup buttermilk
- 2 tablespoons melted butter or margarine
- 5 medium-size ripe apricots (about ¾ lb. *total*), halved and pitted
- 10 blackberries, rinsed and drained
- 2 tablespoons granulated sugar

1. Mix cornmeal, flour, and baking powder in a large bowl. In a small bowl, beat egg, brown sugar, buttermilk, and butter until blended. Add egg mixture to flour mixture; stir until evenly moistened.

2. Pour batter into a greased 8-inch-round cake pan. Press apricot halves, pitted sides up, decoratively into dough. Place a blackberry in hollow of each apricot.

3. Bake in a 350° oven until kuchen feels firm when gently pressed in center (30 to 35 minutes). Sprinkle with granulated sugar. Let cool on a rack. Serve warm or at room temperature. Makes 6 to 8 servings.

Per serving: 189 calories (24% from fat), 4 g protein, 33 g carbohydrates, 5 g total fat (2 g saturated fat), 40 mg cholesterol, 169 mg sodium

CHERRY–CREAM CHEESE COFFEE CAKE

This not-too-sweet cake is so delicious, no one will believe it takes just minutes to prepare. The moist batter, enriched with sour cream and eggs, is filled with cherries and a mellow cream cheese mixture. It's then baked to a soft golden brown.

   Cream Cheese Filling (recipe follows)
- 2 large eggs
- 1 cup sour cream

- ¾ cup sugar
- 2 teaspoons grated lemon peel
- 1½ teaspoons baking powder
- ½ teaspoon baking soda
- 1¾ cups all-purpose flour
- 1¾ cups frozen unsweetened pitted cherries, thawed and drained
- ¼ cup sugar mixed with 1½ teaspoons ground cinnamon

1. Prepare Cream Cheese Filling; set aside.

2. Beat eggs, sour cream, the ¾ cup sugar, lemon peel, baking powder, and baking soda in a large bowl until blended. Add flour; stir until combined.

3. Spread half the batter in a greased 9-inch-square pan. Pour filling over batter; sprinkle with half the cherries and half the cinnamon-sugar. Drop remaining batter in small mounds over cherries and spread evenly over filling. Sprinkle with remaining cherries and cinnamon-sugar.

4. Bake in a 350° oven until cake pulls away from sides of pan (about 50 minutes). Let cool in pan on a rack for 10 minutes. Serve warm or at room temperature. Makes 8 servings.

Cream Cheese Filling. In a small bowl, beat 1 small package (3 oz.) **cream cheese,** at room temperature, and 1 tablespoon **sugar** until blended. Add 1 large **egg;** beat well.

Per serving: 351 calories (32% from fat), 7 g protein, 53 g carbohydrates, 13 g total fat (7 g saturated fat), 104 mg cholesterol, 241 mg sodium

• Pictured on page 110 •

RASPBERRY STREUSEL MUFFIN TOPS

Most muffin fans eat the entire muffin, but there are some who enjoy only the tops. Here's a recipe for muffin tops that are just like big, thick cookies.

- 2½ cups all-purpose flour
- 1 cup firmly packed brown sugar
- ½ cup chopped almonds
- ½ teaspoon ground nutmeg
- ¾ cup (¼ lb. plus ¼ cup) cold butter or margarine, cut into pieces
- 2 teaspoons baking powder
- 1 teaspoon baking soda
- 1 large egg

⅔ cup milk
1 cup fresh or unsweetened frozen,
   thawed raspberries

1. Mix flour, sugar, almonds, and nutmeg in a large bowl. With a pastry blender or 2 knives, cut in butter until mixture resembles coarse crumbs; set aside ¾ cup of the mixture. Add baking powder and baking soda to remaining mixture; stir until blended. Stir in egg and milk until evenly moistened. Gently stir in raspberries.

2. Spoon ¼-cup-size mounds of the batter about 2 inches apart on lightly greased baking sheets. With your fingers, firmly squeeze reserved flour mixture into large lumps. Coarsely break lumps into pea-size chunks and sprinkle over batter.

3. Bake in a 350° oven until well browned (20 to 22 minutes). Let cool in pan on a rack for 5 minutes; transfer muffin tops to rack. Serve warm or at room temperature. Makes 10 or 11 muffin tops.

Per muffin top: 347 calories (45% from fat), 5 g protein, 43 g carbohydrates, 18 g total fat (9 g saturated fat), 55 mg cholesterol, 353 mg sodium

CHOCOLATE MACAROON MUFFINS

Rich, dark chocolate and a creamy coconut filling make these sweet muffins taste almost like candy.

   Macaroon Filling (recipe follows)
¼ **cup butter or margarine**
½ **cup sugar**
1 **teaspoon vanilla**
2 **large eggs**
¾ **cup all-purpose flour**
¼ **cup unsweetened cocoa**
¾ **teaspoon baking powder**

1. Prepare Macaroon Filling; set aside.

2. Beat butter, sugar, and vanilla in a large bowl until fluffy. Add eggs, one at a time, beating well after each addition. In a small bowl, mix flour, cocoa, and baking powder. Add flour mixture to egg mixture; stir until combined.

3. Spoon half the batter equally into 8 greased or paper-lined 2- to 2½-inch muffin cups. Spoon half the filling over batter. Repeat, using remaining batter and filling.

4. Bake in a 350° oven until tops spring back when gently pressed in center and filling is lightly browned (about 25 minutes). Let cool in pan on a rack for 10 minutes; turn out onto rack. Serve warm or at room temperature. Makes 8 muffins.

Macaroon Filling. In a food processor or large bowl, combine ¾ cup (7 oz.) **almond paste** and ½ cup **sugar;** whirl or beat until mixture resembles coarse crumbs. Add 2 large **egg whites,** one at a time, whirling or beating well after each addition. Stir in ¼ cup **sweetened flaked coconut.**

Per muffin: 353 calories (40% from fat), 7 g protein, 48 g carbohydrates, 16 g total fat (6 g saturated fat), 69 mg cholesterol, 143 mg sodium

BANANA BUCKWHEAT MUFFINS

These extra-moist banana muffins are heartier than most. If you can't find buckwheat flour, use all whole wheat flour along with the all-purpose flour.

1 **cup all-purpose flour**
½ **cup *each* buckwheat flour and whole wheat flour**
2 **tablespoons poppy seeds**
2 **teaspoons baking powder**
1 **teaspoon baking soda**
¾ **teaspoon ground nutmeg**
3 **medium-size ripe bananas (about 1 lb. *total*)**
2 **large eggs**
¼ **cup *each* salad oil and honey**

1. Mix all-purpose flour, buckwheat flour, whole wheat flour, poppy seeds, baking powder, baking soda, and nutmeg in a medium-size bowl.

2. Cut bananas into 1-inch chunks. Place in a food processor or blender; add eggs, oil, and honey. Whirl until puréed. Pour banana mixture into flour mixture; stir just until blended. Spoon batter equally into 12 greased 2- to 2½-inch muffin cups.

3. Bake in a 375° oven until muffins are golden and tops spring back when gently pressed in center (about 20 minutes). Turn out onto racks. Serve warm or at room temperature. Makes 12 muffins.

Per muffin: 187 calories (35% from fat), 4 g protein, 27 g carbohydrates, 8 g total fat (1 g saturated fat), 35 mg cholesterol, 198 mg sodium

Moist, tender muffins provide a showcase for a variety of fruits and nuts.
Here, they star in a quartet of delectable choices (clockwise from top left): Heavenly
Pumpkin Gems (facing page), Raspberry Streusel Muffin Tops (page 108), Outstanding
Blueberry Muffins (page 112), and Apricot Granola Muffins (page 112).

• Pictured on facing page •

HEAVENLY PUMPKIN GEMS

A sprinkling of sugar tops these moist pumpkin muffins. Inside, they reveal a tiny golden drop of apricot preserves.

- 2 cups all-purpose flour
- 1 tablespoon baking powder
- 1 teaspoon ground cinnamon
- ¼ teaspoon *each* ground nutmeg, ground ginger, and salt
- ½ cup salad oil; or butter or margarine (¼ lb.), at room temperature
- ½ cup plus 2 tablespoons sugar
- 2 large eggs
- 1 cup canned pumpkin
- ½ cup sour cream
- ¼ cup apricot preserves
- ¼ cup sliced almonds

1. Mix flour, baking powder, cinnamon, nutmeg, ginger, and salt in a large bowl. In another large bowl, beat oil and ½ cup of the sugar until blended. Add eggs, pumpkin, and sour cream; beat until blended. Add pumpkin mixture to flour mixture; stir until evenly moistened.

2. Spoon batter into 12 well-greased or paper-lined 2½-inch muffin cups, filling each half full. Spoon 1 teaspoon of the preserves into each cup; top with remaining batter.

3. Sprinkle evenly with almonds and remaining 2 tablespoons sugar.

4. Bake in a 375° oven until well browned (about 45 minutes). Turn out onto a rack and let cool for 10 minutes. Serve warm or at room temperature. Makes 12 muffins.

Per muffin: 275 calories (46% from fat), 4 g protein, 34 g carbohydrates, 14 g total fat (3 g saturated fat), 40 mg cholesterol, 187 mg sodium

CARROT-NUT MIGHTY MUFFINS

More than mere muffins, these mighty treats can be nearly double the size of most muffins. Spoon the thick batter up to the rims of custard cups or standard muffin cups to achieve the mammoth dimensions. They're especially delicious when served warm with a sweet-flavored butter.

- 1½ cups all-purpose flour
- ¾ cup whole wheat flour
- ½ cup firmly packed brown sugar
- 2½ teaspoons baking powder
- 1 teaspoon ground cinnamon
- ½ teaspoon *each* baking soda and ground nutmeg
- ¼ teaspoon salt
- 1 cup shredded carrots
- ¾ cup chopped walnuts
- ¾ cup milk
- 1 large egg
- ¼ cup butter or margarine, melted and cooled
  Date-Nut Butter (page 124) or Orange Marmalade Butter (page 124), optional

1. Mix all-purpose flour, whole wheat flour, sugar, baking powder, cinnamon, baking soda, nutmeg, and salt in a large bowl. Stir in carrots and nuts. In a small bowl, beat milk, egg, and butter until blended. Add egg mixture to flour mixture; stir just until evenly moistened (batter should be lumpy).

2. Spoon batter equally into 6 greased 2½- to 2¾-inch muffin cups, alternating cups, or 4 greased 6-ounce custard cups (arrange filled cups about 2 inches apart in a large baking pan).

3. Bake muffin cups in a 400° oven or custard cups in a 375° oven until tops spring back when gently pressed in center and a skewer inserted in center comes out clean (about 25 minutes for muffin cups; about 35 minutes for custard cups). Let cool in pan on a rack for 5 minutes; turn out onto rack. Serve warm or at room temperature. Offer with your choice of flavored butter, if desired. Makes 6 large or 4 extra-large muffins.

Per large muffin: 453 calories (41% from fat), 10 g protein, 60 g carbohydrates, 21 g total fat (7 g saturated fat), 60 mg cholesterol, 518 mg sodium

Per extra-large muffin: 679 calories (41% from fat), 15 g protein, 89 g carbohydrates, 31 g total fat (10 g saturated fat), 91 mg cholesterol, 777 mg sodium

• *Pictured on page 110* •

OUTSTANDING BLUEBERRY MUFFINS

The blueberries in these muffins plump and sweeten in the oven, creating an explosion of juicy berry flavor with each bite. To keep the berries blue, mix them into the batter quickly and handle as little as possible; otherwise, the baking soda may turn them green—a harmless but rather unattractive reaction.

- 1½ cups *each* whole wheat flour and all-purpose flour
- 1 cup plus 2 tablespoons firmly packed light brown sugar
- ¼ teaspoon salt
- 2 teaspoons baking soda
- 4 teaspoons baking powder
- 1 tablespoon ground cinnamon
- 2 large eggs
- 1½ cups buttermilk
- ¼ cup salad oil; or butter or margarine, melted and cooled
- 2 cups fresh or unsweetened frozen blueberries

1. Mix whole wheat flour, all-purpose flour, 1 cup of the sugar, salt, baking soda, baking powder, and cinnamon in a large bowl. In a medium-size bowl, beat eggs, buttermilk, and oil until blended. Add egg mixture to flour mixture; stir just until moistened. Quickly stir in blueberries.

2. Spoon batter equally into 12 greased or paper-lined 2½-inch muffin cups (cups will be very full). Sprinkle with remaining 2 tablespoons sugar. Bake in a 375° oven until well browned (about 35 minutes). Let cool in pan on a rack for 5 minutes; turn out onto rack. Serve warm or at room temperature. Makes 12 muffins.

Per muffin: 276 calories (23% from fat), 6 g protein, 49 g carbohydrates, 7 g total fat (1 g saturated fat), 37 mg cholesterol, 471 mg sodium

• *Pictured on page 110* •

APRICOT GRANOLA MUFFINS

These muffins rely on granola, an uncommonly good combination of grains, nuts, and dried fruit. Choose your favorite variety to add to these crunchy treats.

- ¼ cup butter or margarine
- ½ cup firmly packed brown sugar
- 2 large eggs
- ½ cup nonfat milk
- ¼ teaspoon almond extract
- ¾ cup all-purpose flour
- ½ cup whole wheat flour
- 2 teaspoons baking powder
- 1 teaspoon ground cinnamon
- 1 cup granola cereal
- ½ cup dried apricots, chopped
- ½ cup slivered almonds, chopped

1. Beat butter and sugar in a large bowl until smooth. Add eggs, one at a time, beating well after each addition. Stir in milk and almond extract. In a medium-size bowl, mix all-purpose flour, whole wheat flour, baking powder, cinnamon, granola, apricots, and almonds. Add flour mixture to egg mixture; stir just until moistened.

2. Spoon batter equally into 12 greased or paper-lined 2½-inch muffin cups. Bake in a 325° oven until muffins are browned and tops spring back when gently pressed in center (25 to 30 minutes). Turn out onto a rack and let cool. Serve warm or at room temperature. Makes 12 muffins.

Per muffin: 232 calories (41% from fat), 5 g protein, 30 g carbohydrates, 11 g total fat (4 g saturated fat), 46 mg cholesterol, 145 mg sodium

HOMESTEAD BRAN MUFFINS

You can have freshly baked muffins anytime you like with this batter—it keeps for up to 2 weeks in the refrigerator. When you want fresh muffins, just stir the batter and bake!

- 3 cups bran cereal (not flakes)
- ¾ cup boiling water
- 3 tablespoons thawed frozen orange juice concentrate
- ½ cup salad oil
- 2 large eggs
- 2 cups buttermilk
- 2½ cups all-purpose flour
- 1½ cups sugar
- 2½ teaspoons baking soda
- 1 cup dried currants
- ½ cup finely chopped walnuts

1. Combine 1 cup of the bran cereal, water, orange juice concentrate, and oil in a large bowl; stir until blended. Stir in eggs and buttermilk. In another large bowl, mix remaining 2 cups bran cereal, flour, sugar, baking soda, and currants. Add flour mixture to egg mixture; stir until evenly moistened. If made ahead, cover with plastic wrap and refrigerate for up to 2 weeks (stir batter before using).

2. Spoon batter equally into 24 greased or paper-lined 2½-inch muffin cups. Sprinkle with nuts. Bake in a 350° oven until well browned (about 30 minutes). Turn out onto racks and let cool. Serve warm or at room temperature. Makes 24 muffins.

Per muffin: 223 calories (31% from fat), 5 g protein, 37 g carbohydrates, 8 g total fat (1 g saturated fat), 19 mg cholesterol, 257 mg sodium

ORANGE-CURRANT SCONES

These fruit-laced scones are reminiscent of the traditional English teatime treats. Here, you prepare a quick orange butter to spread on top for an extra dose of tangy citrus flavor and a rich, buttery taste.

> About 3 cups **all-purpose flour**
> About ¾ cup **sugar**
> ½ teaspoon **baking powder**
> 1 teaspoon **baking soda**
> 2 teaspoons grated **orange peel**
> ½ cup (¼ lb.) cold **butter** or margarine, cut into pieces
> ¾ cup **dried currants**
> ¾ cup **buttermilk**
> **Orange Butter** (recipe follows)

1. Mix 3 cups of the flour, ¾ cup of the sugar, baking powder, baking soda, and orange peel in a large bowl. With a pastry blender or 2 knives, cut in butter until mixture resembles fine crumbs. Stir in currants. Add buttermilk; stir until evenly moistened.

2. Turn dough out onto a lightly floured board and knead until smooth (about 10 turns). Pat into a 9-inch round and place in a greased 9-inch-round cake pan. Sprinkle lightly with sugar. Bake in a 400° oven until golden brown (about 40 minutes). Meanwhile, prepare Orange Butter.

3. Turn scones out onto a rack; invert onto a serving plate. Cut into 8 wedges. Serve warm or at room temperature with flavored butter. Makes 8 servings.

Per serving: 402 calories (28% from fat), 6 g protein, 67 g carbohydrates, 13 g total fat (7 g saturated fat), 32 mg cholesterol, 331 mg sodium

Orange Butter. In a small bowl, combine ½ cup (¼ lb.) **butter** or margarine, at room temperature; 1 teaspoon grated **orange peel;** and 1 tablespoon **powdered sugar.** Beat until creamy and smoothly blended. Makes about ½ cup.

Per tablespoon: 106 calories (96% from fat), 0.1 g protein, 1 g carbohydrates, 12 g total fat (7 g saturated fat), 31 mg cholesterol, 117 mg sodium

CHOCOLATE CHIP SCONES

In tearooms across Great Britain, scones are traditionally served plain with clotted cream. In the past, the idea of chocolate chip–studded biscuits would probably have horrified even the most liberal-minded teatime lover. These days, however, scones come in many different varieties, chocolate chip being among the favorites.

> 2 cups **all-purpose flour**
> ¼ cup **powdered sugar**
> 1 tablespoon **baking powder**
> 6 tablespoons cold **butter** or margarine, cut into pieces
> 1 large **egg**
> About ½ cup **milk**
> ½ cup **semisweet chocolate chips**
> 1 teaspoon **granulated sugar**

1. Mix flour, powdered sugar, and baking powder in a large bowl. With a pastry blender or 2 knives, cut in butter until mixture resembles fine crumbs (or rub butter into flour mixture with your fingers).

2. Break egg into a glass measuring cup and add enough milk to make ⅔ cup; beat until blended. With a fork, stir milk mixture and chocolate chips into flour mixture until evenly moistened.

3. Shape into a ball and knead on a lightly floured board until dough holds together.

4. Place dough on a greased baking sheet and pat into a 6- by 9-inch rectangle. Sprinkle evenly with granulated sugar. Cut rectangle into 6 squares; then cut each square in half diagonally. Separate wedges, spacing them at least 1 inch apart.

5. Bake in a 450° oven until golden brown (12 to 15 minutes). Transfer to a rack. Serve warm or at room temperature. Makes 12 scones.

Per scone: 187 calories (42% from fat), 3 g protein, 24 g carbohydrates, 9 g total fat (5 g saturated fat), 35 mg cholesterol, 191 mg sodium

BREADS FROM A BREAD MACHINE

For the dedicated bread baker, using a bread machine seems like taking the easy way out. But for those who have succumbed to the ease and speed with which a simple machine can turn out a freshly baked loaf, the bread machine is a dream come true. You simply load ingredients into the bread pan, press a button, and in 3 to 5 hours enjoy a delicious, steaming hot loaf.

As the popularity of bread machines has grown, so has the demand for new recipes. Although each machine comes with a recipe booklet, many bread machine aficionados are turning to other sources for ideas and instructions. The problem is that not all machines work the same way, nor do they consistently achieve the same results.

How Machines Differ

Each bread machine currently on the market has its own set of features and programs. The recipes in this chapter were developed using four machines that are representative of the dozen or so available models: the Panasonic Bread Bakery (virtually interchangeable with the National machine) and Welbilt Bread Oven, both about 1-pound capacity, and the Zojirushi Home Bakery and Hitachi Bread Master, both about 1½-pound capacity (the latter model can be enlarged to accommodate a 2-pound loaf).

The recipes that follow have been developed specifically for each of the machines mentioned above. That's because each machine differs in the order in which ingredients are added, the amounts of the ingredients, the size of the machine, and the length of the cycle. Nearly every model has a delayed baking cycle, which allows you to enjoy a freshly baked loaf

whenever you want. This feature should not be used when recipes contain perishable ingredients, such as eggs or milk, or more than about ¼ cup of added ingredients, such as raisins or nuts.

Adapting Recipes for Your Bread Machine

If your bread machine is not one of those listed here, you can adapt recipes for your model by following a few simple rules: work from a recipe developed for the size machine you have (if you have a 2-pound-capacity model, use the recipes for the 1½-pound-capacity machines), add ingredients in roughly the order given in your manufacturer's recipe booklet, and add the smallest amount of water listed if more than one amount is given.

When you've placed all the ingredients in the bread pan, press the start button. As the machine begins the mixing cycle, watch the dough—it should form a soft ball that pulls cleanly from the sides of the pan. If the dough is too wet, add flour, a tablespoon at a time (or if the dough is dry and crumbly, add water, a tablespoon at a time), until the dough maintains the correct consistency.

Bread machine perfectionists maintain that the ideal loaf has a slightly rounded top and a moist, even interior. But some of the best-tasting breads are not necessarily the most attractive ones. Whole-grain loaves or those using coarsely ground flour, for example, may not rise as high as the breads made only with bread flour, which has more gluten (the more gluten in the flour, the stronger the "framework" for the bread).

*With a bread machine, you can produce a fantastic array of breads with a
minimum of effort. Three examples are (clockwise from top left) Ham & Swiss Bread
(page 119); Bread Machine Sourdough Bread (page 122), shown both in the machine
and as a sandwich; and Dried Cherry & Almond Spice Bread (page 120).*

TROUBLESHOOTING

BREAD MACHINES can't compensate for variations in humidity, heat, altitude, and ingredients. That's why loaves sometimes are overproofed, fail to rise properly, or turn out doughy. It also explains why a recipe that's successful in spring and autumn may not work as well in summer.

The most reliable way to ensure that each recipe produces good results is to check the dough after the mixing cycle has begun, adding water or flour if needed as directed on page 114. (If you're adapting a recipe, you need to be particularly sensitive to the mixing process.)

If results are still not satisfactory, consult the chart below. If more than one solution is suggested, start with the first one; if that doesn't solve the problem, try the second one, and so on.

Problem	Cause	Solutions
Overrises and then sinks	Too much leavening action	1. Decrease liquid. 2. Decrease sugar by 50%. 3. Decrease yeast by 25%. 4. Increase fat by 50%.
Gnarled	Too much flour	1. Increase liquid. 2. Reduce flour. 3. Increase yeast.
Large, uneven holes	Leavening action is too fast for rise cycle	1. Decrease liquid. 2. Decrease yeast. 3. Increase salt by 50%.
Sinks before baking	Improper flour-liquid ratio, resulting in weak gluten structure	1. Increase flour. 2. Decrease sugar.
Too dense	Inadequate gluten structure or insufficient leavening	1. Add wheat gluten (1½ teaspoons per cup whole-grain flour). 2. Substitute bread flour for some of the whole-grain flour. 3. Reduce salt by 50%. 4. Increase sugar by 50%.
Top or sides shriveled	Moisture condensing on bread while cooling	1. Remove loaf from bread pan at beginning of cooling cycle.
Raw in center	Rising time too short or not enough yeast	1. Do not use rapid bake cycle. 2. Increase yeast by 30% to 50%.
Added ingredients clumped	Ingredients not mixed in	1. Add ingredients right after machine beeps. 2. Chop ingredients into smaller pieces.

• *Pictured on page 118* •

DINNER ROLLS

In this versatile recipe, the machine prepares the dough; then you shape it into classic French butterhorns, tiny bowknots, or simple rolls, all of which are baked in a conventional oven.

You can make the rolls plain or in one of three flavorful variations. The savory onion–poppy seed version is slightly crunchy. A handful of chopped green or ripe olives gives the rolls a mild piquancy. Or you can wrap the plain dough around thin strips of prosciutto to make wonderfully tasty and slightly salty breadsticks. To make the dough ahead to bake later, simply follow the directions on page 9.

- **Small Panasonic & National** (*About 1-pound loaf capacity*)

2	cups plus 1 tablespoon bread flour
¼	cup cornmeal
1	tablespoon sugar
1	teaspoon salt
2	tablespoons nonfat dry milk
¼	cup butter or margarine, at room temperature
½	cup water
1	large egg
1½	teaspoons active dry yeast
1	large egg beaten with 1 tablespoon water

1. Set machine on basic dough cycle. Place flour, cornmeal, sugar, salt, milk, butter, water, and egg in bread pan. Place yeast in yeast dispenser. Press start button.

2. Remove dough from bread pan. Shape into butterhorns, bowknots, or rolls as directed below.

To shape into butterhorns, cut dough in half. Shape each half into a smooth ball and roll into a circle about ¼ inch thick. Cut each circle into 6 equal wedges. Starting at curved edge, roll up each wedge.

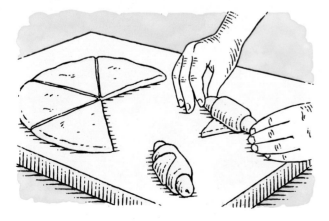

Place point down on a greased baking sheet, spacing rolls at least 2 inches apart.

To shape into bowknots, cut dough into 12 equal pieces. Working with one piece at a time (keep remaining dough covered), roll into a smooth rope about 10 inches long and tie into a loose knot. Place on a greased baking sheet, spacing bowknots at least 2 inches apart.

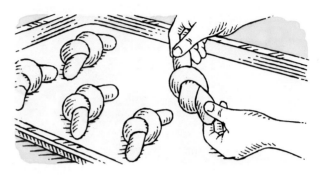

To shape into rolls, cut dough into 12 equal pieces. Shape each piece into a smooth ball and place on a greased baking sheet, spacing rolls at least 2 inches apart.

3. Brush rolls with egg mixture. Bake in a 350° oven until golden (20 to 25 minutes). Transfer to racks and let cool. Serve warm or at room temperature. Makes 12 rolls.

Per roll: 153 calories (33% from fat), 5 g protein, 21 g carbohydrates, 5 g total fat (3 g saturated fat), 46 mg cholesterol, 238 mg sodium

- **Small Welbilt** (*About 1-pound loaf capacity*)

1½	teaspoons active dry yeast
2	cups plus 2 tablespoons bread flour
¼	cup cornmeal
1	teaspoon salt
1	tablespoon sugar
2	tablespoons nonfat dry milk
¼	cup butter or margarine, at room temperature
1	large egg
½	cup warm water (about 110°F)
1	large egg beaten with 1 tablespoon water

1. Set machine on manual cycle. Place yeast, flour, cornmeal, salt, sugar, milk, butter, egg, and warm water in bread pan. Press start button.

2. Follow steps 2–3 for Panasonic and National machines (at left). Makes 12 rolls.

Per roll: 156 calories (32% from fat), 5 g protein, 22 g carbohydrates, 5 g total fat (3 g saturated fat), 46 mg cholesterol, 238 mg sodium

(Continued on page 119)

Once the dough is mixed and kneaded, you can bake it in the machine or shape by hand and bake it in a conventional oven. Dinner Rolls (page 117), shown at left with a variety of added flavorings, are shaped and baked conventionally. Dried Fig & Walnut Wheat Bread (page 121), shown at right, bakes in the machine's removable pan.

- **Zojirushi & Hitachi** (*About 1½-pound loaf capacity*)

   ¾ cup plus 2 tablespoons water
   1 large egg
   3 cups bread flour
   ⅓ cup cornmeal
   1½ teaspoons salt
   1½ tablespoons sugar
   6 tablespoons butter or margarine, at room temperature
   3 tablespoons nonfat dry milk
   1 package active dry yeast
   1 large egg beaten with 1 tablespoon water

1. Set Zojirushi machine on dough setting; set Hitachi machine on knead and first rise cycle. Place water, egg, flour, cornmeal, salt, sugar, butter, milk, and yeast in bread pan. Press start button.

2. Follow step 2 for Panasonic and National machines (page 117), except to shape butterhorns cut each circle into 9 equal wedges; to shape bowknots and rolls, cut dough into 18 equal pieces. Follow step 3. Makes 18 rolls.

Per roll: 144 calories (32% from fat), 4 g protein, 20 g carbohydrates, 5 g total fat (3 g saturated fat), 34 mg cholesterol, 234 mg sodium

Onion-Poppy Seed Rolls

Melt 1 teaspoon **butter** or margarine in a small frying pan over medium heat. Add ¼ cup chopped **onion** (if using a 1-lb. machine) or ⅓ cup chopped onion (if using a 1½-lb. machine); cook, stirring often, until onion is translucent (about 3 minutes).

   Follow step 1 for **Dinner Rolls** for your particular machine (page 117), adding onion and 1 tablespoon **poppy seeds** (if using a 1-lb. machine) or 1½ tablespoons poppy seeds (if using a 1½-lb. machine) to bread pan. Follow steps 2–3.

Per roll (1-lb. machine): 121 calories (34% from fat), 4 g protein, 16 g carbohydrates, 5 g total fat (2 g saturated fat), 35 mg cholesterol, 181 mg sodium

Per roll (1½-lb. machine): 113 calories (34% from fat), 3 g protein, 15 g carbohydrates, 4 g total fat (2 g saturated fat), 26 mg cholesterol, 177 mg sodium

Olive Rolls

Follow step 1 for **Dinner Rolls** for your particular machine (page 117), adding ¼ cup finely chopped **olives** (if using a 1-lb. machine) or ⅓ cup finely chopped olives (if using a 1½-lb. machine) to bread pan. Follow steps 2–3.

Per roll (1-lb. machine): 117 calories (34% from fat), 3 g protein, 16 g carbohydrates, 4 g total fat (2 g saturated fat), 34 mg cholesterol, 229 mg sodium

Per roll (1½-lb. machine): 110 calories (33% from fat), 3 g protein, 15 g carbohydrates, 4 g total fat (2 g saturated fat), 26 mg cholesterol, 220 mg sodium

Prosciutto Twists

Follow step 1 for **Dinner Rolls** for your particular machine (page 117).

   Omit step 2; instead, remove dough from bread pan and cut into 8 equal pieces (if using a 1-lb. machine) or 12 equal pieces (if using a 1½-lb. machine). Roll each piece into a 10-inch rope. Cut 3 ounces **prosciutto** lengthwise into 8 equal strips (if using a 1-lb. machine) or 5 ounces prosciutto into 12 equal strips (if using a 1½-lb. machine). Lay a prosciutto strip over a dough rope. Holding ends, twist in opposite directions. Repeat to shape remaining twists. Place on a greased baking sheet, spacing twists at least 2 inches apart. Follow step 3. Makes 8 or 12 twists.

Per twist (1-lb. machine): 254 calories (35% from fat), 10 g protein, 31 g carbohydrates, 10 g total fat (4 g saturated fat), 77 mg cholesterol, 553 mg sodium

Per twist (1½-lb. machine): 243 calories (34% from fat), 9 g protein, 30 g carbohydrates, 9 g total fat (4 g saturated fat), 61 mg cholesterol, 569 mg sodium

• *Pictured on page 115* •

HAM & SWISS BREAD

This unusual white bread is just like a simple sandwich—each slice is studded with tiny chunks of baked ham and Swiss cheese. Don't worry if the bread fails to rise to the rim of the bread pan during baking; its slightly dense texture and moist, rich interior make it uniquely satisfying.

- **Small Panasonic & National** (*About 1-pound loaf capacity*)

   2¼ cups bread flour
   2 tablespoons cornmeal
   1 tablespoon nonfat dry milk
   1 teaspoon salt
   2 tablespoons butter or margarine, at room temperature

(Continued on next page)

3 tablespoons instant potato flakes
¼ cup *each* diced Swiss cheese and diced ham
1 cup water
1 teaspoon active dry yeast

1. Set machine on medium bake setting. Place flour, cornmeal, milk, salt, butter, potato flakes, cheese, ham, and water in bread pan. Place yeast in yeast dispenser. Press start button. Makes 1 loaf (about 8 servings).

Per serving: 201 calories (22% from fat), 7 g protein, 31 g carbohydrates, 5 g total fat (3 g saturated fat), 14 mg cholesterol, 384 mg sodium

• **Small Welbilt** (*About 1-pound loaf capacity*)

1½ teaspoons active dry yeast
2¼ cups bread flour
2 tablespoons cornmeal
1 teaspoon salt
1 tablespoon nonfat dry milk
2 tablespoons butter or margarine, at room temperature
3 tablespoons instant potato flakes
1 cup plus 1 tablespoon warm water (about 110°F)
¼ cup *each* diced Swiss cheese and diced ham

1. Set machine on medium bake setting. Place yeast, flour, cornmeal, salt, milk, butter, potato flakes, and warm water in bread pan. Press start button.

2. Add cheese and ham when machine beeps (about 25 minutes). Makes 1 loaf (about 8 servings).

Per serving: 201 calories (22% from fat), 7 g protein, 31 g carbohydrates, 5 g total fat (3 g saturated fat), 14 mg cholesterol, 384 mg sodium

• **Zojirushi & Hitachi** (*About 1½-pound loaf capacity*)

1½ cups water
3 cups plus 3 tablespoons bread flour
3 tablespoons cornmeal
1½ teaspoons salt
3 tablespoons butter or margarine, at room temperature
1½ tablespoons nonfat dry milk
¼ cup instant potato flakes
1 package active dry yeast
⅓ cup *each* diced Swiss cheese and diced ham

1. Set machine on medium bake setting. For Zojirushi machine, select raisin bread cycle; for Hitachi machine, select mix bread cycle. Place water, flour, cornmeal, salt, butter, milk, potato flakes, and yeast in bread pan. Press start button.

2. Add cheese and ham when machine beeps (about 30 minutes for Zojirushi machine, 25 minutes for Hitachi machine). Makes 1 loaf (about 12 servings).

Per serving: 190 calories (23% from fat), 7 g protein, 29 g carbohydrates, 5 g total fat (3 g saturated fat), 13 mg cholesterol, 375 mg sodium

• *Pictured on page 115* •

DRIED CHERRY & ALMOND SPICE BREAD

Delicately spiced and laden with almonds and dried cherries, this soft, sweet loaf literally melts in your mouth. If you can't find dried cherries, you can substitute dried apricots or golden raisins.

• **Small Panasonic & National** (*About 1-pound loaf capacity*)

2¼ cups plus 3 tablespoons bread flour
2 tablespoons sugar
¼ teaspoon salt
1 tablespoon nonfat dry milk
¼ cup butter or margarine, at room temperature
2 ounces almond paste, crumbled
1 teaspoon almond extract
1 large egg
1 teaspoon grated lemon peel
½ teaspoon ground cinnamon
¼ teaspoon *each* ground mace and ground cloves
¼ cup *each* chopped dried cherries and chopped blanched almonds
⅔ cup water
1½ teaspoons active dry yeast

1. Set machine on medium bake setting and basic bake cycle. Place flour, sugar, salt, milk, butter, almond paste, almond extract, egg, lemon peel, cinnamon, mace, cloves, cherries, almonds, and water in bread pan. Place yeast in yeast dispenser. Press start button. Makes 1 loaf (about 8 servings).

Per serving: 299 calories (34% from fat), 8 g protein, 41 g carbohydrates, 11 g total fat (4 g saturated fat), 42 mg cholesterol, 140 mg sodium

• **Small Welbilt** (*About 1-pound loaf capacity*)

1½ teaspoons active dry yeast
2¼ cups plus 3 tablespoons bread flour
2 tablespoons sugar
¼ teaspoon salt
1 tablespoon nonfat dry milk

¼ cup butter or margarine, at room temperature
1 large egg
1 teaspoon grated lemon peel
2 ounces almond paste, crumbled
1 teaspoon almond extract
½ teaspoon ground cinnamon
¼ teaspoon *each* ground mace and ground cloves
⅔ cup warm water (about 110°F)
¼ cup *each* chopped dried cherries and chopped blanched almonds

1. Set machine on light bake setting. Place yeast, flour, sugar, salt, milk, butter, egg, lemon peel, almond paste, almond extract, cinnamon, mace, cloves, and water in bread pan. Press start button.

2. Add cherries and almonds when machine beeps (about 25 minutes). Makes 1 loaf (about 8 servings).

Per serving: 299 calories (34% from fat), 8 g protein, 41 g carbohydrates, 11 g total fat (4 g saturated fat), 42 mg cholesterol, 140 mg sodium

• **Zojirushi & Hitachi** (*About 1½-pound loaf capacity*)

1 cup plus 2 tablespoons water
1 large egg
3¾ cups plus 2 tablespoons bread flour (Zojirushi); 3¾ cups bread flour (Hitachi)
¼ teaspoon salt
2 tablespoons sugar (Zojirushi); 3 tablespoons sugar (Hitachi)
6 tablespoons butter or margarine
1½ tablespoons nonfat dry milk
1 teaspoon grated lemon peel
3 ounces almond paste, crumbled
1½ teaspoons almond extract
¾ teaspoon ground cinnamon
½ teaspoon *each* ground cloves and ground mace
1 package active dry yeast
⅓ cup *each* chopped dried cherries and chopped blanched almonds

1. Set machine on medium bake setting. For Zojirushi machine, select raisin bread cycle; for Hitachi machine, select mix bread cycle. Place water, egg, flour, salt, sugar, butter, milk, lemon peel, almond paste, almond extract, cinnamon, cloves, mace, and yeast in bread pan. Press start button.

2. Add cherries and almonds when machine beeps (about 30 minutes for Zojirushi machine, 25 minutes for Hitachi machine). Makes 1 loaf (about 12 servings).

Per serving: 296 calories (33% from fat), 8 g protein, 41 g carbohydrates, 11 g total fat (4 g saturated fat), 33 mg cholesterol, 114 mg sodium

• *Pictured on page 118* •

DRIED FIG & WALNUT WHEAT BREAD

Although this rustic whole-grain loaf may bake to a somewhat ruddy finish, you'll like its light, moist interior, accented by the wonderfully rich flavors of dried figs and walnuts. For most machines, you'll need to add the fruit and nuts after the kneading cycle has begun. If your machine has difficulty incorporating the added ingredients, simply remove the dough, knead briefly on a board until evenly blended, return to the bread pan, and continue to let rise and bake.

• **Small Panasonic & National** (*About 1-pound loaf capacity*)

1½ cups plus 3 tablespoons stone-ground whole wheat flour
½ cup bread flour
2 teaspoons wheat gluten flour
¼ cup wheat germ
1 tablespoon *each* nonfat dry milk and honey
1 teaspoon salt
1 tablespoon butter or margarine
¼ cup *each* chopped dried figs and chopped walnuts
1 cup plus 1 tablespoon water
2 teaspoons active dry yeast

1. Set machine on whole wheat bake cycle. Place whole wheat flour, bread flour, gluten flour, wheat germ, milk, honey, salt, butter, figs, walnuts, and water in bread pan. Place yeast in yeast dispenser. Press start button. Makes 1 loaf (about 8 servings).

Per serving: 188 calories (22% from fat), 6 g protein, 32 g carbohydrates, 5 g total fat (1 g saturated fat), 4 mg cholesterol, 296 mg sodium

• **Small Welbilt** (*About 1-pound loaf capacity*)

2 teaspoons active dry yeast
1½ cups plus 3 tablespoons stone-ground whole wheat flour
½ cup bread flour
2 teaspoons wheat gluten flour
¼ cup wheat germ
1 teaspoon salt
1 tablespoon *each* nonfat dry milk and honey
1 tablespoon butter or margarine
1 cup plus 1 tablespoon warm water (about 110°F)
¼ cup *each* chopped dried figs and chopped walnuts

(Continued on next page)

1. Set machine on medium bake setting. Place yeast, whole wheat flour, bread flour, gluten flour, wheat germ, salt, milk, honey, butter, and warm water in bread pan. Press start button.

2. Add figs and walnuts when machine beeps (about 25 minutes). Makes 1 loaf (about 8 servings).

Per serving: 188 calories (22% from fat), 6 g protein, 32 g carbohydrates, 5 g total fat (1 g saturated fat), 4 mg cholesterol, 296 mg sodium

• **Zojirushi & Hitachi** (*About 1½-pound loaf capacity*)

- 1½ **cups water**
- 1½ **tablespoons** *each* **nonfat dry milk and honey**
- 1½ **tablespoons butter or margarine**
- 1½ **teaspoons salt**
- 2⅓ **cups stone-ground whole wheat flour**
- 1 **cup bread flour**
- 1 **tablespoon wheat gluten flour**
- ⅓ **cup wheat germ**
- 1 **package active dry yeast**
- ⅓ **cup** *each* **chopped dried figs and chopped walnuts**

1. Set machine on medium bake setting. For Zojirushi machine, select raisin bread cycle; for Hitachi machine, select mix bread cycle. Place water, milk, honey, butter, salt, whole wheat flour, bread flour, gluten flour, wheat germ, and yeast in bread pan. Press start button.

2. Add figs and walnuts when machine beeps (about 40 minutes for Zojirushi machine, 25 minutes for Hitachi machine). Makes 1 loaf (about 8 servings).

Per serving: 290 calories (20% from fat), 10 g protein, 51 g carbohydrates, 7 g total fat (2 g saturated fat), 6 mg cholesterol, 442 mg sodium

• *Pictured on page 115* •

BREAD MACHINE SOURDOUGH BREAD

Crisp and golden brown on the outside, chewy and sour-tasting within, this light loaf shares the qualities of the best sourdough loaves. This is a good choice for delayed baking—simply combine the ingredients and program the timer on your machine to complete baking at the desired time. Once cooled and sliced, it makes a terrific sandwich bread. Or serve it in the morning toasted and spread with butter.

• **Small Panasonic & National** (*About 1-pound loaf capacity*)

- 2½ **cups bread flour**
- 2 **teaspoons sugar**
- ¾ **teaspoon salt**
- ¾ **cup sourdough starter (page 54), at room temperature**
- ½ **cup plus 2 tablespoons water**
- 1 **package active dry yeast**

1. Set machine on medium bake setting and basic bake cycle. Place flour, sugar, salt, starter, and water in bread pan. Place yeast in yeast dispenser. Press start button. Makes 1 loaf (about 8 servings).

Per serving: 200 calories (6% from fat), 7 g protein, 39 g carbohydrates, 1 g total fat (0.5 g saturated fat), 2 mg cholesterol, 216 mg sodium

• **Small Welbilt** (*About 1-pound loaf capacity*)

- 1 **package active dry yeast**
- 2½ **cups bread flour**
- ¾ **teaspoon salt**
- 2 **teaspoons sugar**
- ¾ **cup sourdough starter (page 54), at room temperature**
- ½ **cup plus 2 tablespoons warm water (about 110°F)**

1. Set machine on medium bake setting. Place yeast, flour, salt, sugar, starter, and warm water in bread pan. Press start button. Makes 1 loaf (about 8 servings).

Per serving: 200 calories (6% from fat), 7 g protein, 39 g carbohydrates, 1 g total fat (0.5 g saturated fat), 2 mg cholesterol, 216 mg sodium

• **Zojirushi & Hitachi** (*About 1½-pound loaf capacity*)

- 1 **cup water**
- 1 **cup sourdough starter (page 54), at room temperature**
- 3½ **cups bread flour**
- 1 **teaspoon salt**
- 1 **tablespoon sugar**
- 1 **package active dry yeast**

1. Set machine on medium bake setting. For Zojirushi machine, select basic white bread cycle; for Hitachi machine, select basic bread cycle. Place water, starter, flour, salt, sugar, and yeast in bread pan. Press start button. Makes 1 loaf (about 12 servings).

Per serving: 185 calories (6% from fat), 6 g protein, 36 g carbohydrates, 1 g total fat (0.4 g saturated fat), 2 mg cholesterol, 192 mg sodium

Embellish freshly baked breads with the following favorites (clockwise from top left): Spiced Apple Honey, Chile-Cheese Spread, Fresh Mushroom Pâté, Red Radish Cheese Spread, Date-Nut Butter, and Gorgonzola Butter. The recipes are on pages 124–125.

BUTTERS, SPREADS & SYRUPS

BUTTERS, SPREADS, AND SYRUPS make good accompaniments to home-baked breads. If you prefer, offer the butters in curls or balls, the spreads in molded rounds, and the syrups in attractive, small pitchers.

Butters

Orange Marmalade Butter. In a small bowl, combine ½ cup (¼ lb.) **unsalted butter,** at room temperature, and ¼ cup **orange marmalade**; beat until blended. Pack butter mixture into a crock (or place on a piece of plastic wrap or wax paper and shape into a log). Cover and refrigerate until firm. If made ahead, refrigerate for up to 2 weeks. Bring to room temperature before serving. Makes about ¾ cup.

Per tablespoon: 84 calories (79% from fat), 0.1 g protein, 4 g carbohydrates, 8 g total fat (5 g saturated fat), 21 mg cholesterol, 5 mg sodium

Date-Nut Butter. In a small bowl, combine ½ cup (¼ lb.). **unsalted butter,** at room temperature; 3 tablespoons *each* **powdered sugar** and finely chopped **pitted dates;** and ¼ cup finely chopped **pecans** or walnuts; stir until blended. Pack butter mixture into a crock (or place on a piece of plastic wrap or wax paper and shape into a log). Cover and refrigerate until firm. If made ahead, refrigerate for up to a week. Bring to room temperature before serving. Makes about 1 cup.

Per tablespoon: 73 calories (82% from fat), 0.2 g protein, 3 g carbohydrates, 7 g total fat (4 g saturated fat), 16 mg cholesterol, 0.9 mg sodium

Fresh Strawberry Butter. In a small bowl, combine ½ cup **fresh strawberries,** hulled, and 1 tablespoon **sugar.** Mash berries gently with a fork. Reserve about a quarter of the berries. Whirl remaining berries in a food processor or blender until puréed. Add ½ cup (¼ lb.) **unsalted butter,** at room temperature, to puréed strawberries; whirl just until blended (do not overbeat). Scrape butter mixture into bowl, add reserved strawberries, and stir gently until blended. Cover and refrigerate until firm. If made ahead, refrigerate for up to 4 days. Bring to room temperature before serving. Makes about ¾ cup.

Per tablespoon: 74 calories (92% from fat), 0.1 g protein, 1 g carbohydrates, 8 g total fat (5 g saturated fat), 21 mg cholesterol, 1 mg sodium

Macadamia Nut Butter. Remove salt from ¼ cup **macadamia nuts** or cashews by placing them in a kitchen towel and rubbing gently. Spread nuts on a baking sheet and toast in a 350° oven, stirring occasionally, until nuts are lightly browned (about 5 minutes); let cool.

Whirl nuts in a food processor or blender until finely chopped. Combine ½ cup (¼ lb.) **unsalted butter,** at room temperature, and chopped nuts in a small bowl; beat until blended. Pack butter mixture into a crock (or place on a piece of plastic wrap or wax paper and shape into a log). Cover and refrigerate until firm. If made ahead, refrigerate for up to 4 days. Bring to room temperature before serving. Makes about ¾ cup.

Per tablespoon: 87 calories (97% from fat), 0.3 g protein, 0.4 g carbohydrates, 10 g total fat (5 g saturated fat), 21 mg cholesterol, 1 mg sodium

Pesto Butter. In a food processor or blender, combine 2 cups lightly packed **fresh basil,** 1 cup (about 5 oz.) grated **Parmesan cheese,** 2 tablespoons **pine nuts,** and 1 or 2 cloves **garlic.** Add ½ cup (¼ lb.) **unsalted butter,** at room temperature, to pesto mixture in processor; whirl until finely chopped and blended. Pack butter mixture into a crock (or place on a piece of plastic wrap or wax paper and shape into a log). Cover and refrigerate until firm. If made ahead, refrigerate for up to a week. Bring to room temperature before serving. Makes about 1¼ cups.

Per tablespoon: 82 calories (77% from fat), 3 g protein, 2 g carbohydrates, 7 g total fat (4 g saturated fat), 18 mg cholesterol, 133 mg sodium

Gorgonzola Butter. In a small bowl, combine 1 small package (3 oz.) **cream cheese,** at room temperature; 3 ounces **Gorgonzola** or blue-veined cheese, crumbled; and 2 tablespoons finely chopped **walnuts;** stir until evenly blended. Add ½ cup (¼ lb.) **unsalted butter,** at room temperature, to cheese mixture; beat until blended. Pack butter mixture into a crock (or place on a piece of plastic wrap or wax paper and shape into a log). Cover and refrigerate until firm. If made ahead, refrigerate for up to 4 days. Bring to room temperature before serving. Makes about 1¼ cups.

Per tablespoon: 75 calories (91% from fat), 1 g protein, 0.3 g carbohydrates, 8 g total fat (5 g saturated fat), 20 mg cholesterol, 73 mg sodium

Spreads

Chile-Cheese Spread. Combine 1 small package (3 oz.) **cream cheese,** at room temperature, and 4 cups (about 1 lb.) shredded **sharp Cheddar cheese** in large bowl of an electric mixer. Add 1 tablespoon **olive oil,** 1 teaspoon *each* **garlic salt** and **dry mustard,** and 2 tablespoons **brandy;** beat until smooth. Add ½ cup **canned diced green chiles** or chopped pimentos; stir until blended. If made ahead, cover and refrigerate for up to 6 weeks. Bring to room temperature and stir well before serving. Makes 2¾ cups.

Per tablespoon: 53 calories (77% from fat), 3 g protein, 0.3 g carbohydrates, 4 g total fat (3 g saturated fat), 13 mg cholesterol, 112 mg sodium

Red Radish Cheese Spread. In a large bowl, combine 1 large package (8 oz.) **Neufchâtel** or light cream cheese, at room temperature; ½ cup (¼ lb.) **butter** or margarine, at room temperature; 1 tablespoon prepared **horseradish;** and 1 teaspoon **Worcestershire;** beat until blended. Add 1½ cups finely chopped **red radishes** and ¼ cup thinly sliced **green onions;** stir until combined. Season to taste with **salt** or celery salt. If made ahead, cover and refrigerate for up to 4 days. Bring to room temperature before serving. Makes about 2½ cups.

Per tablespoon: 36 calories (89% from fat), 0.6 g protein, 0.4 g carbohydrates, 4 g total fat (2 g saturated fat), 11 mg cholesterol, 49 mg sodium

Ricotta Cheese Spread with Anise Honey. Lightly crush 2 teaspoons **anise seeds** with a mortar and pestle (or back of a wooden spoon). In a small pan, combine seeds and ½ cup **honey;** cook, stirring, over low heat until honey is flavored (about 5 minutes). Let cool briefly and use warm. If made ahead, let cool completely, cover, and refrigerate for up to a month; warm over low heat before using.

Combine 1 pound **ricotta cheese** and 1½ teaspoons grated **orange peel** in a medium-size bowl; stir until blended. Mound on a serving dish and drizzle with honey. Makes about 2 cups.

Per tablespoon: 41 calories (39% from fat), 2 g protein, 5 g carbohydrates, 2 g total fat (1 g saturated fat), 7 mg cholesterol, 12 mg sodium

Fresh Mushroom Pâté. Melt ¼ cup **butter** or margarine in a wide frying pan over medium heat. Add ⅓ pound *each* coarsely chopped fresh **shiitake mushrooms** and finely chopped **onion;** cook, stirring often, until mushrooms are browned (about 15 minutes).

Stir in 1 tablespoon **dry sherry** or chicken broth. Combine 1 small package (3 oz.) **cream cheese,** at room temperature, and ¼ cup minced **parsley** in a medium-size bowl; beat until blended. Add mushroom mixture and stir until combined. If made ahead, cover and refrigerate for up to 3 days. Bring to room temperature before serving. Makes about 1 cup.

Per tablespoon: 52 calories (82% from fat), 1 g protein, 2 g carbohydrates, 5 g total fat (3 g saturated fat), 14 mg cholesterol, 46 mg sodium

Quick Chicken Liver Pâté. Melt 2 teaspoons **butter** or margarine in a wide frying pan over medium-high heat. Add 1 thinly sliced large **green onion** and cook, stirring occasionally, until translucent (about 3 minutes). Add ½ pound **chicken livers** and cook, stirring often, until browned (about 3 more minutes). Stir in ¼ cup **dry red wine,** ⅛ teaspoon **salt,** and a dash *each* **dried thyme** and **pepper;** reduce heat and simmer for 3 minutes.

Stir in 1 tablespoon chopped **parsley.** Transfer mixture to a food processor or blender; whirl until puréed. Dice ½ cup (¼ lb.) **unsalted butter,** at room temperature. With motor running, add butter, a few pieces at a time, and whirl until blended. Cover and refrigerate until firm (about 3 hours). If made ahead, refrigerate for up to 4 days. Makes about 1½ cups.

Per tablespoon: 51 calories (82% from fat), 2 g protein, 0.4 g carbohydrates, 5 g total fat (3 g saturated fat), 53 mg cholesterol, 62 mg sodium

Syrups

Spiced Apple Honey. Combine 1 cup **whipped honey,** 2 tablespoons **spiced apple butter,** and ½ teaspoon *each* **ground nutmeg** and **ground cinnamon** in a small bowl; stir until blended. If made ahead, cover and refrigerate for up to a month. Bring to room temperature before serving. Makes about 1 cup.

Per tablespoon: 67 calories (0.2% from fat), 0.1 g protein, 18 g carbohydrates, 0.02 g total fat (0.01 g saturated fat), 0 mg cholesterol, 1 mg sodium

Blackberry Maple Syrup. Combine ½ cup **blackberry preserves** and 1 cup **maple syrup** in a small pan. Cook, stirring, over medium heat until melted and hot. Serve warm. Makes about 1½ cups.

Per tablespoon: 51 calories (1% from fat), 0 g protein, 13 g carbohydrates, 0 g total fat (0 g saturated fat), 0 mg cholesterol, 4 mg sodium

*Gift giving's a snap with these quick breads, which can be prepared all at once.
Our streamlined technique allows you to bake three different flavor variations in your
choice of pans. Shown are (clockwise from top left) Almond Spice Bread, Pumpkin Nut
Bread, and two loaves of Cranberry Nut Bread. The recipes are on page 100.*

Index
. . . .